A Man of Many Parts

A Man of Many Parts

Essays in Honor of John Westerdale Bowker
on the Occasion of His Eightieth Birthday

Edited by
EUGENE E. LEMCIO

Introduction by
ROWAN WILLIAMS

☙PICKWICK *Publications* · Eugene, Oregon

A MAN OF MANY PARTS
Essays in Honor of John Westerdale Bowker on the Occasion of His Eightieth Birthday

Copyright © 2015 Wipf and Stock Publishers. All rights reserved. Except for brief quotations in critical publications or reviews, no part of this book may be reproduced in any manner without prior written permission from the publisher. Write: Permissions. Wipf and Stock Publishers, 199 W. 8th Ave., Suite 3, Eugene, OR 97401.

Pickwick Publications
An Imprint of Wipf and Stock Publishers
199 W. 8th Ave., Suite 3
Eugene, OR 97401

www.wipfandstock.com

ISBN 13: 978-1-62564-071-0

Cataloguing-in-Publication data:

A man of many parts : essays in honor of John Westerdale Bowker on the occasion of his eightieth birthday / edited by Eugene E. Lemcio.

xiv + 236 p. ; 23 cm. Includes bibliographical references.

ISBN 13: 978-1-62564-071-0

1. Bowker, John, 1935–. 2. Theologians—Great Britain. I. Lemcio, Eugene E. II. Title.

BX4827 B72 M46 2015

Manufactured in the U.S.A.   03/16/2015

Some biblical quotations in chapter 4 are taken from the New Revised Standard Version Bible, copyright 1989, Division of Christian Education of the National Council of the Churches of Christ in the United States of America. Used by permission. All rights reserved.

Some biblical quotations in chapter 4 are taken from *A New English Translation of the Septuagint*, copyright 2007 by the International Organization for Septuagint and Cognate Studies. Used by permission of Oxford University Press. All rights reserved.

"Theodicy," "Midlands Snow," "Prayer," and "Examination Question" are reprinted by permission of the publishers, from "Where Poems Come From: Spirituality, Emotion and *Poiesis*," in *Making Nothing Happen* by Gavin D'Costa, Eleanor Nesbitt, Mark Pryce, Ruth Shelton and Nicola Slee (Farnham: Ashgate, 2014), pp. 127–70. Copyright © 2014.

"For my Tortoise, Joey" © Eleanor Nesbitt. From *Gemini Four*. Reprinted by Permission of Only Connect Publishing.

Excerpts from John Bowker, *Before the Ending of the Day: Life and Love, Death and Redemption: Poems and Translations* (Toronto: The Key Publishing House, 2010), 34, 38. Copyright © 2010. Used with permission of The Key Publishing House.

Contents

Preface | vii
Abbreviations | x
Contributors | xiii

Part 1: Introduction

1. John Bowker: A Theological Overview | 3
   —Rowan Williams

Part 2: Biblical Studies

2. The Teaching of Syriac at Cambridge | 15
   —J. F. Coakley

3. John Bowker and "The Jewish Background to the New Testament": An Essay in *Wirkungsgeschichte* | 30
   —Christopher Rowland

4. Daniel & the Three (Principally in the Old Greek): "Historical" Signs of the Eschatological Son of Man & Saints of the Most High God—a Paradigm for Gospels Christology and Discipleship | 43
   —Eugene E. Lemcio

5. A Pilgrimage of Grace: The Journey Motif in Luke-Acts | 62
   —Martin Forward

Part 3: Theology

6. On Systems, Circles, and Centers: Christianity as a Christocentric "System" | 79
   —Richard Bauckham

7   *"In Persona Christi"*: Who, or Where, is Christ at the Altar? | 95
    —Sarah Coakley

8   The Moral Imagination and a Sense of God | 113
    —Jane Shaw

Part 4: Neuroscience and Theology

9   Brain Battles: Theology and Neuroscience | 131
    —William J. Abraham

10 The Origin of the Sense of God: Causation, Epistemology, and Ontology | 145
    —Quinton Deeley

Part 5: Comparative Religion

11 The Idea of Constraint: A Hindu Example | 169
    —Gavin Flood

12 Al-Ghazālī and the Progress of Islamic Thought | 181
    —David Thomas

13 God, Life, Love, and Religions among Indigenous Peoples of the World | 196
    —Darryl Macer

Part 6: Culture

14 The Word Was Made Flesh: Life without Footnotes. John Bowker as Religious Broadcaster for the BBC | 215
    —David Craig

15 "Such Was the World": A Verse Offering | 222
    —Eleanor Nesbitt

Bibliography of John W. Bowker's Publications | 233

Preface

IN THE AGE OF Internet search engines, it is easy to look up the pedigree of anyone: family, education, professional positions, etc. Readers are thereby free to fill in the gaps that are sure to occur in these more personal remarks.

I first became acquainted with John in 1987, when he was Fellow and Dean of Chapel at Trinity College, Cambridge. In 1984, he had succeeded the late, the Right Reverend Dr. John A. T. Robinson (earlier, my internal examiner—the external one being Robert Morgan). Our Honoree had been educated at Worcester College, Oxford and Rippon Hall. Major appointments followed at the Universities of Cambridge, Lancaster, and London. Prior to his stint at Trinity, he had served as Fellow and Dean of Chapel at Corpus Christi College, Cambridge. From 1977 to 1986, John participated in various commissions for the Church of England, including the Archbishops' Commission on Doctrine. Throughout this era, he gave distinguished lectures at various institutions.

During the Easter Term and Long Vacation in 1987, our family of four was residing in town, thanks to a New Testament Research Fellowship at Tyndale House. Living alongside the Cam on Riverside Street in the Barnwell neighborhood, affectionately known then as "Muesli Town," I would cycle across Midsummer Common, down Jesus Lane, and past Trinity—of which I was a member. So, worshiping there at the beginning of the day came naturally, as it had during my final year of doctoral study in 1973–74. It was in John's sermons and homilies that I first became aware of his wide and deep learning: of the apt quotations from and easy allusions to works in fields other than his own. (Soon, I discovered how many, in the deepest sense, actually *were* his own![1]) That range of John's interests and expertise is only partly reflected in the titles of the following essays, the professional

---

1. See n. 3 below in William ("Billy") J. Abraham's report about the reaction of various specialists to John's 1977 Wilde Lectures at Oxford: "The Sense of God."

positions held by their authors, the bibliography of cited works at the end of each contribution, and by the separate listing of his publications.

During the following decades—at times on trips between Seattle and Ukraine—I had occasion to visit John and Margaret in Cambridge. Based on the west side of town, I usually cycled across Lammas Land (that vast expanse of green at the southern edge of Coe Fen), past the University Press offices, down Hills Road, and alongside [New] Addenbrooke's Hospital to their home nearby. Once, when not themselves serving me lunch (which always seemed like dinner), they hosted me at a pub. Typically, John would begin by reading from a collection of prayers, specially printed and bound by J. F. ("Chip") Coakley—a friend and contributor.[2] Such generous hospitality sometimes occurred while they recuperated from illness or experienced the limitations of various medications. In between visits, John and I (via the marvels of voice recognition technology) exchanged drafts of works in various stages of preparation, mainly about some aspect of the Gospels, especially about the son of man. My debt to him on this subject is reflected in my essay for this volume. How much have I learned from him—and from the authors in this tribute!

Once the decision was made to inform John of our project in advance, so that he and Margaret could derive double pleasure both before and after publication and presentation, he replied with typical modesty:

> I am absolutely unworthy of this—I am not a scholar: in order to rescue the introduction of Religious Studies into Cambridge (when the first of the Government cuts took away a proposed post), I had to change from my early work, and I had to become a Jack-of-all-trades. I have felt like a Victorian explorer cutting through jungles and climbing mountains in order to find new animals and unknown plants without ever quite understanding any of them well! I suppose there is something to be said for trying to show how the different researches of others can belong together and can together be illuminating in a new way, but I could not hope to do research of that kind myself any more. I stand on the sidelines and I admire and cheer on the admirable work that you, and people like you, do. I take delight in it all, and I am grateful for all I have learnt. Anyway, you have knocked me sideways, and I am very, very grateful.

Of course, all of us in this volume respectfully beg to differ! We represent but a sample of those who have been John's colleagues, students, and

---

2. His opening paragraph illustrates how a mentor's "chance" remark can affect the outcome of a student's career.

friends. Each essay in its own way indicates the debt owed to the life and thought of one whose ideas should be more widely known because of their importance for the academy, the church, and the wider culture—facing as they do the challenges of diversity and the impact of the sciences and technology. There are his works of profound reflection and technical erudition. (It will become clear how many of us keep coming back to *The Sense of God* and to *The Religious Imagination and the Sense of God*.) However, in addition to these, John has produced expressions of devotion, imagination, and fancy—among the latter being the delightful *Uncle Bolpenny Tries Things Out*. He has engaged contemporary issues head on. Edited introductions to a variety of related subjects have enabled him to continue teaching beyond the lecture hall or seminar room.

So, it is with a sense of gratitude and immense pleasure that we present to our Colleague, Mentor, and Friend that which can amount only to a mere token of our respect and love for broadening our horizons, deepening our understanding, and elevating our vision.

Eugene E. Lemcio
Seattle, Washington
Ordinary Time, 2015

Abbreviations

AB	Anchor Bible
ABRL	Anchor Bible Reference Library
AGAJU	Arbeiten zur Geschichte des Antiken Judentums und des Urchristentums
Anth and Med	*Anthropology and Medicine*
ASV	American Standard Version
ATR	*Anglican Theological Review*
AV	Authorized Version
BAR	*Biblical Archaeology Review*
Bib	*Biblica*
BCE	Before the Common Era
BR	*Biblical Research*
BRR	*Brain Research Reviews*
CE	Common Era
CBQ	*Catholic Biblical Quarterly*
CRJNT	Compendia Rerum Judaicarum ad Novum Testamentum
Con Cog	*Consciousness and Cognition*
CSML	Cambridge Studies in Medieval Literature
CT	*Christianity Today*
CTR	*Canadian Theological Review*
EJAIB	*Eubios Journal of Asian and International Bioethics*
ET	English translation

Expos	*Expositor*
FHNS	*Frontiers in Human Neuroscience*
HB	Hebrew Bible
HTR	*Harvard Theological Review*
Int	*Interpretation*
ISSJ	*International Social Science Journal*
JB	Jerusalem Bible
JIR	*Journal if Implicit Religion*
JRAS	*Journal of the Royal Asiatic Society*
JRDH	*Journal of Religion, Disability & Health*
JSOTSup	Journal for the Study of the Old Testament Supplement Series
JSS	*Journal of Semitic Studies*
JTS	*Journal of Theological Studies*
Jud	*Judaica*
KJV	King James Version
KHN	*Kosmos: Handweiser für Naturfreunde*
LB	*Living Bible*
LHGR	*Law and Human Genome Review*
LXX	Septuagint of the Greek Old Testament (=OG)
MT	Masoretic Text of the Hebrew Bible
NEB	New English Bible
NETS	New English Translation of the Septuagint
NICNT	New International Commentary on the New Testament
NRSV	New Revised Standard Version
NT	New Testament
NTS	*New Testament Studies*
NZFP	*New Zealand Family Physician*
OG	Old Greek (=LXX)
OED	*Oxford English Dictionary*
OSB	Orthodox Study Bible

OT	Old Testament
PLoS ONE	Public Library of Science ONE
PSCF	*Perspectives on Science and Christian Faith*
Psych Med	*Psychological Medicine*
RASD	*Research in Autism Spectrum Disorders*
RS	*Religious Studies*
RB	*Revue Biblique*
RSV	Revised Standard Version
SBLDS	Society of Biblical Literature Dissertation Series
SNTSMS	Society for New Testament Studies Monograph Series
SWBA	Social World of Biblical Antiquity
TynBul	*Tyndale Bulletin*
TS	*Theological Studies*
TSAJ	*Texte und Studien zum antiken Judentum*
VT	*Vetus Testamentum*
WUNT	Wissenschaftliche Untersuchungen zum Neuen Testament

Contributors

William J. Abraham, Albert Cook Outler Professor of Wesley Studies in the Perkins School of Theology at Southern Methodist University

Richard Bauckham, Senior Scholar at Ridley Hall, Cambridge and Emeritus Professor of New Testament Studies, University of St Andrews, Scotland

J. F. Coakley has lectured at Harvard, Lancaster, and Cambridge Universities

Sarah Coakley, Norris-Hulse Professor of Divinity in the Faculty of Divinity in the University of Cambridge and Fellow of Murray Edwards College, Cambridge

David Craig, former Head of Religious Broadcasting for the BBC World Service

Quinton Deeley, Senior Lecturer in Social Behavior and Neurodevelopment, Institute of Psychiatry, Psychology, and Neuroscience, Kings College London. Honorary Consultant Psychiatrist, South London and Maudsley NHS Trust

Gavin Flood, Professor of Hindu Studies and Comparative Religion in the University of Oxford and Academic Director, Oxford Center for Hindu Studies

Martin Forward, Professor of History in the College of Arts and Sciences at Aurora University, Aurora, Illinois

Eugene E. Lemcio, Editor and Emeritus Professor of New Testament at Seattle Pacific University

Darryl Macer, Provost, American University of Sovereign Nations, Scottsdale, Arizona; Director, Eubios Ethics Institute, New Zealand, Japan, and Thailand; Director, International Peace and Development Ethics Center, Kaeng Krachan, Thailand

Eleanor Nesbitt, Professor Emeritus, Warwick Religions and Education Research Unit, Centre for Education Studies, University of Warwick, Coventry (UK)

Christopher Rowland, Emeritus Dean Ireland's Professor of the Exegesis of Holy Scripture in the University of Oxford

Jane Shaw, Professor of Religious Studies and Dean for Religious Life at Stanford University

David Thomas, Professor of Christianity & Islam and Nadir Dinshaw Professor of Interreligious Relations at the University of Birmingham

Rowan Williams, Master of Magdalene College, Cambridge and formerly Archbishop of Canterbury

Part 1

Introduction

1

John Bowker
A Theological Overview

—ROWAN WILLIAMS

JOHN BOWKER SHARES WITH that other great Anglican thinker Austin Farrer the twin disadvantages of being interested in too much for comfort and being congenitally independent of parties and schools in philosophy or theology. Both write out of an enormous erudition, both have no qualms about following through connections of thought even when they lead well beyond what most people would regard as intellectual comfort zones. And the unhappy result has all too often been that they are regarded with a mixture of patronizing mild praise on the one hand, and, on the other, a sort of awed reluctance to engage and argue. Both have had an impact whose depth is hard to calculate on countless individuals; but because neither is the creator of a "school," it is hard to quantify. The fashionable and deplorable concern with measurable "impact" in the academic world of today would find it difficult to manage writers who were so ready (recklessly or generously or both) to spread their genius over such diverse fields. Both are in many ways very distinctively Anglican; both manage to produce deeply persuasive versions of classical orthodoxy almost in passing, with a few lines of radically illuminating analogy or with a single fresh concept; yet the constructive dogmatic work is offered in the most unsystematic way, embedded in a rich fabric of imaginative prose and poetic allusion. For both, the exercise of creative imagination is inseparable from trying to think seriously about God—to *think*, not just to illustrate with apt quotation or decorative charm.

John Bowker's earliest work as writer and teacher was much concerned with pushing the envelope in the study of the Jewish elements of Christian Scripture; an early paper on Targumic forms[1] and a more sustained essay on Jesus and Pharisaism[2] sketched out—in ways that readers at that time could not have fully predicted—a future intellectual trajectory which would embrace a monumentally careful reading of non-Christian religious texts and traditions and also an abiding concern with locating Christology in a new way. The 1970 monograph on the theodicies of different religions was far more than a textbook listing diverse approaches to "the problem of suffering": it conveyed, as few works in what was then still called "comparative religion" did, a full sense of the interiority of each religious world. Anyone studying this remarkable work will have emerged convinced of the need to read every tradition's reflections in the context of its prayer and poetry. One of its concluding insights is that differences between religious idioms are differences over "the nature of the joy attainable by men"[3]: it is a typically unexpected perception, one of those observations which radically but unobtrusively change the way in which a reader frames the issues of interfaith engagement.

And the same originality of understanding and intensity of attention are conspicuous in the Wilde Lectures given in Oxford in the early seventies on "The Sense of God." The two books that came out of these lectures[4] have been shamefully neglected in subsequent decades. They begin to define a quite distinctive approach to the theology of interfaith encounter (bypassing the clichés around exclusivism, inclusivism, and pluralism that still dominate too many introductions to the field), while also outlining a new approach to natural theology and a radical repristination of Chalcedonian Christology. Perhaps—again—because they ranged too widely for the comfort of some, and undoubtedly because they demand very close reading, they have yet to enter the mainstream of theological discussion; but to reread them now is to see how much they do to clear the ground for the revolution in religious studies that has overtaken the subject since the seventies, and to put in place the philosophical resources that are going to be needed in the face of an aggressive antireligious polemic in the last couple of decades.

---

1. Later appearing in *Targums*.
2. *Jesus and the Pharisees*.
3. *Problems of Suffering*, 290.
4. *Sense of God* and *Religious Imagination*.

Central to all of this—in a sense the key concept in a great deal of Bowker's thinking—is the idea of "constraint."[5] It is an interesting choice of word: it is meant to avoid the potential crudities (and the unhelpful polysemy) of talking about causes for things. What is, is as it is because of the constraints within which it lives: it is as it is because of the pressures upon it. Every substance in the universe is a bounded system of information, and we are always as metaphysical or scientific enquirers seeking better to understand what specifies those boundaries. The pressures which do so, however, are unmanageably diverse, and we must avoid like the plague the persistent temptation to ask what the real or fundamental forms of constraint are, as if somewhere you could track down the one causal nexus that really mattered. The question of God is thus one about how far the human mind can and should go in imagining constraint: if all specific constraints are themselves constrained by a constraining context, active in and with every specific pressure at work in the universe, then at some level the "constraint" of God is what makes each element in the universe what it is—not as an extra force exercised but as the ground of intelligible convergence between all specific finite constraints; as that which makes action or energy at the same time *information*.

The classical confession of Christ's divinity, Bowker argues, reflects a recognition that the life of Jesus of Nazareth was one in which the constraint of God's underlying intelligent agency was uninterruptedly present in human awareness and responded to in human action: this is a life uniquely "informed" by the constraint of unconditional agency. And if this is a large and abstract claim, it is located painstakingly in an analysis of the precise kinds of challenge posed by Jesus to the religious and political consensus of the first Christian century, in which one of the focal issues was a crisis of transcendence, a systemic bafflement as to where and how divine action could be recognized.

A full summary of the discussion would not be appropriate here; but part of its brilliance and originality is—paradoxically—that it is set in the middle of a series of analyses of how religious discourses or cultures come to crisis point and how those crises are resolved. What we might call the christological solution to the problem of lost transcendence becomes more intelligible if seen in the context of a global range of crises and resolutions in the world of religious language—crises and resolutions which make it plain that communities of faith are not, as a superficial critic will claim, immune to the pressures of immediate experience and cultural fluidity. The

---

5. This is explored in various ways in *Sense of God*, in the introduction to *Religious Imagination*, and in *Is God a Virus?*, especially chapters 10–12 and 16–18.

question of how and when a language loses credibility and what it takes to recover that credibility is always built in to religious self-awareness. When it fades or is obscured, religions become more than usually damaging in their environments.

So, this is a natural theology which does not look to produce watertight chains of evidence but invites us to entertain a perfectly coherent model of the world's construction as a world of interlocking clusters of intelligibles, appealing to the fundamental idea of a basic constraint within—or around—all constraints. What makes religion interesting—to say the very least—is its capacity to negotiate crises of plausibility and to recover transmittable and continuous tradition, constraining individual thoughts and behaviors in turn. Of course, religions reinvent themselves—as do all traditions of thought. Once we are over the crude surprise or triumph that such a recognition brings, we can begin to grasp why religion is so perennially engaging. Credibility may falter or practically fail; yet managing that moment uncovers resources hitherto unsuspected, a deeper level at which the constraint of God's truth works.

In the light of this, Bowker can be found in the nineties and later constructing a very sophisticated response to the antireligious writings of Richard Dawkins. With the cooperation of his student, Quinton Deeley,[6] himself a strikingly original mind, Bowker dismantles, not only the very amateur philosophy behind the scientistic determinism of the "selfish-gene" generation, but much of the scientific argument itself, tracing the significantly different theories deployed simultaneously without recognition of their divergences by Dawkins and others, and returning once more to the fundamental themes of his earlier discussions of how causality insists on being read as information exchange and what this entails for the interpretation of genetic and neuroscientific research. The closer we look at the working of the human brain, the more it should be clear that we are examining a system of information processing which builds up to increasingly sophisticated and ambitious levels of receptivity; rather than reducing the operations of the brain to the reactive and recursive strategies characteristic of primitive responses—"fight or flight," or whatever the fashionable formula may be—we have to learn to see how we become open to ever-deeper levels and kinds of "constraint."

We do not need to appeal to these for the resolution of routine and context-specific questions; but the substantive point is that, if we do not need reference to God for sorting out local causal puzzles, identifying immediately relevant constraints, that is not a reason for assuming that such

---

6. Particularly in *Is God a Virus?* and *Sacred Neuron*.

reference is otiose at other levels—any more than it would be sensible to claim, say, that chemical properties could have no pertinence to biological ones, because the latter could work admirably well in resolving immediate questions about the world of life systems. But—and this is both a complicating and a simplifying qualification—the point at which reference to the ultimate constraint of God comes in is not like the opening up of a new set of causal problems and solutions: it is "the constant practice of the presence of God, of God as constraint over the outcomes of our behaviour, moving them constantly in the direction of love."[7]

The coherence offered by reference to the constraint of God is not that of a theoretical system but that of an intelligibly ordered life which transmits the fundamental information about the nature of the ultimate constraint; which is why Christians say of Jesus Christ that he is both divine and human, in the sense that the constraint of God, the unsurpassably active character of divine love, is made "specific and continuous" in this human life without any interference in the routine causal processes that make up a human existence.[8] The incarnation is reimagined as the continuous embodying in a human biography of the "information" of God's way of being.[9] Although Bowker does not draw this out, the shape of his Christology echoes the style of late patristic and early Byzantine discussion, for which the central categories were to do with how a unique mode, *tropos*, of divine life could be seen as the ultimately determining agency shaping (constraining) a human individuality.

Bowker is consistently modest in his doctrinal formulations and properly critical of any triumphalism in approaches to faiths other than Christianity; yet he speaks from an unabashedly traditional Christian base in many ways. How does this sit with his broader interests in interfaith encounter? To this question, he will not give a simple answer—chiefly because he is insistent (as the great constructive work of the midseventies shows) that no religious discourse can be effectively renewed except from its own internal critical resources: there is little point in staging arguments between traditions aimed at showing where another faith is inadequate or inconsistent. What is interesting about any discourse of faith is that it represents a continuous effort to be open to actual constraint (i.e., to what it has not itself generated or succeeded in controlling)—to truth.

---

7. *Is God a Virus?*, 117.

8. Ibid.

9. See especially *Religious Imagination*, 184–91, on constructing a modern translation of Chalcedonian Christology.

Thus the significant questions in a discourse will be about how it negotiates the challenge of sustaining continuity and identity while attending to and deploying its self-critical elements in the name of an intensified truthfulness, an intensified submission to the fundamental constraint to which it looks. This helps us see why what is deeply dangerous in religious discourse is also what is deeply positive and humane: the passion to preserve continuity, at its best a passion for distinctive and life-giving truth, may become violent and exclusive; but what we need to do is not to soften the contours of the distinctiveness but simply to become more intelligent in understanding the nature of the disagreements. Looking back to Bowker's earliest reflections, we can say that if we have a disagreement about "the nature of the joy attainable" by human beings, violent conflict and mutual threat are logically inadmissible ways of resolving this. I cannot be made to be happy in your way; yet if my own religious conviction assumes, as the major traditions do, that in some sense the holy makes for the well-being of all, a resort to violence against you will necessarily entail betraying or trivializing the basic grammar of that conviction. Not an academic point, as will readily be grasped.

It is a sophisticated and fresh approach to interfaith engagement, avoiding very effectively the banalities of those various essays in "global" religion for which the historical and specific elements in any faith are treated as embarrassing surface phenomena. I would only add—a point elaborated elsewhere—that the more serious we are about the transcendent liberty (the unconstrainedness) of the divine constraint to which we seek to attend, the less anxious we should be to defend it (as if it were vulnerable to finite assault or competition). This might connect with one of Bowker's bolder and more controversial speculations. He argues that the basic stance for interfaith engagement has to be what he calls "differentialism": we cannot find a vantage point from which to assess and grade the diverse accounts offered by religions of ultimate human fulfilment. "There may be equal outcomes of value which cannot be translated into each other."[10] And if each of these outcomes is the result of a sustained effort to be obedient to the ultimate constraint of sacred truth, can we hope that God, or whatever ultimate point of reference we assume, "endorses" such outcomes? To put it differently, if God is beyond constraint, God is beyond anxiety or self-defense; and so it might be that God could or would perfect the particular happiness each tradition looks to, without some kind of insistence that all be drawn into the same fulfilment.

---

10. *Is God a Virus?*, 182.

But I confess to finding some difficulties with this. It is certainly true that the world's faiths are not a set of rival answers to the same questions; true also that there is no Archimedean point from which to judge, and no translation programme to render diverse accounts of human fulfilment into universal terms; true again that we cannot compel any other to accept or aspire to an alien vision of joy or fulfilment. All that being said, there is still a case for saying that, if there is supposed to be some ground for supposing universal human kinship and universal mutual obligations of a certain kind, the varieties of human joy cannot be diverse to the point of mutual contradiction or flat incompatibility. Each faith makes claims about fundamental and defining features of human identity, and, as Bowker freely allows, this entails argument—properly civil, properly attentive and open to learning, but nonetheless argument; and this surely allows us to say not simply that God "endorses" a simple variety of final ends, but that those ends need to be convergent if humanity is one.

And if so, the argument is about the point of convergence; about what will ultimately appear as the category which knits all the others together. A Christian might say that this is the hope that all human beings will find themselves caught up in the identity of the Divine Son, fulfilled in the intimate relation-without-duality that is at the heart of the Trinitarian life. A Muslim might say that the ultimate inclusive category was that of perfected obedience to divine will, a Buddhist that it was the radical abandonment of the illusion of self-subsisting ego. It is not difficult to imagine any of these saying of any of the others, "I see and value the goal you propose, but for me it has to be finally instrumental to the realizing of the goal I believe to be most basic for human subjects." It is certainly not a zero-sum game; but there are questions about too simple a reading of the idea of a divine "endorsement" of seriously divergent human ends; and such a simple reading could in clumsy hands reinstate just those forms of mutual exclusivism that Bowker's entire work struggles to set aside.

But whatever we make of this specific point, there can be little doubt that Bowker's work lays the groundwork for a theology of religions that is substantially different from and a good deal more interesting than a lot of what has been produced under that heading. In this brief exposition of some of his recurrent concerns, I have been trying to show how the apparently centrifugal forces in his writing are in fact profoundly interlaced. The theology of religions is built on the fundamental idea of religious systems as *bounded* discourses, necessarily committed to questions about continuity and identity because of the belief that they are not humanly self-generated schemata but responses to a constraining agency as much given and nonnegotiable as the local constraints that specify the various discourses of the sciences.

And this same basic set of principles is what allows Bowker to sketch, tantalizingly but persuasively, a reworking of Chalcedonian Christology in terms of the unrestricted human "absorption" of divine constraint. The controlling models of information theory which underlie this are an essential part of what he brings to the debate with deterministic philosophies of science; and it is no accident that in *Is God a Virus?* he moves from discussion of genetics and genetic information-carrying to a particularly rich account of what interfaith argument might be, and thence to a case-study on continuity and change in the context of the modern Church of England (analyzing arguments around the ordination of women), in which he reaffirms the crucial principle that theologically serious changes in religious discourse and practice happen when some hitherto occluded aspect of a basic set of convictions is explored afresh—in such a way that the inner logic of the scheme comes to be seen differently and new conclusions are drawn. The way in which this subject is handled in the final section of the book thus points back unmistakably to the phenomenology of internal religious revolutions spelled out in *The Religious Imagination*.

In short, the superficial impression of a theologian whose interests are simply too disparate for comfort is misleading. The point could be reinforced by reference to shorter works, more devotional in intent, or more deliberately broad-brush; but it should be clear that there is a connecting thread in the major works of scholarship and apologetic discussed here. John Bowker has never claimed to be a system builder in theology or religious studies— and in this respect too he stands close to other great Anglican figures like Farrer. But not being a system-builder is by no means the same as being an unsystematic or merely occasional thinker, a superior journalist; and what I have attempted to do very briefly in this introductory sketch is to display Bowker as a thinker who consistently addresses a tightly connected series of questions. How do religious discourses change and under what pressures? How do we make sense of that notion of a "pressure" in the first place, if we do not want to reduce it to the vague pushings and pullings of contemporary intellectual fashion? How is the vision of a world shaped by immensely complex networks of constraint fleshed out in the various discourses of the sciences?

In tackling these basic issues, John Bowker lays the foundations for reconstructing two crucially important areas of reflection, the theology of interfaith engagement and the theological response to challenges articulated by popularized science. In both these areas, it is hard not to feel that much of the theological world is still catching up with what Bowker has long since mapped out. And the tantalizing proposals around a new vocabulary for Christology still await further and fuller exploration from other theologians: the reaffirmation of the Chalcedonian settlement in the seventies, at a time when the tide seemed to be running so strongly against a robust incarnational theology in many ways, was a characteristic bit of intellectual courage and independence; it was one of the things that helped at least some younger theologians at that time to believe that there was more to the doctrinal tradition than many leading voices were then claiming, and that this "more" had rich and significant implications for a religiously informed anthropology and a new metaphysic capable of intelligent conversation with the philosophy of science.

And all of this has also been framed within a distinctive language and style of exposition, often very complex but at the same time shot through with glimpses of personal vulnerability and personal passion. I said earlier that the broad range of poetic reference in the books is something other than decorative: it is a way of thinking. Unobtrusively, Bowker slips into many of his books poetry of his own, always moving and demanding; he refuses to write *about* "constraint" without illustrating something of what it means in the actual way the writing gets done, so that we cannot come away with any illusions about the cost of thinking under constraint. Poetry is one of the ways in which constraint is deliberately invited and intensified in human speech; so it should be no surprise to find it deployed in this context. Understanding this is to understand why Bowker's mode of theological thinking is as important and as formative as its content; yet another point at which he touches Farrer, whose conversational, footnote-free style shows the process of ideas coming to birth rather just than a polished, bullet-pointed product—yet whose sermons and meditations display a tightly-focused passion in their wording that gives a sense of near inevitability to their theological conclusions.

I do not want to overplay the parallels; Farrer and Bowker are very diverse thinkers, Farrer largely indifferent, like most of his generation, to the world or religious plurality, Bowker working at a distance from the mainstream philosophical arguments that preoccupied Farrer. Their work on biblical questions shares an interest in rabbinical exegesis, but Bowker's contributions represent a very much more historically acute and informed hinterland as regards the cultural and linguistic detail of the field. But there are some illuminations to the comparison; perhaps most importantly, both remind us of the unhelpfulness of enclosing writers too tightly in ready-made categories ("biblical scholar," "apologist," "interfaith expert," "systematician"). If Christian theology is what the greatest theologians assume it is, a genuine thinking of the range of human experience in the light of God's gift in Jesus, we ought to expect different areas of discourse to connect; we ought to expect the questions of one area to open out on to the questions of another. It is not by any means a uniquely Anglican affair, either: how do we place Augustine or Newman within the conventional markers of territory? But the Anglican tradition has fairly consistently acknowledged a responsibility to look for ways of conversing with its ambient culture that do not fit neatly on the map's grids, and it is one of this tradition's gifts to the wider Christian world that it has nurtured minds capable of these deceptively informal and seemingly loosely structured conversations. All this brief essay intends is to alert us to some of the ways in which deeper consistencies may be hidden, and accordingly to alert us to the risks of ignoring writers like John Bowker, who have the patience and courage to follow tracks from discipline to discipline in the faith that all these paths lead to the ultimate constraint of truth, loving, active, and unbounded intelligence.

BIBLIOGRAPHY OF JOHN BOWKER'S WORKS (IN CHRONOLOGICAL ORDER)

The Targums and Rabbinic Literature: An Introduction to Jewish Interpretations of Scripture. Cambridge: Cambridge University Press, 1969.

Problems of Suffering in Religions of the World. Cambridge: Cambridge University Press, 1970.

Jesus and the Pharisees. Cambridge: Cambridge University Press, 1973.

The Sense of God: Sociological, Anthropological and Psychological Approaches to the Origin of the Sense of God. Oxford: Clarendon, 1973.

The Religious Imagination and the Sense of God. Oxford: Clarendon, 1978.

Is God a Virus? Genes, Culture and Religion. Gresham Lectures 1992–93. London: SPCK, 1995.

The Sacred Neuron: The Extraordinary New Discoveries Linking Science and Religion. London: Tauris, 2005.

Part 2

Biblical Studies

2

The Teaching of Syriac at Cambridge

—J. F. Coakley

In 2003 John Bowker made me a present of a book from his library, William Wright's edition of the *Chronicle of Joshua the Stylite* (1882). In this copy, long before J. B. acquired it in 1963, the Syriac text of the *Chronicle* had been marked with vowel signs on every single word. The marks were not difficult to explain: this *Chronicle* was for many years a set text for the Cambridge Oriental Languages tripos, and a teacher will have marked the words for some beginning student to ease his first reading of this not altogether easy text. Thoughts of this teacher and student, and the occasion of my own retirement from teaching Syriac in 2013, suggested the following sketch as an appropriate tribute to my sometime head of department and still advisor and friend.

SYRIAC IN CAMBRIDGE BEFORE 1871

Syriac scholarship in Cambridge began, and continued for a long time, as a servant to the study of the Bible. In 1587, the Regius Professor of Hebrew, Edward Lively (c. 1545–1605), cited the New Testament (NT) in Syriac in his commentary on the Minor Prophets. This was, even then, not a display of rare erudition,[1] the Syriac NT having been in print for more than thirty

---

1. And worse, the citation is garbled. On Hosea 2.14 ודברתי על־לבה, wishing to

years; and by 1611 the King James Bible translators could say that "the Syrian translation of the New Testament is in most learned mens Libraries."[2] But later in the century Cambridge established a more particular association with Syriac scholarship. This can be traced to the acquisition by the University Library of its first ten Syriac manuscripts in 1628,[3] and then to Brian Walton's polyglot Bible published in six volumes in 1653–58[4] containing the Old and New Testaments in Syriac. Work on the Syriac text, including collation of one of the new manuscripts, was carried out by Cambridge men: Herbert Thorndike,[5] Abraham Wheelock,[6] Edmund Castell,[7] and Thomas Hyde.[8] Arising out of the Polyglot were Castell's great *Lexicon Heptaglotton* and two Syriac-related works by William Beveridge.[9]

How most of these scholars *learned* Syriac is not recorded, but some certainly did so as students in Cambridge, whether helped by a tutor or alone. It is worth recording that Thomas Comber (1575–1653), a fellow (and later master) of Trinity, was "dexterous" and "accomplished" in Syriac (among many other languages) according to his biographer, and an "excellent

---

confirm the meaning "I shall console her," Lively says: "1 ad. Thess.2.11. in Syriaco testamento dicitur מלין על לב loquentes ad cor" (*Annotationes*, 6). But the Syriac text is different: ומלין הוין בלבבון; and מלין does not come from מלל "speak."

2. Wright, *Authorized Version*, 17.

3. Wright and Cook, *Catalogue*, 1:viii–xii.

4. Walton was himself acquainted with Syriac, but although a Cambridge graduate, he probably met it first at Oxford. Vol. 1 of the Bible has Walton's Prolegomena, including "De lingua Syriaca et versionibus Syriacis." He also published *Introductio ad lectionem linguarum orientalium* (1655), in which a section sets out the Syriac alphabet and other reading signs (pp. 39–55). The story of the Polyglot and all the persons involved is documented in Todd, *Memoirs of the Life and Writings*, 1:77–81, 163–318.

5. Todd, *Memoirs of the Life and Writings*, 1:209–15. Thorndike (1598–1672) was a fellow of Trinity and also author of (besides many theological writings) *Epitome lexici Hebraici, Syriaci, rabinici et Arabici* (1635).

6. Ibid., 1:230–43. Wheelock (1593–1653) became University librarian in 1629 and the first Sir Thomas Adams Professor of Arabic in 1632.

7. Ibid., 1:163–79. Castell (1606–85) was Wheelock's successor in 1666 as Sir Thomas Adams Professor. His *Lexicon heptaglotton: hebraicum, chaldaicum, syriacum*, [etc.] was published in 1669. His own knowledge of Syriac is shown by his (not very inspired) verses in *Sol Angliae Oriens* (1660).

8. Ibid., 1:261–68. Hyde (1636–1703) was later Bodley's Librarian and professor at Oxford.

9. Beveridge (1637–1708) was later Bishop of St Asaph. His two early books (both from 1658) were *De linguarum orientalium, præsertim Hebraicæ, Chaldaicæ, Syriacæ, Arabicæ, & Samaritanæ præstantia, necessitate, & utilitate quam & theologis præstant & philosophis* (38 pp.), and *Grammatica linguæ Domini nostri Jesu Christi, sive Grammatica Syriaca*.

tutor";[10] but we do not know if he taught Syriac to anyone. Conceivably he, or more likely Wheelock, encouraged Henry Dunster (matriculated from Magdalene in 1627), who in 1640 emigrated to Massachusetts to become president of Harvard College. Hebrew and Syriac were, remarkably, required subjects at Harvard under his presidency, and the Harvard historian S. E. Morison reasonably concluded that Dunster's special interest in these languages went back to his student days at Cambridge.[11] Somewhat later, Thomas Hyde, who worked on the Polyglot while still an undergraduate at King's, was a pupil of Wheelock. Another scholar who must have learned Syriac at Cambridge at this time was Beveridge, whose grammar and apology for Syriac studies were published just two years after he graduated BA.

For a long subsequent period, including the whole eighteenth century, there is little evidence of interest in Syriac at Cambridge, and still less of its being taught. A single exceptional figure is Simon Ockley (1678–1720), Sir Thomas Adams Professor of Arabic 1711–20, whose *Introductio ad linguas orientales* (Cambridge 1706)[12] exhorts young scholars to take up oriental languages. But all he can do is recommend grammars, dictionaries, and editions of the Bible for self-tuition.[13] Other holders of Ockley's chair, or of the Regius chair of Hebrew, or of the Lord Almoner's chair of Arabic founded in 1724, did not publish, or—as far as the anecdotal evidence can show[14]—lecture, on subjects involving Syriac.

At the end of this period comes Samuel Lee (1783–1852), Sir Thomas Adams Professor of Arabic 1819–31 and Regius Professor of Hebrew 1831–48. Lee was famous for his command of many languages, and Syriac was one of them. He edited the whole Syriac Bible,[15] assisted in the design of

---

10. Lloyd, *Memoirs*, 447–48.

11. On Thursdays at 10 President Dunster lectured to the third-year men on Syriac grammar; and at 4 they practised reading the New Testament from Martin Trost's edition (Köthen 1622). See *New Englands First Fruits* (London, 1643), 28–30; Morison, *Founding of Harvard College*, 113; and Morison, *Harvard in the Seventeenth Century*, 141–42, 204.

12. On this book, containing one word in Syriac type which the Cambridge press had to borrow, see McKenzie, *Cambridge University Press*, 2:279.

13. "Methodum itaque planam & facillimam docui; insigniores auctores indigitavi, quo denique ordine legendi sint, monstravi, ut nihil jam deesse videatur, nisi industria vestra" (preface captioned "Juventuti academicae"). Syriac is discussed in part of a chapter, pp. 62–67, including an argument for the antiquity of the Syriac version of the Bible. There are three chapters on Arabic: this was Ockley's principal interest.

14. Wordsworth, *Scholiae academicae*, ch. 13 "Oriental Studies," 162–70.

15. The Old Testament in 1823 and the New Testament twice in 1816 and 1831: see Darlow, *Historical Catalogue*, numbers 8981, 8979, and 1455 respectively.

two Syriac typefaces,[16] and lived long enough to publish a newly recovered text from the Egyptian library of Dayr al-Suryan. But his recorded pupils were all students of Arabic and Hebrew, and there is nothing to show that his Syriac learning was passed on to others.[17]

The first traces of Syriac as a subject for teaching and examination at Cambridge appear in connection with Tyrwhitt's Hebrew Scholarships. These scholarships, set up from the bequest of the Reverend Robert Tyrwhitt in 1818, became the principal university prizes in the study of the Hebrew Bible. The examination was taken in May by candidates who already had the degree of BA. It was "primarily in the Hebrew Scriptures of the Old Testament [and] secondarily in such other Hebrew Works and in such exercises as the Examiners shall judge most likely to assist and advance the knowledge of the sacred Writings."[18] Printed question papers survive from 1824 on.[19] In the earliest of these, Syriac appears only in questions about variant readings and etymology; but from 1835 there appear Syriac passages for translation. (The Syriac type used to print the passage on the 1835 paper was no doubt acquired by the University Press for just this purpose.[20]) The fact that these are usually taken from the NT and occasionally nonbiblical works suggests that candidates had been assigned a special preparation in Syriac, apart from reference to the Hebrew Bible.[21]

This modest emergence of Syriac as an examination subject in 1835 needs some explanation, and probably we should seek this in the person of George Phillips (1804–92). Phillips became a tutor at Queens' College in 1831, where he convened a Hebrew class—"and ardently welcomed each new student," as one of his obituarists said. The same writer continues:

---

16. Coakley, *Typography*, 110, 114.

17. Lee's pupils are mentioned in Lee, *Scholar of a Past Generation*, 22, 24, 48, 160, 162, 217. It seems at least possible that Thomas Pell Platt (1798–1852; BA Trinity 1820, Tyrwhitt scholar 1821), Secretary of the British and Foreign Bible Society and editor of a Syriac New Testament in 1829, was also Lee's pupil at Cambridge; but I cannot verify this. Lee's prefaces to his edition and translation of the Syriac version of Eusebius on the Theophany (1842 and 1843) make his work out to be quite solitary.

18. Clark, *Endowments*, 309–14; quotation p. 312.

19. University Library, class-mark L952.b.5.1ff.

20. For this type see Coakley, *Typography*, 98–99 (W31). It must have been considered unacceptable, and another type (W36, much superior) replaced it three years later.

21. A later student's preparation for the Tyrwhitt Scholarship is described in Sinker, *Memorials*, 46. He mentions that "pieces of Syriac are also occasionally set." This anomaly was eventually addressed in 1907 by a change in the rules: "That notwithstanding the nature of these Scholarships it shall be competent for the Examiners to set simple passages for translation from Aramaic into English together with questions arising out of the same": *Reporter* (19 Feb. 1907), 577.

Beginning with the old system of the study of Hebrew, which was limited by the traditional knowledge of Jewish teachers, who were seldom familiar with the cognate languages, he soon satisfied himself that for the understanding of the language of the Old Testament the Syriac and the Arabic must be known. He worked earnestly to impress this view upon Semitic students and aided them by publishing a Syriac grammar and other works illustrative of that language.[22]

Phillips published his *Elements of Syriac Grammar* in 1837. It was indeed aimed at students of Hebrew and its introductory apology for Syriac studies is first of all for the elucidation of the OT, although the NT and Syriac literature are also mentioned as reasons for acquiring the language. There is a short "appendix" consisting of John 2 with detailed grammatical analysis by way of a chrestomathy. The need for a second edition in 1845 suggests that the book had been bought by students; and it has the kind of scattered revisions and expansions that would have been made in the course of teaching. The chrestomathy is also enlarged to include other biblical passages and selections from Bar Hebraeus. It would seem that even after Phillips became president of Queens' (after an absence as a parish priest, 1846–57), he continued to teach Syriac. A third edition, now titled *A Syriac Grammar*, was published in 1866, incidentally showing an increase in sophistication compared with the first two editions, with less emphasis on the OT and fuller grammar (notably a longer section on syntax, and on poetic meters) to serve the "riper student"—one, that is, whose interest in Syriac might have gone beyond the Bible.

THE SEMITIC LANGUAGES TRIPOS, 1871–93

Whatever Syriac teaching took place in Cambridge before 1871 was in the colleges, and has left only the indirect evidence that we have seen. This changed with the establishment by the University of a Semitic Languages tripos. A Syndicate appointed in December 1871 "to consider the best means of promoting the study of the Oriental Languages" made the proposal; their report was approved in May 1872; and regulations for the new tripos were published in the *Reporter* in advance of the first examinations planned for 1875.[23]

The tripos consisted of seven days of examinations, morning and afternoon. The fifth and sixth days were occupied by Aramaic:

22. *Cambridge Review* (11 Feb. 1892), 192, an obituary of Phillips signed W. M. C.
23. *Reporter* (15 May 1872), 296–300.

Friday	
9 to 12	Translation into Syriac; selected books of the Syriac Versions of the New Testament.
1½ to 4½	Biblical Chaldee, and selected books of the Targums and of the Syriac Versions of the Old Testament.
Saturday	
9 to 12	Selected Syriac works.
1½ to 4½	Passages for translation into English from unspecified Syriac works.[24]

The prominent place of Syriac in the new tripos had an explanation in principle, and another explanation in terms of the Cambridge professoriate of the time. In principle, Syriac served the study of church history. The Syndicate's report stated:

> The connection of Syriac with the early Christian Literature, and the revival of its study in the present generation, to which the large addition of Syriac MSS. to the British Museum has in no slight degree contributed, would justify the position proposed for it in a Semitic examination.[25]

An introduction to the tripos written ten years later by E. H. Palmer (professor of Arabic and one of the original Syndicate) makes the connection between Semitic languages and Christian studies—specifically, to prepare for ordination—more generally:

> The Semitic Languages Tripos commends itself more particularly and obviously to the intending Divinity Student, and it is not too much to say that if only a small proportion of those who take Holy Orders were to go through the course of reading prescribed in the accompanying lists it would lay the foundation of a much wider school of Theological criticism. Seeing that it is from the University that the ranks of the Church are recruited, this is surely a consideration that should have very great weight with all who have her interests at heart.[26]

The other explanation for the advent of Syriac as an undergraduate course of studies at this time is the appointment of William Wright (1830–89)

---

24. Quoted here from *Ordinances of the University of Cambridge* (1888), 79. The scheme is unchanged from 1872, except that originally the examinations went from Wednesday to Wednesday.

25. *Reporter* (15 Nov. 1871), 57–58.

26. *Student's Guide*, 21–22.

to the Sir Thomas Adams chair of Arabic in October 1870. Wright had studied in Germany, and the perceived taint of German biblical criticism had caused him to be passed over for a chair at Oxford in 1861. But George Phillips (whose own critical views were less advanced) secured him an honorary fellowship at Queens' in 1868 while Wright was still working at the British Museum on his catalogue of Syriac manuscripts; and then he was instrumental in Wright's election to the chair of Arabic. The new tripos would also have the services of Robert Bensly (1831–93), a Tyrwhitt scholar (1857) and like Wright a former pupil of Emil Roediger in Halle, who was a lecturer in Hebrew at Gonville and Caius College and under-librarian at the University Library.

Starting in 1872–73, Wright and Bensly presided over a demanding course of studies. According to the *Reporter*, Wright taught Syriac grammar and Roediger's *Chrestomathia* throughout the year 1872–73 on Wednesdays and Fridays at 11, and Aphrahat at 12; and similar timetables are found for the following years. Bensly's classes in Caius on other set texts are mentioned in the *Reporter* in 1878–79 and then more consistently from 1883–84 on, when the *Reporter* started to publish a fuller lecture list. E. A. Wallis Budge describes the plan of study given to him by Wright in 1879:

> Certain set books in Syriac and Arabic he would read with me himself; Syriac works which were translations from the Greek were to be read with Mr. R. L. Bensly, who would help me in translating English into Syriac; and the Hebrew and Chaldee books were to be read with the Rev. W. H. Lowe, who would direct me in Hebrew composition.[27]

To say the least, neither Wright nor Bensly cultivated a reputation as a teacher. In his letters to German correspondents, Wright speaks of teaching as one of the tiresome and distracting duties of his post. For example:

> Really when I look back upon the 5 years which I have spent at Cambridge, I am woefully disappointed & vexed. In fact, I have done less for Oriental Literature during these 5 years than during any similar period in my earlier life . . . . But my time has gone in teaching and writing lectures (for which I had no previous preparation) and in attending University Syndicates and College meetings.[28]

Other letters speak of the number of hours, fifteen or more per week, spent with students mostly "mere beginners."[29] No doubt too Wright discouraged

27. Budge, *By Nile and Tigris*, 1:56.
28. Wright to H. Fleischer, 23 Dec. 1877: Maier, *Semitic Studies*, 264.
29. Maier, *Semitic Studies*, 287, 302; and similarly in other unpublished letters in

students who he thought were not fully committed to the subject. Nor, perhaps, should we leave out of account Wright's view of Syriac literature as unattractive, which may have kept some pupils away.[30] But Wright's language to his correspondents was surely no more than what research-minded scholars typically say to their colleagues; and Budge makes clear his devotion to students who did persist.

> He carefully explained to me that there was still time for me to abandon Semitic Languages, because, as he said, the man who took them up to gain a living by them was a fool, but, of course, if I persisted in my foolish idea, he was there to help me, and he would do so.... He expected his pupils to follow his example, and for those who did he could never do enough. He spared neither time nor pains in teaching me to work at Syriac, Arabic, and Ethiopic.[31]

Wright's evidently favorite pupil, Ion Keith-Falconer, likewise appears in a number of his letters, latterly with dismay when he decided to leave his Cambridge post for the mission field.[32] Bensly's few publications, editions of biblical and parabiblical texts, have an esoteric quality unlikely to have inspired many students. Wright thought him "a thoroughly sound man in Syriac"[33] but "horribly slow."[34] But if not charismatic, he did his duty by his students. Budge recalls that with Bensly he translated most of *Pilgrim's Progress* into Syriac as an exercise for the Syriac composition paper of the tripos.[35]

Under Wright and Bensly it is accordingly not surprising that the Semitic Languages tripos had few takers. Class-lists between 1875 and 1894 yield a total of twenty-four names, most years showing a single name or none. However, perhaps half these names are of future scholars, and seven

Prof. Maier's files. I thank him for sharing this information with me.

30. For Wright's well-known verdict on Syriac literature, see his *Short History*, 1. Before coming to Cambridge Wright had, it seems, the curious view that intending students of Syriac were likely to be careerists: "You must understand that *Syriac*, having a closer connection with *Biblical* studies than Arabic, pays better and attracts more notice to a man in this country—and after all, *one must live*" (Wright to M. J. de Goeje, 15 Jan. 1866: Maier, *Semitic Studies*, 53).

31. Budge, *By Nile and Tigris*, 1:55, 56.

32. Maier, *Semitic Studies*, 331, 335.

33. That Bensly had an "exhaustive knowledge of Syriac literature" (C. Bendall, *Dictionary of National Biography* [supplement volume, 1909], 171) would hardly be inferred from his published work, but might be from his collection of books acquired after his death for the University Library (and kept together in class Bensly).

34. Maier, *Semitic Studies*, 301. Cf. Soskice, *Sisters of Sinai*, 175. Mrs. Lewis and Mrs. Gibson did not find him easy (pp. 156 etc.).

35. Budge, *By Nile and Tigris*, 1:60.

of them are men whose later careers in teaching or research were connected with Syriac: I. Keith-Falconer (1880, Tyrwhitt scholar 1879); E. A. Wallis Budge (1882); R. H. Kennett (1886, Tyrwhitt scholar 1887); A. A. Bevan (1887, Tyrwhitt scholar 1888); Norman McLean (1890, Tyrwhitt scholar 1891); George Margoliouth (1890, Tyrwhitt scholar 1891); and S. A. Cook (1894, Tyrwhitt scholar 1895). F. C. Burkitt (Tyrwhitt scholar 1889) did not take the tripos but has to be added to this list as a pupil of Bensly.[36] The same is probably true for W. E. Barnes (Tyrwhitt scholar 1882), who edited Bensly's *The Fourth Book of Maccabees and Kindred Documents in Syriac* (1895).[37]

The Syriac texts set by the examiners for the Saturday morning paper (that is, texts other than the Bible) were wide-ranging, and included many that were newly edited at the time.[38] The texts set for 1874 were taken from Aphrahat (Wright's edition of 1869), Edessan martyr acts, Jacob of Serug on Habib the martyr, *Book of the Laws of Countries*, and John of Ephesus. In subsequent years, Aphrahat was always assigned, only the particular selection of *Demonstrations* changing. Other texts came and went, and down to 1893 they included parts of the following works: Bar Hebraeus's *Chronicon Syriacum*, the *Doctrina Addai* (Phillips's edition of 1876), the *Chronicle of Joshua the Stylite* (Martin's edition, but then Wright's from 1888), the *Acts of Thomas* (Wright's edition of 1871), *memre* on the Blessed Virgin Mary by Jacob of Serug, *memre* on solitaries by Ephrem, the *Julian Romance*, the *Carmina Nisibena* of Ephrem, and Eusebius on the Theophany.

LECTURERS IN ARAMAIC, 1893–2001

Wright died, at age fifty-nine, in 1889. Bensly, assisted by R. H. Kennett, took over the teaching of Syriac for the tripos until Bensly's own early death four years later in 1893. In the same year, a University lectureship was

---

36. Francis, *In Memoriam*, 6. According to J. F. Bethune-Baker, Burkitt was a member of Wright's "seminar" ("Frances Crawford Burkitt," 450); but this statement has to be understood broadly: there is nothing else to show that Wright presided over a seminar (as Burkitt later did). Burkitt was an examiner for the Oriental Languages tripos in 1901–1902, but that was his last contact with it, as far as I can tell. Although preeminent among Cambridge Syriac scholars in his day, Burkitt was never exactly a "teacher of Syriac" and will not be mentioned again here.

37. Barnes, *Fourth Book of Maccabees*, viii, says, "I had not the privilege of knowing Professor Bensly for a long time, but it was long enough to have felt his kindness and helpfulness."

38. Names of set texts are taken here and later in this article from lists published annually in the *Reporter*.

created "in order to provide for the teaching of Aramaic." It was the holders of this lectureship, and later other lecturers "in Aramaic," who carried on the teaching of Syriac to undergraduates. The history of the tripos under these *epigonoi* is hardly eventful, and the number taking the Aramaic papers in the Oriental Languages tripos (into which the Semitic Languages tripos was folded after 1893[39]) was rarely more than one a year and usually less.

The first holder of the lectureship in Aramaic was Robert H. Kennett, who had been sharing the teaching of set texts already before 1893 with Bensly and A. A. Bevan.[40] Kennett edited Bensly's *Epistles of S. Clement to the Corinthians in Syriac* (1899); but otherwise, "successful and ever-stimulating teacher" as he was,[41] his publications and research interests were in the Hebrew OT; and, once he became Regius Professor of Hebrew in 1903, he never taught Syriac again.

Kennett's successor in that year was Norman McLean (1865–1947), then a lecturer in Hebrew at Christ's College. McLean was one of Wright's last pupils, and he had edited his *History of Syriac Literature* (1894) and *Ecclesiastical History of Eusebius in Syriac* (1898); but these were his last publications in the field. McLean's work in the background was as one of the editors of the larger Cambridge Septuagint. He also became Master of Christ's in 1927 while still the University lecturer in Aramaic. McLean held the lectureship for twenty-eight years in all, retiring in 1931.

At McLean's retirement, the lectureship lost some of its definition, being no longer treated like an endowed position. The Faculty did continue to have lecturers "in Aramaic,"[42] although for the next four years, the teaching of Syriac, or at least classes on the set texts, were the business of Fred Shipley Marsh (Tyrwhitt scholar 1907), a fellow of Selwyn College who did not then have a university appointment.[43] In the meantime, a new lecturer

---

39. The name was changed to Oriental Studies in 1958. The division of the tripos into parts 1 and 2, in which Aramaic became a "half-subject" usually paired with Hebrew, dates from 1920. Other more or less technical changes to the regulations of the tripos can be followed in the University ordinances (see the successive editions, annual since 1949, of *Statutes and Ordinances of the University of Cambridge*), but will not be recorded here.

40. Bevan is listed in the *Reporter* as teaching classes on the *Carmina Nisibena* 1892–98, after which he became Professor of Arabic and did not teach Syriac again.

41. Cook, "Kennett."

42. Including Stanley A. Cook, 1926–32 (before he became Regius Professor of Hebrew). I cannot make out whether Cook ever taught Syriac or, more probably, only Jewish Aramaic.

43. Marsh became Lady Margaret's Professor of Divinity in 1935 and moved away from Syriac studies. His papers in the archives of Selwyn College contain his teaching notes on the set texts and on passages for translation in the tripos. Others of his papers

in Aramaic came in 1933. This was Alan Edward Goodman. Goodman was a graduate of the tripos (1st. cl. 1927) and Tyrwhitt scholar (1928) who had gone on to ordination and a curacy in London. After sharing the teaching with Marsh for two years, he took it over in 1935 and was the sole teacher of Syriac for almost forty years. (There was no Aramaic teaching between 1943 and 1946 during his war service.) Goodman was not what Kennett and McLean had been, specialists in other subjects for whom Syriac was a second string; but neither did he have a college post, and he combined his lectureship with parish duties during much of his tenure of it (1940–43 and 1950–63).[44] Goodman's few publications were all related to the David Jenks collection of Syriac manuscripts given to Pembroke College in 1935. He compiled a detailed catalogue of these manuscripts in 1937,[45] and at the end of his career collaborated with Luise Abramowski on an edition of one of them published in 1972 as *A Nestorian Collection of Christological Texts*.

Sebastian Brock, appointed lecturer in Hebrew in 1967, had "Aramaic" added to his title in 1970, and took up the teaching of Syriac on the retirement of Goodman. Dr. Brock, whose special place in Syriac studies does not need to be described here,[46] stayed in Cambridge for only four more years, leaving in 1974 for a lectureship "in Aramaic and Syriac" at Oxford. At this point, the teaching of Syriac devolved chiefly upon John Snaith, who had been appointed lecturer in Hebrew and Aramaic in 1971. Some was also borne by the incumbent Regius Professor of Hebrew, John Emerton, until his retirement in 1995. Syriac classes appear in the lecture-list for the last time in 2000–1, the year before Mr. Snaith's retirement.

The Syriac texts set for examination in the tripos included some new ones in the early years of this period: the *Book of Governors* by Thomas of Marga, the *History of Joseph*, the story of Ahikar, *memre* of Isaac of Antioch, the *Ecclesiastical History* of Eusebius (Wright and McLean's edition), the *Life of Simeon the Stylite*, and the *Life of Rabbula*; and texts from Brockelmann's chrestomathy and Burkitt's edition of *Euphemia and the Goth*. Some reforms were made by Dr. Brock in 1972–73, notably replacing texts in old

relate to his major Syriac publication *The Book of Hierotheos* (1927).

44. Details may be seen in *Crockford's Clerical Directory*. No doubt the lecturer's salary was insufficient by itself for a married man.

45. The manuscripts were all but one transferred to the University Library. Goodman's handwritten catalogue, dated 2 Feb. 1937, is in the files of the Near and Middle Eastern Department of the Library. A summary of this catalogue is his article "The Jenks collection of Syriac Manuscripts in the University Library, Cambridge." (I hope to bring his good work to publication at last as part of a future catalogue of Syriac manuscripts in Cambridge acquired since Wright's time.)

46. See the festschrift edited by G. A Kiraz entitled *Malphono w-rabo d-malphone* (approximately "teacher and teacher of teachers").

editions with the *Odes of Solomon,* the *Martyrdom of Pusai,* prose works of Ephrem, and commentaries of Isho'dad of Merv. Such texts as Aphrahat, the *Acts of Thomas,* Ephrem's *Carmina Nisibena,* and *Joshua the Stylite* kept their canonical status.[47]

The history of the tripos, taken by itself, does not give the impression of a lively pursuit of Syriac studies at Cambridge over this long period; but among those who took at least one part of the tripos in "Hebrew and Aramaic" were many future scholars. These included H. M. J. Loewe (1904), C. W. Mitchell (1904), C. P. T. Winckworth (part 1 1920), E. C. Ratcliff (part 1 1920), T. W. Manson (1923), L. H. Titterton (1923), A. E. Goodman (1927), F. D. Coggan (1931), J. B. Segal (part 1 1934), H. St. J. Hart (part 1 1935), A. S. Eban (part 1 1937), F. C. Lindars (part 1 1943), L. R. Wickham (part 1 1957), J. V. M. Sturdy (1958), S. P. Brock (part 1 1962), M. P. Weitzman (1967), R. P. Gordon (1968), and P. J. Williams (part 1 1993).

Of course, some learning of Syriac must always have gone on outside the tripos. The story is now well known that Mrs. Lewis and Mrs. Gibson, the "Sisters of Sinai," learned Syriac from Kennett privately, since women were not in their day allowed to attend University classes.[48] Beside that special case, F. C. Burkitt and W. E. Barnes have already been mentioned. F. S. Marsh was perhaps prepared for the Tyrwhitt Scholarship by McLean, but we do not know.[49] A very few postgraduate students in more recent times should also be recorded.[50]

PROSPECTUS

In 2004, all but one of the Aramaic papers in the Oriental Studies tripos were "suspended until further notice."[51] (Paper Am 1, covering biblical and targumic Aramaic, survived briefly as part of Hebrew Studies.) This was also the year in which the General Board of the University authorized a review of the Faculty, resulting three years later in its restructuring. The review did not fail to notice the low numbers of undergraduates in some parts of the

---

47. In the 1960s and 70s, the specifications for all the triposes, including details of set texts, were published for the world in annual editions of the *Cambridge University Handbook.*

48. Soskice, *Sisters of Sinai,* 116, 207.

49. Marsh papers (n. 43 above), box 9/5 is an exercise book containing notes on grammar which give the impression of being made in a class or supervision.

50. The present author, who first learned Syriac with Sebastian Brock in 1973–74, is one. Another is Brian McNeil, whose 1978 PhD thesis was on "The Provenance of the Odes of Solomon."

51. *Reporter* (12 Jan 2004).

tripos. (Just four students had taken any part of the tripos in Hebrew and Aramaic since 1988.) One of the consequences of what was a much larger reform—including a change of name of the Faculty from Oriental Studies to Asian and Middle Eastern Studies, "FAMES"—was a new specification for the tripos. From this tripos, now in place, Syriac has entirely vanished.[52]

The disappearance of Syriac from the undergraduate curriculum at Cambridge is, of course, lamentable. Although its original justification as a useful preparation for Holy Orders probably never counted for much, the tripos provided a solid foundation for a number of academic careers over the 130 years in which Syriac was included in it. But those who know that they wish to study Syriac as part of their first degree are now, as in the past, very few; and for them there is happily still Oxford.[53] What is new, however, since 1871 is the emergence of postgraduate degree programs. The field of Syriac studies is now usually a discovery made by graduate students, whether in Late Antiquity, Bible, patristics, or philology. It is for these students that a university like Cambridge needs to make provision, if not with dedicated master's programs, then at least with language and reading classes. Unfortunately, such things are not part of the mandatory teaching for which budgets and teaching posts exist. In recent years FAMES and the Faculty of Divinity have made use of available scholars in non-established posts to teach Syriac and Syriac-related subjects to graduate students. Dr. Erica C. D. Hunter and the present author kept the subject alive in different ways from 2002 until 2013.[54] But until such time as a position in Syriac studies can be established with outside funds,[55] this endeavor will always require some resourcefulness. Anyone observing the state of affairs at the moment of this writing will notice that the needful teaching is in abeyance. Still, I feel sure that the want will be addressed, and that this article will not turn out to be an elegy for the teaching of Syriac in Cambridge.

---

52. See *Reporter* (13 Feb. 2008): "Report of the Faculty Board of Ancient and Middle Eastern Studies on a new Asian and Middle Eastern Studies Tripos." The last students under the old Oriental Studies tripos finished in 2010–11.

53. Aramaic, including Syriac, is an "additional language option" for undergraduate students in Egyptology and Ancient Near East Studies, Jewish Studies, Arabic, or Persian.

54. Dr. Hunter notably supervised four MPhil and two PhD theses on Syriac subjects.

55. A member of the Syriac, or Assyrian, community who was able to make such an endowment could do a work of abiding value to Syriac studies.

BIBLIOGRAPHY

Bendall, C. "Bensly, Robert Lubbock." In *Dictionary of National Biography*, edited by S. Lee, 22:171. London: Smith, Elder, 1909.

Bensly, R. L. *The Fourth Book of Maccabees and Kindred Documents in Syriac*. Cambridge: Cambridge University Press, 1895.

Bethune-Baker, J. F. "Francis Crawford Burkitt, 1864–1935." *Proceedings of the British Academy* 22 (1936) 445–84.

Budge, E. A. Wallis. *By Nile and Tigris: A Narrative of Journeys in Egypt and Mesopotamia on Behalf of the British Museum between the Years 1886 and 1913*. 2 vols. London: Murray, 1920.

Cambridge University Reporter. Cambridge, 1870–.

Castell, Edmund. *Lexicon heptaglotton: hebraicum, chaldaicum, syriacum, samaritanum, æthiopicum, arabicum, conjunctim; et persicum, separatim*. London: Roycroft, 1686.

Clark, John Willis. *Endowments of the University of Cambridge*. Cambridge: Cambridge University Press, 1904.

Coakley, J. F. *The Typography of Syriac*. New Castle, DE: Oak Knoll, 2006.

Cook, S. A. "Robert Hatch Kennett." *JTS* 33 (1932) 225–36.

Darlow, T. H., and H. F. Moule, compilers. *Historical Catalogue of the Printed Editions of Holy Scripture in the Library of the British and Foreign Bible Society*. 2 vols. in 4. London: Bible House, 1903–11.

Francis, H. T. *In Memoriam R. L. Bensly*. Cambridge: privately printed, 1893.

Goodman, Alan Edward. "The Jenks collection of Syriac Manuscripts in the University Library, Cambridge." *JRAS* (Oct. 1939) 581–600.

Kiraz, George A., ed. *Malphono w-Rabo d-Malphone*. Gorgias Eastern Christian Studies 3. Piscataway, NJ: Gorgias, 2008.

Lee, Anna Mary, *A Scholar of a Past Generation: A Brief Memoir of Samuel Lee*. London: Seeley, 1896.

Lively, Edward. *Annotationes in Quinque Priores ex Minoribus Prophetis*. London: George Bishop, 1587.

Lloyd, David. *Memoires of the lives, actions, sufferings & deaths of those noble, reverend and excellent personages that suffered by death, sequestration, decimation, or otherwise, for the Protestant religion* [etc.]. London: Speed et al., 1668.

Maier, Bernhard. *Semitic Studies in Victorian Britain: A Portrait of William Wright and His World through His Letters*. Arbeitsmaterialien zum Orient 26. Würzburg: Ergon, 2011.

McKenzie, D. F. *The Cambridge University Press, 1696–1712: A Bibliographical Study*. 2 vols. Cambridge: Cambridge University Press, 1966.

McNeil, Brian. "The Provenance of the Odes of Solomon." PhD diss. University of Cambridge, 1977.

Morison, Samuel Eliot. *The Founding of Harvard College*. The Tercentennial History of Harvard College and University, 1636–1936. Cambridge: Harvard University Press, 1935.

———. *Harvard College in the Seventeenth Century*. 2 vols. The Tercentennial History of Harvard College and University, 1636–1936. Cambridge: Harvard University Press, 1936.

Ockley, Simon. *Introductio ad Linguas Orientales*. Cambridge: Cambridge University Press, 1706.

Ordinances of the University of Cambridge. 1858–1948; continued by *Statues and Ordinances of the University of Cambridge*. 1949–.

Sinker, Robert. *Memorials of the Hon. Ion Keith-Falconer, M.A.* 6th ed. Cambridge: Deighton Bell, 1890.

Soskice, J. *The Sisters of Sinai: How Two Lady Adventurers Found the Hidden Gospels*. London: Chatto & Windus, 2009.

The Student's Guide to the University of Cambridge. 4th ed. part ix. Cambridge: Deighton Bell, 1882.

Todd, Henry John. *Memoirs of the Life and Writings of the Right Rev. Brian Walton*. 2 vols. London: Rivington, 1821.

Walton, Brian, ed. *Biblia Sacra Polyglotta : Complectentia Textus Originales, Hebraicum cum Pentateucho Samaritano, Chaldaicum, Græcum; Versionumque Antiquarum Samaritanæ Græcæ LXXII interp., Chaldaicæ, Syriacæ*, [etc.]. 6 vols. London: Roycroft, 1655–7.

Wordsworth, Christopher. *Scholiae Academicae: Some Account of the University Studies in the Eighteenth Century*. Cambridge: Cambridge University Press, 1877.

Wright, William, ed. *The Chronicle of Joshua the Stylite*. Cambridge: Cambridge University Press, 1882.

———. *A Short History of Syriac Literature*. London: Black, 1894.

Wright, William, and Stanley Arthur Cook, eds. *A Catalogue of the Syriac Manuscripts in the Library of the University of Cambridge*. 2 vols. Cambridge: Cambridge University Press, 1901.

Wright, W. Aldis, ed. *The Authorized Version of the English Bible 1611*. Cambridge: Cambridge University Press, 1909.

3

John Bowker and "The Jewish Background to the New Testament"

An Essay in *Wirkungsgeschichte*

—Christopher Rowland

THIS IS AN ESSAY on *Wirkungsgeschichte*, principally the history of the effects of a person, albeit in one small area of the remarkable intellectual career of John Bowker, but also of the texts, primarily Ezekiel's *merkabah* vision, on later interpreters and the way, as John Bowker puts it, "the attempt to understand the meaning of the passages (particularly the 'chariot' chapters) might lead the exegete to 'see again' the vision of the original prophet."[1] The essay begins with some scene-setting in the form of a reminiscence of the Faculty of Divinity, Cambridge in 1968–69 when I first heard John Bowker. It then examines John's early work on "The Jewish Background to the New Testament" (to quote the title of his lecture course from 1968, which I attended). In particular, out of this extraordinarily varied and mind-expanding course, there was the suggestion that Paul may have been a practitioner of *merkabah* mysticism, which made a brief appearance in those lectures in his consideration of the Dead Sea Scrolls and in particular *The Songs of the Sabbath Sacrifice*. In other words, Paul was one of those "who saw again" the vision of the prophet Ezekiel. Paul was not alone in so

---

1. Bowker, "Merkabah Visions," 158.

doing. The evidence of Revelation 4–5 shows that for John the visionary, "in the Spirit," the *merkabah* vision was central to his visionary imagination and had similar mind-blowing effects in its christological impact, as happened to Paul on the Damascus road. The essay develops in two ways. The personal impact of John Bowker's interest in early Jewish mysticism is then explored in its significance for my own intellectual development, how this informed my doctoral dissertation, and the publication of my first book about the nature of apocalypticism.

CAMBRIDGE IN 1966–1970

To understand the impact of John Bowker, we need to get some sense of Cambridge theology in the 1960s when I first met John. I hope that John will forgive this rather autobiographical reflection. I hope that it not only gives some indication of my debt to him but also the importance of his presence and work in helping to form the kind of New Testament study which is commonplace today.

New Testament in the late 1960s was dominated by Charlie Moule, the Lady Margaret Professor of Divinity from 1951 to 1976. Like the understanding of many others, my understanding of the New Testament was conditioned by his lectures on the Theology and Ethics of the New Testament. In an extraordinary theological exposition, three hours a week for two terms, a schedule which must have been very demanding, and would be unthinkable these days, Charlie Moule explored most facets of New Testament theology. There were nods in the direction of the Dead Sea Scrolls and other historical and background questions, but the basic interpretative framework was that formed by a previous generation of scholarship, with all its great strengths, especially familiarity with the biblical languages. It was dominated by a conservative attitude to history and the interpretative tradition, which, as I was later to discern, was very English, not least the corporate interpretation of the "one like a son of man" figure of Dan 7:13. Charlie made no bones about his aversion to apocalyptic. Indeed, his New Testament colleague and my supervisor in New Testament, John Sweet (1927–2009), gave the lectures on Revelation in Charlie's Theology and Ethics of the New Testament after 1968. I went to Charlie's lecture course in my second and third years as an undergraduate, but it was only in 1967 that I heard him lecture on apocalyptic and the book of Revelation, with wisdom and insight, let it be said. The following year, he left that part of the course to John Sweet. The heart of New Testament theology was for Charlie "the corporate Christ," in which the Son of Man was the key: in so far as Charlie and I argued about anything it was about the Son of Man, where I've always dissented from his corporate interpretation and its effects on early Christianity; in due course, I became part of promoting the "apocalyptic son of man tradition" that he utterly repudiated. In retrospect, what was almost completely lacking from his lectures was any reference to the contribution of Schweitzer to the discussion of eschatology. There were things on the kingdom of God, but that pervasiveness of eschatology and apocalypticism in the New Testament was almost completely absent. I remained unaware of the Weiss–Schweitzer tradition on early Christian eschatology until much later in my academic development.

On the other hand, there was a very different kind of approach to the New Testament from Dennis Nineham, who at the time when I was an undergraduate in Cambridge was Regius Professor of Divinity in Cambridge. He was a representative of an Oxford group of New Testament scholars, referred to by Charlie Moule as "R. H. Lightfoot's boys," which included Dennis, C. F. Evans, Austin Farrer, Leslie Houlden, Michael Goulder, and John Drury. Their approach was marked by a greater historical skepticism, and an interest in redaction criticism. I came to realize that there was a Cambridge and an Oxford tradition. The former was represented by C. H. Dodd, C. F. D. Moule, T. W. Manson, C. K. Barrett, Morna Hooker, J. A. T. Robinson, G. B. Caird, and more recently by Tom Wright (the last two both from Oxford but more in line with the Dodd/Manson/Moule approach).

What Charlie also brought to his study of the New Testament was evident piety and a formidable knowledge of Greek and Latin texts. In retrospect, there was a clear contemporary theological agenda though he, and indeed many of us students, was unaware of such hermeneutical issues in the 1960s. It was very Anglican, reflecting the hegemony of Anglicanism in Oxbridge because of the 1871 University Tests Act. There were prayers before Charlie's lectures, and he always wore clerical dress. There was a tacit assumption that theologians, not exegetes, did hermeneutics, and an assumption that if only one interpreted text correctly, it would speak directly to today. John O'Neill, who was much more philosophically aware, was in this, as in so much else, an exception.

I have often wondered what John Bowker now thinks as he considers the Cambridge Theology Tripos which he did so much to renovate and to push in a direction which adequately took account of the issues of the modern world. Those familiar with the contemporary scene in the UK would not be aware of the sea change that was taking place, heralded by Religious Studies in Lancaster. In some ways, John did not appear out on a limb. Indeed, I never sensed that he has ever been opposed to traditional theology but instead has always been determined to see that the syllabus reflect contemporary questions, and it is these questions which have in their various ways driven his work over the years. As I think back to what I was taught in New Testament as an undergraduate and a graduate, I can see very clearly what was not there as I embarked on the course, even from a historical perspective. John's work on "The Jewish Background to the New Testament" was the obvious hiatus. As I look back over my notes on those lectures that he gave, there were many themes that made their appearance in later publications, such as the *JSS* article, which I will discuss below, and in the books on the *targumim*[2] and the Pharisees.[3] But there was much else, including a fascinating discussion of the Jewish background to the cultic language in the Letter to the Hebrews.

"MERKABAH" VISIONS AND THE VISIONS OF PAUL

So, John (JB) was a breath of fresh air in biblical studies in the Cambridge Divinity Faculty. The world of ancient Judaism illuminated the biblical text in ways that we had never been able to comprehend. JB's lectures were called "Background to the New Testament," but this wasn't by way of the odd illuminating reference, to show the authenticity of a NT text or to give it historical credibility. In listening to him, we were asked to really get to grips with this extraordinary textual legacy. If this essay concentrates mainly on the essay on *merkabah* speculation in Paul's visions, this should not detract from the remarkable achievement of the book on the *targumim*, the content of which reflects themes from some of his lectures. Apart from anything else, it offered a concise introduction to the world of rabbinic literature, which was indispensable not only for a young New Testament scholar. (It was published in the year that I finished my undergraduate degree.) But there was much more. Time and again over the years, I have returned to the commentary on the selected passages, not least the discussion of Gen 5:24,[4] and the extraordinary varied traditions which developed in both Judaism and Christianity on the figure of Enoch based on the enigmatic reference, "that Enoch was not, for God took him."[5] Even forty years later, this commentary remains a model of its kind, and is an extraordinary mine of information and insight. The world of ancient Jewish scriptural interpretation, its inventiveness and its legacy is set out within the form of sources which take one far and wide in the literature of ancient Judaism and Christianity.

2. Bowker, *Targums*.
3. Bowker, *Jesus and the Pharisees*.
4. E.g., in Rowland and Morray-Jones, *Mystery of God*, 33–62.
5. Bowker, *Targums*, 143–50.

There was nothing quite like this going on in a conservative Faculty. With the exception of Ernst Bammel, whose lectures were largely confined to textual criticism and the Gospel of John, and the younger William Horbury, the approach to the New Testament was largely in the context of the Bible as a whole. When Charlie Moule referred to a pseudepigraphical text like *1 Enoch*, it was to distinguish it from the New Testament and play down its value for New Testament study as being an inferior kind of theological text. The situation was different with JB. Here for the first time we were introduced to the Mishnah, to *halakah* and *haggadah* and the Aramaic *targumim*. In the midst of all of it were a couple of remarkable lectures about *merkabah* mysticism. Looking back at the notes that I kept, I clearly found it difficult to spell, not to mention understand, what JB was saying! What was much clearer, however, was JB's conviction that this phenomenon was crucial to our understanding of Paul's conversion as recorded in Acts 9, 22 and 26. The general outline offered in the lectures was eventually published as "Merkabah Visions and the Visions of Paul."[6]

Life could never be the same again for those of us who listened to those remarkable lectures. The same was true in terms of pedagogy. Those of us who were fortunate enough to be part of it had the opportunity to enjoy our first experience of seminar teaching, with project work, being introduced to concordances of the *targumim* and rabbinic texts, as we studied messianism in a collaborative venture, being taught to study these texts for ourselves. This I found daunting at first, but it empowered me in ways that I never experienced in any other part of the course. It is no surprise in the light of this that the direction of my future interests were already set. I chart the beginnings of my interest in Jewish mysticism and the New Testament to those lectures in the late 1960s when the strange world of *merkabah* mysticism, of the patriarch Enoch's rapture (Gen 5:24), and the *'aqedah*, "The Binding of Isaac," were opened to me.

In "Merkabah Visions and the Visions of Paul," we have a detailed analysis of the different versions of Eleazar ben Arak's exposition of the *merkabah* chapter of Ezekiel before his teacher Rabban Yohanan ben Zakkai. In the comparison with Paul, the bulk of the discussion focuses on the account of Saul's vision on the road to Damascus (Acts 9, 22, and 26). JB points to similar features: the journey motif; the time; the light from heaven; falling to the ground; the voice speaking—though what Saul heard made more of an impact on his life than seems to be the case in the rabbinic accounts. Paul believed he heard a voice that had to identify itself as the voice of Jesus, although it makes it possible that *initially* Paul might have expected

6. Bowker, "Merkabah Visions."

to hear the voice of an angel, and that his *first*, though rapidly changed, estimate of Jesus was as an emissary in that particular role—exactly the interpretation of the basis of Paul's position suggested by the Pharisees in Acts 23:9 ("certain scribes of the Pharisees' group stood up and contended, 'We find nothing wrong with this man. What if a spirit or an angel has spoken to him?'"). The differences as to whether the traveling companions heard the voice but saw no one (9:7), or saw the light but did not hear the voice (22:9 and probably 26:13–14) may reflect the concern in the rabbinic tradition to restrict the vision, and confine it to the adept, trance condition. On the basis of comparison, JB suggests a general similarity. The lack of reference to the *merkabah* in the testimonies about Paul is the result of the fact that Saul's occupation at the time of the vision paled into insignificance compared with the transformative effects of the vision itself. JB suggests that what may have happened is that Ezekiel 1–2 offered a coherent context for the sudden reversal of his beliefs. Ezekiel 2 took on a dramatic new meaning. JB notes that Ezek 2:1 and 3 is quoted in part in Acts 26:16. Paul in the "perfectly ordinary process of *merkabah* contemplation reflected the voice of commission to Ezekiel in Ezek 2:3. Whereas Ezekiel was told to go not to strangers but the house of Israel, Paul became convinced that it was not the Christians who were the rebellious people but the Jews who had commissioned him.[7]

There is an important section of the article in which JB points out that although visions were often regarded with suspicion, these were part of rabbinic orthodoxy, a form of "higher education," to be undertaken only by the very well trained (as stated in the Mishnah Hagigah 2:1: "the Account of the Chariot [may not be expounded] before one alone, unless he is a sage that already understands of his own knowledge"). The engagement with the *merkabah* chapter was exegetical as much as it was visionary, but

> obviously the attempt to understand the meaning of the passages (particularly the "chariot" chapters, Ezekiel 1 & 10) might lead the exegete to "see again" the vision of the original prophet: in a sense, the vision is the meaning of the passage. The "seeing again" of the vision might well arise from contemplation on the "chariot" chapters, but it did not necessarily do so on every occasion that the chapters were contemplated. . . . the answer to uncontrolled and privately inventive apocalyptic was apocalypse which arose from a total exegesis of scripture, with the part remaining a part, and not becoming an independent end in itself.[8]

---

7. Ibid., 172.
8. Ibid., 158.

But herein lies the problem posed by Paul. A passage that JB does not mention but which is a reference to that dramatic turn of events in Paul's life mentioned on three occasions in the Acts of the Apostles is Gal 1:12 (cf. 1:16, though there is an echo of 1:12 in JB's words "revelation of Jesus"). Here, Paul writes about the "apocalypse of Jesus Christ," which, Paul wrote, turned his world upside down. What Paul chooses to share with his readers about the experience is that whatever the origin of the moment when God was pleased "to reveal his son to me" (ἀποκαλύψαι τὸν υἱὸν αὐτοῦ ἐν ἐμοί [1:16]), it is of a piece with language used of prophetic calls, and indeed is the same words used at the opening of the New Testament's primary visionary and prophetic text, the book of Revelation. According to Gal 1:16, Paul now proclaims good news to strangers—the reverse of Ezekiel. There are obvious links with Isa 49:1 and Jer 1:5 in Gal 1:15. Such linking of different parts of Scripture should not surprise us in the imaginative engagement of Saul the exegete. Rightly, as already mentioned, JB goes on to comment, "in a sense, the vision is the meaning of the passage." Yes, indeed. Saul now understood that the glorious human figure seated on the throne was Jesus.[9]

The affinity of Paul's views with those ascribed to an early second-century teacher, Elisha ben Abuyah, often known in rabbinic sources by his alias, *Aher*, "an other one"—almost as if he was such a renegade that he could not be named—may reflect theological currents that affected Paul, Jesus, and John the visionary.[10] In the version of the legend about Elisha in the Babylonian *talmudim*, as one of the notorious Four who entered *pardes*, we read that Elisha (mistakenly in view of the rabbinic editors, of course) declared that there were two powers in heaven. Whether Aher is a cipher for Paul or was an actual rabbi of the late first or early second century CE, as I still believe, the rabbinic tradition manifests its enormous fear of views where a second power is given authority alongside God. These were exactly the views that were typical of the early Christians, including Paul, who on the basis of Psalm 110 ("The LORD said to my lord, Sit at my right hand") gave the exalted Christ a position of prominence and divine authority, albeit derived from God the Father (1 Cor 15:24-28; cf. Matt 22:44).

The problem posed for contemporaries by Paul, was that he seemed to have engaged in "uncontrolled and privately inventive apocalyptic" which did *not* arise from a total exegesis of Scripture, and certainly not from that which was handed down from the "fathers," with the part remaining a part, and not becoming an independent end in itself. For Paul, the part had become an end in itself, and the law of Moses and the culture in which he had

---

9. Kim, *Origin*, especially 241–53, drawing on Rowland, "Influence."
10. Hengel, *Son of God*; Chester, *Messiah*, 82–3; 393–94; Ashton, *Religion of Paul*.

been brought up took a subordinate place. The remembered stories in the early rabbinic tradition about the teachers who "went off the rails" could well have been told about Jesus, especially the Jesus of the Gospel of John, or Paul. However much Paul may have protested, as the accounts in Acts suggest that he did, the basic challenge he posed was that it was not the tradition handed down from Moses through the elders and teachers to the attested authoritative teachers which mattered but the exercise of "religious imagination" in the present understanding of "the sense of God" which was decisive. It may have authenticated that tradition, but that was the decisive move: first experience, then the tradition. It was this emphasis on visionary experience that made such an impact on me and was a catalyst for much of my subsequent work.

FROM "MERKABAH VISIONS" TO THE OPEN HEAVEN AND THE MYSTERY OF GOD

So, that article was the framework of my formation and an inspiration, but then I engaged with the work of Gershom Scholem, as a result of an essay on the Letter to the Ephesians I wrote for William Horbury for the old Cambridge Part III Tripos in New Testament. Scholem was the great pioneer student of the study of Jewish mysticism from the earliest times to the messianic mysticism of Sabbatai Sevi.[11] Scholem introduced me to the origins of the Kabbalah, but much more, to the world of claims to heavenly ascents, of the formulae needed to achieve celestial bliss, to the visions of the anthropomorphic deity seated on the throne of glory, inspired by Ezek 1:26–7, and the deity's angelic attendants, the seven heavens through which the mystic ascends to view the enthroned divinity and the qualities needed to engage in such dangerous religious activity. In a sense, I have never recovered from my discovery of Scholem! It was like having been infected with a bug, which compelled me to explore, from Jesus to William Blake and beyond! The New Testament has never seemed the same again—and never will. It was then that it became obvious that what JB had introduced me to had wider ramifications for the New Testament and Christian origins than the Acts of the Apostles: the cosmology of Ephesians and Colossians, the letter to the Hebrews, the apocalyptic world, and even the Gospel of John, where, as John Ashton has more recently put it, we find "Intimations of Apocalyptic."[12]

11. Scholem, *Major Trends*; Scholem, *Jewish Gnosticism*; Scholem, *Sabbatai Sevi*.
12. Ashton, *Understanding*, 307–29.

Ernst Bammel had insisted that I should research on Enoch, but then took a term's sabbatical leave. Thus, it transpired that during the first year of my research I was supervised by JB, whom I discovered to be a challenging supervisor who questioned Bammel's advice. I had two meetings with JB in his home in Sylvester Road, Cambridge. By the time of the end of the second session, I had immersed myself in the subject to his satisfaction. But the subject of my research had changed. JB endorsed my inkling that there was a research topic linking the NT and Jewish apocalyptic and mystical sources. So I told Ernst Bammel that I did not want to do the subject he had given me. Bammel said graciously, "You must go where the Spirit leads you." That first term of work under JB's oversight has been crucial for much of what I have worked on since. What the study of Jewish mysticism gave me was the tentative discovery of my own intellectual voice. What JB, and then Scholem's books, opened up to me was another world of thought that revolutionized my understanding of the New Testament and gave me a register to sing in and a contrapuntal melody to the main theme of Cambridge New Testament studies. It meant struggles; I was on my own, and had my own song to sing—however lonely that felt at times.

This led to my doctoral thesis, "The Influence of the First Chapter of Ezekiel on Judaism and Early Christianity" (1975).[13] JB had much to do with the choice of this subject. Discrete parts of it (a detailed commentary on *1 Enoch* 14; the beginnings of engagement with Ezek 1:26–7 and its contribution to Christology; the earliest testimonies about *merkabah* mystics among the circle of Rabban Yohanan ben Zakkai and Rabbi Akiba, (including a discussion of the story of the Four who entered *pardes*) trace their origins to papers I wrote for JB, using his synoptic methodology. Indeed, it was JB's synopsis of the accounts of Eleazar ben Arak's exposition of the *merkabah* before Rabban Yohanan ben Zakkai in the Tosefta the two Talmuds and the Mekilta of Rabbi Simeon ben Yohai that, with his permission, I included in my dissertation.

Such a history-of-religions framework helped me to explain aspects of the theology of the New Testament—particularly the importance of dreams, visions, and auditions in understanding the character of early Christianity. The pervasiveness of these elements in the New Testament, and the possible link with the major texts of the early Jewish mystical tradition, plus the first chapter of Ezekiel, formed the centre part of my doctoral research. Out of this in 1982 emerged *The Open Heaven*.[14] That book has a simple thesis, which I would summarize as follows: it challenged the notion that

13. Rowland, "Influence."
14. Rowland, *Open Heaven*.

apocalypse/apocalypticism was about the end of the world; and that the way in which the term *apocalyptic* was used could be understood by reference to the confusion between a definition of *apocalyptic*, which concentrated on the form of the Book of Revelation (revelatory) and one which concentrated on the content of Revelation (the cataclysmic events, the angelic beings, the symbolism, numerology, and a predetermined series of disasters that had to precede the new age). Such a reappraisal not only enabled a link between that which was categorized as apocalyptic and that categorized as mystical, but also questioned whether apocalyptic texts were primarily about eschatology and should rather be considered a peculiar form of theological epistemology alongside other ways of discerning the divine will.

In some examples of the interpretation of Ezekiel 1, the meaning of the text may have come about as the result of the interpreter's own creative and experiential appropriation of the text, a "seeing again" of what Ezekiel had seen. In this, the visionary's own experience of what had appeared to Ezekiel becomes itself the context for a creative interpretation of the text. I have already quoted JB's words on this: "the attempt to understand the meaning of the passages (particularly the 'chariot' chapters) might lead the exegete to 'see again' the vision of the original prophet." Hence, the "seeing again" of the vision might well arise from contemplation on the "chariot chapters," and the exegesis of its mysteries come through such visionary contemplation. There are many peculiarities, not least the meaning, as the rabbis pointed out, of the word חשמל, which makes a brief appearance in the opening chapters of Ezekiel but whose meaning is obscure. Nearly twenty years later, David Halperin could have been quoting JB when he captured this aspect of *merkabah* exegesis when he wrote: "When the apocalyptic visionary 'sees' something that looks like Ezekiel's *merkabah*, we may assume that he is seeing the *merkabah* vision as he has persuaded himself it really was, as Ezekiel would have seen it, had he been inspired wholly and not in part."[15]

The simple distinction between exegesis and visionary experience, which I presupposed when I wrote The *Open Heaven*, I now doubt. A decade or so ago, I discovered the work of Mary Carruthers on memory, rhetoric, and *ekphrasis* in the medieval period and in antiquity, which showed me how the exercise of imagination, which included the visualization in the mind of objects, has been an important part of the reading of Scripture."[16] The creative process of interaction of images in monastic practice, she suggests, may have derived both from Jewish spirituality, including meditation on the *merkabah*. The emphasis she points to upon interpreters' "pictur-

---

15. Halperin, *Faces*, 71; Stone, "Lists," 167–80.
16. Carruthers, *Craft of Thought*, 68–69; and Wolfson, *Through a Speculum*, 1994.

ing" what they recall or hear, and then using these for further thinking, is a striking and continuous feature of medieval monastic hermeneutics.[17] So, ancient readers and hearers of texts could seek to "visualize" what they read (or heard), and that seeing or listening would frequently involve the creation of mental images. "Painting in the heart" (to quote words of Jerome) the images of the scriptural texts was a way of seeing what one was reading and facilitating the process of application. Such meditative practice was the result of a sophisticated process of memorization of scriptural texts, in which, in imitation of Ezekiel's and John's "digestion" of the scroll passages (often mentioned in medieval treatises on the reading and interpretation of Scripture), the one meditating was able to recall and envision.

It was part of the exegetical culture in which I was raised to want to illuminate the Bible by being able to relate documents and individual verses to particular "parallel" texts. This was the motor behind the method I learnt. So, it mattered greatly to demonstrate that, for example, later rabbinic mystical texts reflected earlier ideas, which could have influenced the New Testament. When I wrote *The Open Heaven*, and at the start of writing *The Mystery of God*,[18] I was more interested in being able to trace genealogical relationships between ancient Jewish and Christian texts, even if, as is the case with many Jewish texts, these came from centuries later than the Christian texts. I do not want to deny the importance of this method. But now my interest has moved to a different kind of diachronic perspective, which concentrates less on antecedents and more on effects. Strangely, this has taken me back to where I started as a graduate student, when I was interested to explore how far early Christian texts were a part of the *Wirkungsgeschichte* of the *merkabah*, though I did not at that time see it in those terms! This story, as Michael Lieb has shown in *The Visionary Mode*, from the Apocalypse via Dante to Boehme and Blake is in its way also a part of the history of *merkabah* mysticism.[19]

IN CONCLUSION

Those lectures by John Bowker forty-five years ago anticipated not only so much of what has been important for me, but also opened the eyes of English-speaking scholarship to the riches of the Jewish tradition. As far as I am concerned, it has only been with the discovery of William Blake that I have been able to appreciate as fully as I would like the profundity of

---

17. Ibid., 304.
18. Rowland and Morray-Jones, *Mystery of God*.
19. Lieb, *The Visionary Mode*; Rowland, *Blake*.

JB's discussion of religious imagination. The study of Blake, linked with the historical input from Mary Carruthers on imaginative exegesis in the late medieval period, has been the cornerstone for my understanding of early Christianity—along with eschatology. JB's theological method has indirectly always been a companion for me as I discovered Marx and Freud. *The Sense of God*[20] offered a model for a theologically aware engagement with these modern masters. Understanding liberation theology, for example, would not have happened so easily, without the pioneering theological methodology in that book. JB's initial research and writing on ancient Judaism was part of a much broader contribution to the Cambridge Faculty. Without him much of the new theology and religious studies of the early 1970s, certainly in Cambridge, would have been unthinkable. All that I have done in this essay is sketch one small aspect of JB's remarkable intellectual contribution to the study of theology and religion over the last fifty years, but it is illustrative of so much more, which his other friends and colleagues outline in this tribute to a remarkable scholar.

BIBLIOGRAPHY

Ashton, John. *Understanding the Fourth Gospel*. 2nd ed. Oxford: Oxford University Press, 2007.

———. *The Religion of Paul the Apostle*. New Haven: Yale University Press, 2000.

Bowker, John, *The Targums and Rabbinic Literature: An Introduction to Jewish Interpretations of Scripture*. Cambridge: Cambridge University Press, 1969.

———. "Merkabah Visions and the Visions of Paul." *JSS* 16/2 (1971) 157–73.

———. *Jesus and the Pharisees*. Cambridge: Cambridge University Press, 1973.

———. *The Sense of God: Sociological, Anthropological, and Psychological Approaches to the Origin of the Sense of God*. 2nd ed. Oxford: Oneworld (first edition Oxford University Press, 1973), 1995.

Carruthers, Mary. *The Craft of Thought: Meditation, Rhetoric, and the Making of Images, 400–1200*. CSML 34; Cambridge: Cambridge University Press, 1998.

Chester, A. *Messiah and Exaltation: Jewish Messianic and Visionary Traditions and New Testament Christology*. WUNT 207. Tübingen: Mohr/Siebeck, 2007.

Halperin, David J. *The Faces of the Chariot: Early Jewish Responses to Ezekiel's Vision*. TSAJ 16. Tübingen: Mohr/Siebeck, 1988.

Hengel, Martin. *The Son of God: The Origin of Christology and the History of Jewish-Hellenistic Religion*. 1976. Eugene, OR: Wipf & Stock, 2007.

Kim, Seyoon. *The Origin of Paul's Gospel*. WUNT 2/4; Tübingen: Mohr/Siebeck, 1981.

Lieb, M. *The Visionary Mode: Biblical Prophecy, Hermeneutics, and Cultural Change*. Ithaca: Cornell University Press, 1991.

Rowland, Christopher. "The Influence of the First Chapter of Ezekiel on Jewish and Early Christian Literature." PhD diss., University of Cambridge, 1975.

---

20. Bowker, *Sense of God*.

———. *The Open Heaven: A Study of Apocalyptic in Judaism and Early Christianity.* London: SPCK, 1982.

Rowland, Christopher, and C. Morray-Jones. *The Mystery of God: Early Jewish Mysticism and the New Testament.* CRJNT 12. Leiden: Brill, 2009.

———. *Blake and the Bible.* London: Yale University Press, 2010.

Scholem, Gershom. *Major Trends in Jewish Mysticism.* New York: Schocken, 1955.

———. *Jewish Gnosticism, Merkabah Mysticism, and Talmudic Tradition.* New York: Jewish Theological Seminary of America, 1960.

———. *Sabbatai Sevi: The Mystical Messiah, 1626–1676.* The Littman Library of Jewish Civilization. Bollingen Series 93. London: Routledge & Kegan Paul, 1973.

Stone, Michael E. "Lists of Revealed Things in Apocalyptic Literature." In *Magnalia Dei, the Mighty Acts of God: Essays on the Bible and Archaeology in Memory of G. Ernest Wright*, edited by Frank Moore Cross et al., 414–52. Garden City, NY: Doubleday, 1976.

Wolfson, Eliot R. *Through a Speculum that Shines: Vision and Imagination in Medieval Jewish Mysticism.* Princeton: Princeton University Press, 1994.

4

Daniel & the Three (Principally in the Old Greek[1])

"Historical" Signs of the Eschatological Son of Man & Saints of the Most High God—a Paradigm for Gospels Christology and Discipleship

—EUGENE E. LEMCIO

INTRODUCTION

IN HIS BOOK *THE Religious Imagination and the Sense of God*, our Honoree addressed the sense of God in Christianity[2] in part by reiterating his thesis about "son of man." (I have retained in this instance what appears to be gender specificity because the expression has become something of a technical term in Scripture, which "human" or "mortal" obscures.) In an earlier publication,[3] John argued for the meaning of this Semitic idiom as "man

---

1. With most, I use OG and LXX interchangeably. For a recent treatment of the manuscript evidence, see Reynolds, "The 'One Like a Son of Man,'" 70–73. See nn. 24–26, below, for instances where critical texts differ.

2. Bowker, *Religious Imagination*, 139–69.

3. Bowker, "The Son of Man," 19–48.

born to die." Subsequently, he expressed it in contemporary, cosmological categories: being "subject . . . to entropy and the laws of thermodynamics as any other organic system."[4] I found myself won over by his appeal to a wide range of supporting data.[5]

However, it occurred to me that this designation could too easily be confined to the start and finish of one's life. And he had by-passed the witness of Hellenistic Judaism. Consequently, I tried making the case that the period between one's beginning and end was also covered by the term, especially its frailty and vulnerability: the downside of human existence—its being at risk.[6] Yet, our point was essentially the same: it was precisely through this fragile, grave-bound creature that God was pleased to accomplish the great work of deliverance and transformation—both in this age and in the age to come. In the end, one could speak both about the sense of God in Judaism and the sense of man (i.e., humanity) in Judaism—and in Christianity. My contribution to our thinking in this essay attempts to move the discussion forward by taking a step backward: that, according to the book of Daniel, especially in its Greek translation, Daniel and his Friends gave "historical" expression to such convictions.[7] It provided, a century or so before the Common Era, a literary-theological model, paradigm, or type for subsequent appropriation, modification, and application.

Two Earlier Attempts at Association

The inclination to attempt a connection between "son of man" and Daniel is understandable because the only two instances of the term occur in back-to-back chapters of the eponymous book: in a dream envisioned by the Seer (7:13–14) and in a visitation by Gabriel, who addresses him as such (8:17). Forty years ago, Herbert Schmid tried to associate the two texts (with some attention to the Greek). But he did so by means of a complex (and, to my mind, very vulnerable) traditio-historical argument.[8] John J. Collins found

---

4. Bowker, *A Year to Live*, 89. This makes potential suffering inherent in the term itself.

5. Such evidence provided additional support for an interpretation going back at least five centuries. See Burkett, *Son of Man Debate*, 14–17.

6. Conveyed in the Old Greek (OG) of Daniel as well: Lemcio, "'Son of Man,'" 43–60. In other words, it is not simply an equivalent of the more generic אדם or ἄνθρωπος. Kenneth Taylor, in the *LB*—his paraphrase of the ASV (1901)—gets at the idea by rendering the expression in Ezekiel as "son of dust."

7. Although not dependent upon our (admittedly contested) understanding of "son of man," aspects of the thesis defended in this essay are congenial with it.

8. Schmid, "Daniel, der Menschensohn," 192–220.

fault with this identification because the Daniel of the second passage exercises no eschatological leadership role.⁹

Herman Waetjen (who ignores the Greek translations) concluded:

> Since the designation *ben adam* refers to him as he is living in the end-time, he must also be identifiable with the *bar enash* of 7.13, regardless of the difference between the Aramaic *bar enash* of 7.13 and the [Hebrew] *ben adam* of 8.17. For both terms are bearers of the same distinguished qualities and attributes. The *bar enash* of 7.13 is given the rulership, glory, and kingdom that the Hebrew Scriptures associate with *ben adam*.¹⁰

Because such widespread dominion is not exercised by Daniel (as son of man) in 8:17, Waetjen appeals to Ps 8:4–6. However, in making this move, he leaves the terrain of the book. Rather than do this, I attempt to develop internally, in a chapter-by-chapter analysis, the implicit analogical relationship that exists between personages in an "historical" narrative concerning the nature of political sovereignty¹¹ and the *dramatis personae* envisioned in a dream full of symbols belonging to an apocalyptic myth about the future, where the same issue is at stake: who rules—really—how, and through whom?¹² Finally, I argue towards the end of this essay that the message of Daniel would not have been lost on Hellenistic Jews reading the book in Greek a century or so before the Common Era—both throughout the Diaspora and on Roman-occupied Palestinian territory.

MY PROPOSAL

I contend that the OG translator enhanced an already-existing Semitic pattern and vocabulary in a manner that more fully promoted the general conviction—expressed most explicitly and frequently in chapter 4 (see below)—that God rules human kingdoms and grants them according to the

---

9. Collins, *Commentary on Daniel*, 309.
10. Waetjen, "Millenarism," 237.
11. By *politics*, I mean a strategy for distributing power within human community.
12. Fewell, working solely with the MT, notes the ironic nature of this rise to power: *Circle of Sovereignty*, 119–36. She also contends, as I do, that a central question (if not *the* central one) is about sovereignty, especially political sovereignty. I expand the issue to include the *manner* of that rule. Whereas God's raising up the lowly is a common enough theme in Scripture, it is raising them up to new heights of *political* power that becomes a particular species of this genus. Sometimes, a reversal of fortunes takes place: first, bringing down those currently in charge—as in the "songs" of Hannah (1 Sam [=1 Kingdoms] 2:4–10) and Mary (Luke 1:52–53).

divine will, even to the unlikeliest of candidates. Both the author[13] (and especially our translator)[14] developed this theme (in narratives about Daniel and his Three Companions) within each chapter, among chapters 1–6, and between them and chapter 7 (pertaining to one like a son of man and the saints or holy ones of the Most High). Specifically, author and translator consistently incorporated most (if not all) of the following six elements and characteristic terminology—whose sequence varies: (1) a human or divine ruler [various emperors or the Ancient of Days or Most High God] (2) gives [נתן, יהב; δίδωμι] or appoints [הקם, καθίστημι] a (3) subordinate/inferior figure [variously described] (4) authoritative status [שׁלט/י, ἐξουσία], (5) glory [יקר, δόξα], and a (6) kingdom [מלכו/תא, βασιλεία]. Daniel and the Three (all prisoners of war exiled from the fallen kingdom of Judah) gain promotions after overcoming ordeals—two of them leading to a death sentence. The same pattern and vocabulary holds for one like a son of man and the saints or holy ones of the Most High.

The persistence of these similarities (reflecting a "template" or "form"?) is all the more noteworthy, given differences between chapters 1–6 and 7 in genre ("historical" narrative vs. apocalyptic vision), time (past vs. future), place (earth vs. heaven/sky), scope (local vs. global), demography (ethnic vs. international), and character (human vs. supernatural). The result is a comprehensive literary and theological integration of chapters 1–7. I do not claim, as Schmid and Waetjen have, that Daniel *is* the son-of-man figure of the vision (or that the Three *are* the saints or holy ones of the Most High of the dream). Rather, the former function as "historical" signs or models or paradigms, or even types of the latter. By narrating the local, "political" past of these four loyalists, the author (and especially the translator) enabled readers to glimpse the global, "political" future promised to God's faithful remnant. Daniel and the Three in chapters 1–6 act as a lens by which to view the eschatological outcome conveyed by the symbols of an apocalyptic myth (chapter 7). Their trials and successes in this age are a signal of their destiny in the age to come. Readers are not exhorted, "Dare to be a Daniel" (or his Friends); rather, they are to dare being "signs" of God's future in the present. Or, one might say, "The experiences of Daniel and his comrades in chapters 1–6 are the *already* of which the experiences of one like a son of man and the saints or holy ones of the Most High in chapter 7 are the *not*

---

13. For the MT, I have used Elliger and Rudolf, *Biblia Hebraica Stuttgartensia*. All English translations are from the NRSV (unless otherwise indicated).

14. Geissen, *Der Septuaginta-Text*; Rahlfs, *Septuaginta*; and Ziegler and Munnich *Susanna. Daniel. Bel et Draco*. All translations of the OG and Θ are (unless otherwise indicated) from Pietersma and Wright, *A New English Translation of the Septuagint* [NETS].

yet." These motifs were available for Jesus and his followers to adopt, adapt, and arrange according to their convictions about the Word and Deed of God in their own day.[15]

ANALYSIS

Chapter 1

Both the MT and Greek translations report that Daniel and the Three belonged to the royal family[16] and the nobility (1:3)—backgrounds that had made them, even as exiles, eligible for training and service in Nebuchadnezzar's house. Θ notes that they were (3) "from the sons of the captivity of Israel" (v. 3). This designation will identify them throughout their careers, regardless of the political heights that they scale during the reigns of four emperors and in the affairs of three empires. OG mentions (v. 10) that they were reared among (3) the "foreign born" [ἀλλογένων]. Each label indicates an absence of power, though not qualification or potential. But here the similarities end. The OG (following an alternate Semitic *Vorlage*?) makes significant additions to v. 20—the additions indicated by numbered parentheses according to the elements of the recital identified earlier. After these (3) candidates for the king's service maintain faithfulness to kosher law and being examined by none other than the king himself, (1) Nabouchodonosor (5) glorified [ἐδόξασεν] them and (2a) appointed [κατέστησεν] them as (6a) rulers [ἄρχοντας] in his (6) kingdom [ἐν τ. βασιλείᾳ]. This pattern and vocabulary will characterize their subsequent rise within the system. However, such promotions are to come at great cost: they undergo various ordeals that, in two explicit instances (chapters 3 and 6), threaten their lives.

---

15. The possibility exists that the fuller features of OG translator are not always "additions" to MT. Rather, he may be reflecting emphases that are (at least at points) present in another Semitic source available to him. Therefore, because the state of investigation into other *Vorlagen* is too contested to enable anything more than speculation about what the translator might have done with them, I shall simply acknowledge throughout that the OG may not in every instance be simply embellishing or enhancing MT. See especially Meadowcroft, *Aramaic Daniel and Greek Daniel*. Of particular significance is his examination of chapter 4 (pp. 30–56). An earlier study of this material is Pierre Grelot, "La Septante de Daniel iv," 5–23.

16. As such, each is at least a potential anointed one, a messiah-in-waiting, a christ candidate (so far as Jewish thinking and expectation is concerned). This is particularly the case as they are promoted to ever-higher positions of responsibility while in captivity, even ruling over parts of the Babylonian kingdom itself. See also n. 20 below.

Chapter 2

This is the only instance where OG adds very little to a two-part account rendered in Aramaic—the first part, ironically, with reference to the king himself. Perhaps the translator felt that the original was already full enough of the typical terminology. Daniel's interpretation of the dream about the fourfold composite statue reminds the Babylonian ruler of the time when he was (3) without his present majesty, informing the despot about the Originator of his glorious and universal reign (vv. 37–38). The (1) God of the heavens had (2) given (3) the "King of Kings" [before he was such] the (6) kingdom and the (5) glory. He had made him (6a) ruler over all humans and animals [reminiscent of the assignment given to the First Couple in Gen 1:26–28].

The second passage occurs later in the chapter when the (1) king (2a) appointed (3) Daniel—identified as "from among the sons of the captivity" (v. 25)—over the affairs of Babylon, designating him (6a) ruler of all the savants in the city for successfully revealing the dream's mysterious meaning (vv. 47–48). OG adds that he was also made (6a) leader [ἡγούμενον] of those wise men. On Daniel's petition, (1) the king (2a) appointed his (3) three Friends over the affairs of the (6) kingdom of Babylon (v. 49). (1) Nebuchadnezzar had earlier promised that his dream's (3) interpreters would be (5) glorified (v. 6).

Chapter 3

Nothing in the Aramaic corresponds to the longer text of the OG and Θ, containing as they do "The Prayer of Azarias" and "The Song of the Three" during their consignment to the fiery furnace. Only OG records their promotion by Nabouchodonosor in language that is emerging as stereotypical (30[97]): (1) the king (2a) appointed [κατέστησεν] (3) Sedrach, Misach, and Abdenago (6a) [ἄρχοντας] (2) giving [δοὺς] them (4) authority [ἐξουσίαν] over all of the region.

Chapter 4

Although Daniel himself is not the subject of elevation here, he repeatedly makes to Nebuchadnezzar the foundational point driving the pattern both before and after this chapter—the universal principle from which all of the particular "historical" and eschatological expressions of it derive: God rules human kingdoms and gives them according to the divine will—even to a despised/rejected person: vv. 14[17], 22-23 [25-26], 28[31], 34[37]. This frequency itself indicates how important the notion was to the author and translators. However, the rendering in the MT (followed by Θ) and the OG is diverse. The third of these four expressions deserves closer attention. Nowhere else is evidence for the thesis that I have been proposing more apparent, so far as the completeness of the pattern and vocabulary is concerned.

> The (6) kingdom [ἡ βασιλεία] of Babylon is being taken from you and (2) is being given [δέδοται] to another, (3) a despised/rejected man [ἐξουθενημένῳ ἀνθρώπων] in your house. See, (1) I am (2a) appointing [καθίστημι] him to your (6) kingdom [ἐπὶ τ. βασιλείας] and your (4) authority [ἐξουσίαν] and your (5) glory [δόξαν] and your luxury he (2b) will receive [παραλήψεται] until you recognize that (1) the God of heaven has (4) authority [ἐξουσίαν] over the (6) kingdom [ἐν τ. βασιλείᾳ] of men and to whomever he wishes (1) God (2) will give [δώσει] it.[17]

So thoroughgoing is the phenomenon that, for a while, the king himself became its subject. For seven years, Nabouchodonosor experienced the status of a (3) despised/rejected person (an irrational animal grazing in the field instead of a ruler feasting at the royal table). Afterwards, however, reversal occurred. In language more vivid than in Θ (vv. 32[35]–33[36]), OG reports, that an angel urged the king (in the formulaic language), to "(2) give [δός] (5) glory [δόξαν] to (1) the Highest. The (6) palace [βασίλειον] of your nation (2) is being given back [ἀποδίδοται] to you. 'In that hour, my (6) kingdom [βασιλεία] (2a) was restored [ἀποκατεστάθη] to me and my (5) glory [δόξα] (2) was given back [ἀπεδόθη] to me'." Having committed the gravest offense, Nabouchodonosor received the harshest of sentences. After expressing the most profound repentance, the king was rewarded in the most lavish manner (the latter especially evident in v. 34[37a–b]).

Chapter 5

As was the case with chapter 2, so the original of chapter 5 is already largely up-to-speed (as it were) with the pattern and vocabulary characteristic of the recital. Two mininarratives are devoted to Belshazzar's/Baltasar's feast. The first recounts (1) the king's promise to (2) grant (4) authority over half of his (6) kingdom to (3) Daniel—still regarded as belonging to the exiles of Judah (v. 10)—on learning from the queen of his reputation as a sage (vv.

---

17. Fragments of this thinking and terminology occur in the original and both translations at 4:14[17].

11–12). After Daniel successfully interprets the writing on the wall, the (1) monarch (2) gave [OG: ἔδωκεν] (3) Daniel (4) authority over a third of his (6) kingdom (v. 29).

Chapter 6

The familiar story about "Daniel in the Lions' Den" recounts the ironic twist that, at the zenith of his career and favor with Darius the Mede, the Seer nevertheless experiences its nemesis—being condemned to death in the beasts' cave because of his rivals' power play. Semitic original and both translations tell of (1) the king's attempt to (2) appoint (3) Daniel over the entirety of his (6) kingdom (vv. 1–3). Unique to OG is the use of (4) authority [ἐξουσίαν] in connection with the appointment. Furthermore, OG alone describes (1) the king (v. 1) as being "full of days [πλήρης τ. ἡμερῶν] and esteemed/glorious in old age" [ἔνδοξος ἐν γήρει]. Only this translator (or an alternative Semitic *Vorlage*?) mentions again that Darius desired (2) to appoint [καταστῆσαι] (3) Daniel (twice described, like the king, as (5) esteemed/glorious [ἔνδοξος])—perhaps because of previous promotions?—over all of his (6) kingdom [ἐπὶ πάσης τ. βασιλείας] (vv. 4–5). After Daniel's being vindicated through his ordeal, only in the OG do we read that Daniel was (finally) (2) appointed [κατεστάθη] over the (6) kingdom [ἐπὶ τ. βασιλείας] of Darius (v. 29). Thus, all six categories of the pattern appear in typical terminology being enhanced by the translator.[18]

Chapter 7:9–14

Both the author and translators of this chapter maintain these phenomena. (One is tempted to speculate that earlier expressions of them might have been driven by this chapter.) After four unnatural and destructive beasts from the sea exercise their authority [vv. 1–10], a (1) majestic Ancient of Days strips them (especially the fourth) of it [vv. 11–12]. He (2) gives (4) authority, (5) glory, and (6) kingdom to (3) one like a son of man [vv. 13–14]—a human figure of some kind whose identity is contested by scholars working with both the MT and the Greek. Whether this figure is a collective

---

18. It is tempting to suggest that in noting Darius's esteemed and glorious old age and in recounting his efforts to promote Daniel, the OG translator meant to portray in this final "historical" narrative a foretaste of the majestic Ancient of Days' elevation of one like a son of man, envisioned in the following chapter.

symbol for the saints or holy ones of the Most High,[19] or their (messianic?[20]) representative or champion,[21] or the angel Michael[22] is beside the point, so far as my thesis is concerned. What matters is that as in the earlier "historical" instances cited, a *subordinate figure* occupies category 3. So it is with this mysterious beneficiary: prior to arriving, he had been without authority. Previously, the one like a ["frail/vulnerable"?] human had lacked glory. Earlier, "he" had not possessed a kingdom. Each of these legacies is derivative; none originates with him. Even if this personage were to be regarded as a celestial being with human features, he would still have to be seen as coming from the lower ranks.[23]

At first blush, one could get the impression that OG neutralizes category 3 by appearing to upgrade him. Whereas the Aramaic, Θ, and the earliest codices of the Christian Bible (mid-fourth and fifth centuries)[24] read that one like a son of man came on the clouds of heaven *to* the Ancient of Days [עד, ἕως],[25] OG reads that he came and was present *as* [ὡς] the Ancient of Days.[26] The debate as to whether the likeness relates to his "nature" or to his having an entourage as well[27] must not become a distraction. Further, a more significant point will be missed if one narrowly focuses (as most do) on the *result* of the minidrama related by both original and translations rather than on the *process or dynamics* of it. Whatever [the] son of man's identity (and however comparable he is with the Ancient of Days), it is still

---

19. For those holding this view, see Burkett, *Son of Man Debate*, 35–37.

20. Receiving authority, glory, and a kingdom implies becoming ruler over it. Thus, there is at least an implicit messianism at work here. See also comments in n. 16 regarding 1:3, where Daniel and the Three are identified as belonging to the royal family. By this time in the story, all four will have been promoted to increasingly important positions within the realm.

21. Reynolds "The 'One Like a Son of Man,'" 77–78.

22. Collins, *Commentary on Daniel*, 10, 317–18; and Rowland, "Apocalyptic Literature," 176; and Rowland, *The Open Heaven*, 180–83.

23. Some scholars speak of this experience as [the] son of man's "vindication," in a forensic sense: he, not the beasts, was deemed to be in the right. This certainly fits with the statement that "a court sat in judgment" (7:10) However, the focus in v. 14 seems to be upon "awarding damages" to the defendant.

24. Sinaiticus, Vaticanus, and Alexandrinus are foundational to the critical reconstruction of the LXX.

25. Followed by Ziegler and Munnich, *Susanna. Daniel. Bel et Draco*, in their critical text.

26. Followed by Rahlfs in his *Septuaginta*. Reynolds fully treats the Greek traditions in "The 'One Like a Son of Man,'" 70–80.

27. Reynolds, "The 'One Like a Son of Man,'" 72–74.

the case in the OG that prior to his cloud-borne arrival,[28] the enigmatic figure had lacked authority, glory, and kingdom. The absence of these endowments thus complicates the nature of [the] son of man's similarity with the Ancient of Days in the OG. The fundamental point is this: despite the OG's enhancement, category 3 is still represented by a lesser or subordinate candidate.

So, one may conclude—on the basis of the consistency of the sixfold pattern and terminology, even into chapter 7 (or extending forwards from it?)—that Daniel has been to each of his political superiors as one like a son of man will be to the Ancient of Days. However, one could object that—unlike the eschatological son of man—the "historical" Daniel was not in any way "served" [λατρεύουσα] by "all nations, according to their posterity" [πάντα τ. ἔθνη τ. γῆς κατὰ γένη] (7:14). Nor is the vocabulary of λατρεύειν in Daniel ever applied to a human—although it is elsewhere.[29]

Nevertheless, at 2:46 is OG's unique version of the stunning account of Nabouchodonosor's attempt to offer sacrifices to Daniel in the wake of his successful interpretation of the ruler's dream about the four kingdoms. Neither the Aramaic nor Θ goes as far as the OG translator in recounting a kind of devotion ordinarily reserved for the divine. Whereas both versions, like the MT, relate that the king fell face down before the Seer and "did obeisance" to him [προσεκύνησε], OG reads κ. ἐπέταξε θυσίας κ. σπονδὰς ποιῆσαι αὐτῷ ["and ordered that sacrifices and libations be carried out to him"]. Θ has κ. μαναα κ. εὐωδίας εἶπεν σπεῖσαι αὐτῷ ["and ordered manaa [מנחה] ('grain offering') and fragrances be poured out to him"]. Surprisingly, nothing is said about the Sage's shrinking back in horror at such reverential treatment. Furthermore, this king who did obeisance [προσκυνεῖν] to Daniel is said later to rule over people of all languages, tribes, and nations (4:[37b]34. Cf. v. 21)—a point made in OG alone. Were the sovereign to be regarded as embodying the realm, may it be said that in receiving such homage, Daniel

---

28. One regularly encounters the observation that cloud conveyance is a mark of divinity or the supernatural. However, so far as the Greek is concerned, contact with a cloud is not in every case a mark of God-likeness. For example, in a passage laden with "messianic" overtones and undertones, the LXX alone at Ps 88:7 (=MT 89) reads, "Who in the clouds will be equaled to the Lord?" [τίς ἐν νεφέλαις ἰσωθήσεται τ. κυρίῳ;]. The text continues, "Who among the sons of God [angels?] will be likened to the Lord?" [τίς ὁμοιωθήσεται τ. κυρίῳ ἐν υἱοῖς θεοῦ;]. The expected answer is a negative one.

29. See 2 Suppl [=2 Chr] 35:3, where Iosias commands the Leuites to serve both God and the people. However, λατρεύειν and προσκυνεῖν are used interchangeably at Dan 3:10 and 18 in connection with τ. εἰκόνι and τ. εἰδώλῳ. At v. 95 [in Greek translations only], τ. θεῷ is the object of both verbs—as it is in 6:27 (but not in Θ).

was functioning as a "historical" sign of that which the eschatological son of man would experience?[30]

Chapter 7:15–27

This section consists of three interpretations of the original dream—each containing some or all of the terms belonging to the six categories encountered so far, and each becoming more detailed as the mystified Daniel requests additional clarification. The four beasts are said to represent four kingdoms that are to arise from the earth (v. 17), a horn (=king) of the fourth fighting against the saints or holy ones of the Most High (v. 21). However, (1) the Ancient of Days or Most High [God] (vv. 22, 25) (2) gave (vv. 22, 27) to the (3) saints or holy ones of the Most High (vv. 22, 27) (4) authority (vv. 26–27) and a (6) kingdom (vv. 18, 22, 27). Except in one significant detail, original and Greek translations largely agree. Just as some interpreters of the Aramaic regard "one like a son of man" in vv. 13–14 to be an angel (perhaps Michael?), so they view the saints or holy ones as the heavenly patrons of God's people on earth.

However, whereas such a case might be made from the Semitic, it cannot be argued from the OG because forms of αγ- in Daniel are never associated with angels. In other words, the latter per se are never modified by "holy." Instead (significantly), the adjective modifies "people" in 7:27 [λαῷ ἁγίῳ ὑψίστου], as it does elsewhere in Daniel.[31] Thus, just as the same pattern and terms have been used regarding the elevation of both Daniel and one like a son of man, so the same recital and vocabulary has been employed

30. Problematic for some might be the displacement in P[967] (the earliest witness to the OG [second–third century CE]) of chapters 5 and 6 to the end of chapter 8. This is usually regarded as an attempt by the copyist to maintain a stricter chronological sequence, since the events take place after Nabouchodonosor (during whose time Daniel had his vision) and Baltasar are deposed by Darius the Mede and Cyrus the Persian. However, two things need to be kept in mind. Because of the shift, the fulsome presence of the phenomena under examination in chapter 4 immediately abut chapter 7. The latter then becomes a kind of watershed for the six categories and their vocabulary. Chapters 5 and 6 continue to maintain in this position the six-part recital under consideration, culminating (as we saw) in Daniel's highest elevation to date. Furthermore, in this arrangement, Gabriel addresses Daniel as "son of man" in 8:17 (fallen face to the ground and needing to be raised up!) immediately after one like a son of man is empowered by the Ancient of Days in 7:13–14. So, that which appears to be a loss at one level is a gain at another.

31 Adjectival forms of the root αγ- occur four times in the OG (three in Θ) with the people of God: Ισραηλ τ. ἅγιόν σου at 3:35 [also Θ but not MT]; τ. λαοῦ τ. ἡγιασμένου at 4:19[22], but without parallels in Θ or MT; δῆμον ἅγιον at 8:24 [λαὸν in Θ]; and λαοῦ ἁγίου at 12:7 [Θ has λαοῦ ἡγιασμένου].

with regard to Daniel's Three Friends and the saints or holy ones of the Most High. While both the dynamics and the terminology appear throughout chapters 1–7 in the MT, their enhancement in the OG leads me to believe that the translator wanted to depict the past promotions—preceded by trials—of "The Babylonian Four" as a foretaste of the elevation—preceded by tests of loyalty—to be experienced by God's people and their symbol or representative in the future. Of course, establishing with precision the relationship within chapter 7 between one like a son of man and the saints or holy ones is important. But it can become too narrow a concern. More broadly, one should be obliged to identify the relationship between them and the *dramatis personae* of chapters 1–6: principally, with Daniel and the Three.

SOME IMPLICATIONS FOR GOSPELS CHRISTOLOGY & DISCIPLESHIP

Although these conclusions can stand alone, the profound influence of Daniel upon the Gospels—especially in its supply of data for son-of-man Christology and kingdom theology—obliges me to say something about the implications of this study for Christology and discipleship.

Whatever their views about the historicity of the Son of Man sayings in the Gospels, scholars acknowledge these characteristics about them at the literary level: "the Son of Man" was Jesus's favorite self-reference, he alone making use of it.[32] This is the supremely narrative term. Never part of a confession, like "Christ" and "Son of God," it is one of action, covering all aspects of Jesus's ministry: earthly authority, suffering, death, resurrection, and glorious appearance.[33] Whenever human or supernatural agents address him by one of the other categories, Jesus either suppresses them outright (e.g., Mark 3:11–12[34]) or shifts to the term "the Son of Man" (e.g., Mark 8:29, 31; 9:7, 9; 13:24, 26; 14:61). In short, since the term "the Son

---

32. My late, beloved doctoral supervisor, the Reverend Professor C. F. D. Moule, never tired of reminding all who would listen that "son of man" becomes articular (in the singular) for the first time in the Gospels, where it functions as a mild demonstrative pronoun. In effect, Jesus was saying, "If you want to know what *this* son of man ['frail human'?] is about, refer to *that* son of man ['frail human'?] in Daniel 7." For a technical discussion of the grammar, see Moule, *Idiom Book*, 111. His latest, published statement of the position appears in *Origin of Christology*, 13.

33. In the Gospels, the "coming" of the Son of Man is never explicitly a downward movement. This being the case, Jesus may be referring to the scene in Dan 7, with the "lateral" coming of the son-of-man figure to the Ancient of Days for elevation and endowment.

34. The imperfective form of the verbs indicates customary action.

of Man" does the "heavy lifting" of Gospels' Christology, getting right the significance of this reported self-designation is vital for the understanding of Jesus and those who originally followed in his train.[35] Now, it remains for me to indicate how Greek Daniel might help in the endeavor.

Which Language Shall We Borrow?

If my particular appeal to Greek Daniel for Gospels Christology and discipleship is to be justified, then the matter of language has to be taken up. More often than not, discussions about "Second Temple Judaism" exclude "Hellenistic Judaism," a category that is regularly reserved for the Greek-speaking Jewish Diaspora. Rarely does either expression embrace *Greek-speaking Judaism on Palestinian soil*. This remains largely the case despite the lip service paid to the indisputable fact that both Galilee and Judea (including Jerusalem) had been Hellenized (with varying degrees of effort and success) for three centuries before the Common Era.[36] In this essay, I want to do justice to the fact that the message of Daniel (as expressed by the thesis) would not have been lost on Hellenistic Jews reading the book in Greek a century or so before the Common Era during the Second Temple period—both throughout the Diaspora and on Roman-occupied Galilee, Judea, and Jerusalem itself.

As a result, OG Daniel 1–7 (and not exclusively chapter 7) can be taken seriously as a potential source for shaping the thought and teaching of Jesus—and for its transmission among the earliest Christians.[37] Although he argues that Jesus at least on some occasions spoke in Greek, Joseph Fitzmyer doubts that he had taught in it.[38] Since Professor Fitzmyer does not support his doubts with contrary evidence and argument, I would like to adduce some of both to suggest at least a possibility. Two of Jesus's disciples bore Greek names: Andrew and Philip (Mark 3:18 and the other three gospels).

---

35. Equivalent Christology and ethics can be discerned elsewhere in the New Testament—most vividly in passages such as Phil 2:1–11.

36. A mountain of evidence in support of this view has been marshaled by M. Hengel, chiefly through his magisterial work, *Judaism and Hellenism*. Lesser known is the author's smaller survey of the three-hundred-year gap between this and the Bar Kochba revolt (*"Hellenization" of Judaea*). Before Hengel, J. Sevenster had come to similar conclusions: *Do You Know Greek?* A. Millard took up the matter in *Reading and Writing*. For the most recent amassing of the data (including for Galilee, Judea, and Jerusalem itself), see Cotton, *Corpus Inscriptionum*.

37. I attempt to demonstrate this in Lemcio, "Son of Man's Rejection," 1–12.

38. See his short but heavily documented popular article "Did Jesus Speak Greek?," 58–63, 76–77. The latter two pages consist solely of footnote references to primary and secondary material.

Jesus's teachings, if not sometimes originally conveyed in Greek as well as in Aramaic, would soon have taken on a bilingual character, if Acts can be trusted. The Mother Church in Jerusalem was home to Jewish converts, both Aramaic- and Hebrew- as well as Greek-speaking (6:1–7).[39] So, while it is beyond the scope of this essay to attempt a historical reconstruction of Jesus's life or the transmission history of his teachings, the potential impact of Greek in general and of OG Daniel in particular cannot be ignored.

Life, (Near-) Death, and "Resurrection": of Daniel and of [the] Son of Man

Some (mainly) Anglo American interpreters have attempted to link the *experience* of suffering by the holy ones ("saints," their preferred term) of the Most High in chapter 7 with one like a son of man, whom these scholars regard as the saints' collective symbol. (He has no independent existence outside of the vision.)[40] However, the researchers who take this route (and those who criticize them for it) limit themselves to the vocabulary and dynamics of the Aramaic in this chapter alone. They point to the three explanations (vv. 15–27) about the rewarding of the saints politically because of their loyalty to the Most High, despite assaults by a horn (=king) of the fourth beast (=fourth kingdom). These are then related to the same or similar vocabulary used in the original vision for the endowment of one like a son of man with the attributes of political rule. Rewarding the saints with such a legacy in the wake of their suffering (say these scholars) is collectively symbolized by (the) son of man's receiving a virtually identical inheritance for undergoing his (implied) ordeal.[41]

Such an interpretation can be supported by the OG at 7:8c, where the oppression of the saints or holy ones by that horn of the fourth beast

---

39. The Theodotus synagogue inscription (first century CE) from The Ophel in the Old City provides dramatic evidence of reading and teaching the Law in Greek for pilgrims in the heart of Jerusalem. A photograph and edited text may be found in Frey, *Corpus Inscriptionum Judaicarum*, #1404, 332–35. The inscription is discussed in Meyers and Chancery, *Alexander to Constantine*, 208–9.

40. Burkett, *Son of Man Debate*, 35–37, 48–49.

41. Rarely is the nature of suffering discussed. What do we mean by it, precisely? Πάσχειν occurs only at 11:17 (and that only in the OG [חלה, ni.]). Does suffering necessarily involve physical (and other kinds of) pain? We need to look behind such symptoms to their causes: the loss (or absence) of control over health, wealth, security, interpersonal relations, career, the course of one's life, etc. Individuals and groups may experience [another meaning of πάσχειν] loss of control as a result of accidents, natural disasters, deliberate acts of ill will, etc.

belongs to part of the original dream as well as to its interpretation at v. 21.[42] Although Collins regards 7:8c as "clearly intrusive in the present context,"[43] I allow for the clause's having a deliberate, interpretive effect: "sandwiching" one like a son of man between two statements about the saints' suffering—thereby creating a double synonymous parallelism, fore and aft—implying that "he," as their individual representative or collective symbol, underwent it as well. In so contending, I do not suggest that the Greek rendition necessarily justifies reading Aramaic son of man as a suffering figure.

Furthermore, if the relationship between Daniel and son of man that I have proposed is sound, then the following might also be supportive of the above. Both Greek translations narrate in Bel et Draco a second set of circumstances leading to Daniel's death sentence (the first recounted by all in chapter 6). We saw that the Prophet had been regularly identified throughout the body of the work as a vulnerable member of the Jewish captivity—despite his scaling the heights of political power within the empire (1:3 [Θ], 2:25, 5:10 [5:14 Θ], 6:13 [Θ]). As in the case of the first instance, the Sage emerges in this "Addition" as the ultimate insider: "a companion of the king" [συμβιωτὴς τ. βασιλέως]. (Θ goes farther: "and was honored beyond all his friends" [κ. ἔνδοξος ὑπὲρ πάντας τ. φίλους αὐτοῦ].) Nevertheless, Daniel is still at risk: condemned yet a second time to destruction by lions (vv. 31–36)—the fate of any official who might fall into disfavor with his sovereign. But the king's favorite is in double jeopardy: not only as one who strikes at the heart of Babylonian religious and political institutions (by destroying both the idol Bel and its dragon)[44] but also as a supremely effective representative of the Other: one who was perceived as able to convert the pagan king into a Jew, thereby precipitating an additional political crisis within the realm (v. 28). The Prophet's belonging to an influential minority makes his threat a twofold one.

In all likelihood, debate about [the] son of man's suffering, if confined to the dynamics of 7:13–27, will continue to remain at an impasse. However, if the phenomena of this chapter are read within the larger context of the preceding six (and supplemented by Bel et Draco), then the thesis of Daniel's signaling in "history" the son of man's fate in the future[45] will

---

42. The language employed is similar: ἐποίει πόλημον πρὸς τ. ἁγίους and πόλημον συνιστάμενον πρὸς τ. ἁγίους, respectively.

43. Collins, *Commentary on Daniel*, 299n199.

44. In another related study, I have argued that by these acts (and by accepting the king's worship in 2:46 of the OG) Daniel is also being portrayed in the OG as an "historical" sign of the eschatological Ancient of Days or Most High God. See Lemcio, "Daniel as 'Historical' Sign."

45. Or, conversely, one might say that the son of man figure and the saints/holy ones

liberate and deepen the discussion. Furthermore, this approach will provide a broader framework from within which to discuss the nature, cause, and (perhaps) the purpose of the suffering.

The Costs (& Rewards) of Discipleship

There is something awkwardly "materialistic" in the synoptists' account of the man who had decided to keep his great possessions rather than leaving them to the poor so as to follow Jesus and receive treasure in heaven (Matt 19:16–30//Mark 10:17–31//Luke 18:18–30). Subsequently, Jesus warns his disciples about the barrier that riches place against entering the kingdom of God. In Mark's version (the fullest), Peter exclaims, "Look, we have left everything and followed you" (v. 28), to which Jesus responds,

> Truly I tell you, there is no one who has left house or brothers or sisters or mother or father or children or fields, for my sake and for the sake of the good news, who will not receive a hundredfold now in this age—houses, brothers and sisters, mothers and children, and fields, *with persecutions* [Mark alone, italics mine]—and in the age to come eternal life. But many who are first will be last, and the last will be first (vv. 29–31).

It makes one wonder if the account of Daniel and the Three provides the backdrop for approved, materialistic thinking of this sort. Just as these four did in their story, so followers of Jesus might well achieve a level of domestic and economic success in this age. However, the threat of persecution (and sometimes death) as realistic possibilities must always be taken into account as the "cost" of discipleship. Jesus's closing comment reflects the pattern of reversal that had characterized the Daniel story.

Type or Sign?

In a little-known article, J. D. M. Derrett has argued (from the MT alone) that "Luke himself saw Christ before Pilate and Herod as a parallel to Daniel and Cyrus."[46] Furthermore, he also noted that "second- and third-century

---

in chapter 7 epitomize the full experiences of Daniel and the Three in the preceding narratives. If the latter suffered, then—by implication—those for whom they are types will also have suffered.

46. Derrett, "Daniel and Salvation History," 132–37. The author cites parallels (only from the MT) between Daniel before Darius and Cyrus, and Jesus before Pilate and Herod as indications of a Daniel-as-Messiah prototype for Jesus. However, he does not work with the son of man category, which does not appear in either of the two gospel

fathers took it for granted that Daniel was a 'type' of Jesus."[47] Without denying this, I would add that, before becoming such a messianic model for the future, Daniel (and his Friends) had functioned as "historical" signs of the eschatological son of man and of the saints or holy ones of the Most High. If Daniel came to be regarded as a type of Christ by Luke and (more explicitly) in later Christianity, he had first been portrayed as a "historical" paradigm of the eschatological son of man in the book bearing his name. Even though one could fault Derrett for bypassing this intermediate step, he was correct to see Christology more broadly—in terms of type rather (or more) than title.

Furthermore, New Testament scholars have tended to be too limited in their appeal to the Aramaic of Daniel 7. Rarely, if ever, is the larger setting of chapters 1–6 brought to bear on the interpretation of chapter 7.[48] So far as I am aware, no one has suggested that the Daniel who recounts his dream about the eschatological son of man is that figure's own "historical sign"—that The Three Friends function in the same manner relative to the saints or holy ones of the Most High. Put another way, in the "historical" narrative, all four "embody" and anticipate the eschatological myth of chapter 7. The apocalyptic vision *by* Daniel epitomizes the experiences *of* Daniel and his comrades. We are provided not only with a vision recounted in a single chapter (whose individual words and phrases might be cited) but also with an extended narrative of a life (and lives) lived. Furthermore, unique is my argument that the OG highlights these motifs. If both the Semitic and Greek traditions are taken into account, then Jesus and his followers had available (at least a century preceding them) a paradigm upon which to draw in their formulation of a son-of-man Christology and to shape their convictions about the price to be paid for being a disciple during exile and occupation.[49]

---

episodes anyway.

47. Ibid., 137 and n. 15. Derrett notes (134) that, according to Josephus, "the book was immensely popular in the first century" (*Antiquities* 10.266–267).

48. E.g., the four kingdoms of chapter 4 are regularly associated with the four beasts (=kingdoms) of chapter 7; but these are limited connections between vocabulary and theme.

49. So as to avoid allowing confessional commitments to affect scholarly judgment in this instance, I (a Protestant) remind myself that for Jews who no longer knew Hebrew or Aramaic and for Christians reading their Scriptures in Greek—and later, Latin (and translations made from both)—the Prayer of Azariah and the Song of the Three; Susanna; and Bel et Draco would not have been regarded as "Additions" to Daniel. Nor would they have been judged as "Apocryphal" in the pejorative sense used by Jerome (against Augustine's majority view) and appropriated by the Reformers five centuries ago.

BIBLIOGRAPHY

Bowker, John. *The Religious Imagination and the Sense of God.* Oxford: Oxford University Press, 1978.

———. "The Son of Man." *JTS* 28 (1977) 19–48.

Burkett, Delbert. *The Son of Man Debate: A History and Evaluation.* SNTSMS 107. Cambridge: Cambridge University Press, 1999.

Collins, John J. *Daniel: A Commentary on the Book of Daniel.* Hermeneia. Minneapolis: Fortress, 1993.

Cotton, Hannah et al., eds. *Corpus Inscriptionum Judaeae/Palestinae.* Vol. 1, pt. 1, *Jerusalem*, 1–704. Berlin: de Gruyter, 2010.

Derrett, J. Duncan M. "Daniel and Salvation History." In *Studies in the New Testament.* Vol. 4, *Midrash: The Composition of the Gospels, and Discipline*, 132–38. 6 vols. Leiden: Brill, 1986.

Elliger, K., and W. Rudolph, eds. *Biblia Hebraica Stuttgartensia.* 3rd rev ed. Stuttgart: Deutsche Bibelgesellschaft, 1997.

Fewell, Danna Nolan. *Circle of Sovereignty: Plotting Politics in the Book of Daniel.* Nashville: Abingdon, 1991.

Fitzmyer, Joseph A. "Did Jesus Speak Greek?" *BAR* 18/5 (October, 1992) 58–77.

Frey, Jean-Baptiste. *Corpus Inscriptionum Judaicarum. Receuil Des Inscriptions Juives Qui Vont Du IIIe Siècle Avant Jésus-Christ Au VIIe Siècle de Notre Ère.* Vol. 2, *Asie-Afrique*. Sussidi allo studio delle antichità cristiane 3. Rome: Pontifico Instituto di Archeologica Cristiana, 1952.

Geissen, Angelo, ed. *Der Septuaginta-Text Des Buches Daniel.* 3 vols. Bonn: Habelt, 1968. http://www.uni-koeln.de/phil-fak/ifa/NRWakademie/papyrologie/PTheol2.html/.

Grelot, Pierre. "La Septante de Daniel iv et son substrat sémitique." *RB* 81 (1974) 5–23.

Hengel, Martin. *The "Hellenization" of Judaea in the First Century after Christ.* 1989. Reprinted, Eugene, OR: Wipf & Stock, 2003.

———. *Judaism and Hellenism. Studies of the Encounter in Palestine in the Early Hellenistic Period.* Philadelphia: Fortress, 1974.

Law, Timothy Michael. *When God Spoke Greek: The Septuagint and the Making of the Christian Bible.* Oxford: Oxford University Press, 2013.

Lemcio, Eugene E. "Daniel as an 'Historical' Sign of the Eschatological Ancient of Days/God Most High? *Bel et Draco* in its Eschatological Contexts: Apocalyptic (Daniel 7), Prophetic (Esaias 27:1), and Sapiential (Wisdom of Salomon 14:11–14)." In *Festschrift for Paul Livermore*, edited by J. Richard Middleton, n.p. Toronto: Clements, 2015.

———. "'Son of Man,' 'Pitiable Man,' 'Rejected Man': Equivalent Expressions in the Old Greek of Daniel." *TynBul* 56/1 (2005) 43–60.

———. "Where (More Precisely) Is It Written about the Son of Man's Rejection? Mark 9:12b—a Midrash upon Daniel 4 and 7?" *CTR* 2 (Winter 2012) 1–12.

Meadowcroft, T. J. *Aramaic Daniel and Greek Daniel: A Literary Comparison.* JSOTSup 198. Sheffield: Sheffield Academic, 1995.

Meyers, Eric. M., and Mark A. Chancery. *Archaeology of the Land of the Bible.* Vol. 3, *Alexander to Constantine.* ABRL. New Haven: Yale University Press, 2012.

Millard, Alan R. *Reading and Writing in the Time of Jesus.* New York: New York University Press, 2000.

Moule, C. F. D. *An Idiom Book of New Testament Greek.* 2nd ed. Cambridge: Cambridge University Press, 1963.

———. *The Origin of Christology.* Cambridge: Cambridge University Press, 1977.

Pietersma, Albert, and Benjamin E. Wright, eds. *The New English Translation of the Septuagint.* Oxford: Oxford University Press, 2007.

Rahlfs, Alfred, ed. *Septuaginta.* 7th ed. Stuttgart: Württembergische Bibelanstalt, 1962.

Reynolds, Benjamin. "The 'One Like a Son of Man' according to the Old Greek of Daniel 7,13–14." *Bib* 89 (2000) 70–80.

Rowland, Christopher. "Apocalyptic Literature." In *It Is Written: Scripture Citing Scripture; Essays in Honour of Barnabas Lindars, SSF,* edited by D. A. Carson and H. G. M. Williamson, 170–89. Cambridge: Cambridge University Press, 1988.

———. *The Open Heaven: A Study of Apocalyptic in Judaism and Early Christianity.* New York: Crossroad, 1982.

Schmid, Herbert. "Daniel, der Menschensohn." *Jud* 27 (1971) 192–220.

Sevenster, Jan Nicolaas. *Do You Know Greek? How Much Greek Could the First Jewish Christians Have Known?* VTSup 19. Leiden: Brill, 1968.

Waetjen, Herman C. "Millenarism, God's Reign, and Daniel as the Bar-Enosh." In *To Break Every Yoke: Essays in Honor of Marvin L. Chaney,* edited by Robert B. Coote and Norman K. Gottwald, 236–61. SWBA, 2nd ser., 3. Sheffield: Phoenix, 2007.

Ziegler, Joseph et al., eds. *Susanna. Daniel. Bel et Draco.* 2nd ed. Septuaginta: Vetus Testamentum Graecum 16/2. Göttingen: Vandenhoeck & Ruprecht, 1999.

5

A Pilgrimage of Grace
The Journey Motif in Luke-Acts

—Martin Forward

John Bowker was an inspirational figure to me when I was a young seminarian and then a part-time graduate student, trying to make sense of God in the religiously plural settings of England and India in the 1970s. I was fascinated by his willingness and eagerness to relate issues in the new discipline of religious studies to the interrogations of the natural and social sciences, and found my Christian faith tested yet strengthened by his masterly survey of the extraordinarily powerful insights of religions and ideologies into the meanings of human suffering. I was much taken by his engagement with sacred scriptures, especially his interpretations of the parable of the Sower, and of the concept of intercession in the Qur'an. One of the things I most admired about him was his willingness to be a jack-of-all-trades for the sake of truth, yet I was also amazed by the breadth of his learning: this Jack seems to be master of all he surveys!

Before I became John's student, I had encountered his wife Margaret's work. As an undergraduate reading History at Manchester University, I had written a dissertation on John Longland, Bishop of Lincoln under Henry VIII and the king's confessor, and was indebted to her work on early Tudor England, and even corresponded with her about it. So it was a delight, when from 1995 to 2001, I was on the staff of the Cambridge Theological

FORWARD—A Pilgrimage of Grace   63

Federation, and got to know her, and to have some of my students benefit from her remarkable gifts as a spiritual director.

I learned from John that God isn't contained within our own academic specialties; rather, God expects us to look outwards at the wider world of truth rather than obsessing with our own narrow concerns and specialties. So, in a spirit of academic filial piety, I propose to look, for the sake of truth, at an area far outside my scholarly comfort zone. Long years ago, I moved my eyes away from books and manuscripts about the ups and downs and ins and outs of Islamic modernism in British India and turned them instead to gaze upon the Gospel of Luke and what it can teach us about being a follower of Jesus in a world of many faiths. In much older age, I return to that gospel to record my further reflections. I cannot begin to match John's wide-ranging knowledge of many subjects. I can, however, offer a magpie mind that likes to play around with shiny things and finds quirkiness to be a more interesting academic quality than the search for assured results.

Academic discussions about traveling in Luke have for the most part focused on the gospel's central section, the so-called travel narrative, from when Jesus set his face towards Jerusalem (9:51) to his arrival in that city in chapter 19. Some scholars attempt a chronological approach to the material,[1] but then have to explain the fact that it is almost impossible to chart a convincing map of how he got there. Indeed, Jesus's saunter through Samaria (9:52), Bethany (10:38–52), somewhere "between Samaria and Galilee" (17:11), and then Jericho (19:11) before finally reaching Jerusalem is so convoluted an itinerary that some scholars claim that the evangelist had no clear idea of the geography of the Holy Land. Other scholars offer an overtly theological interpretation of the material. Conzelmann, for example, pointed out Jesus's gradual awareness that he must suffer.[2] A third approach has been to locate the influence of particular books or literary patterns upon Luke as he shaped his travel narrative. C. F. Evans, for example, noted the influence of words and phrases from the Septuagint translation of Deuteronomy (especially chapters 1–26) upon the central section of Luke.[3] Other scholars explore and underline the importance of particular topics in the travel narrative.

One result of this long-standing scholarly discussion has been to cast doubt on Luke's ability as a historian. Almost a century ago, J. A. Robertson wrote: "There is no portion of the writings of Luke which presents a more forbidding obstacle to our acceptance of the claims of the evangelist to be an

1. E.g., Fitzmyer, *Gospel according to Luke*.
2. Conzelmann, *Theology of St. Luke*.
3. Evans, "Central Section," 37–53.

accurate and orderly historian than the section of the Third Gospel which is sometimes called 'the Travel Narrative.' It is the happy hunting ground of the detractors of the historian."[4] In fact, it would be anachronistic to assume that Luke aspired to be a historian according to modern understandings of that profession. Rather, his orderly account attempts to persuade Theophilus of the "firmness" or "certainty" (τὴν ἀσφάλειν) of the things he had been taught (1:3–4). Like many Greek historians since Herodotus and Thucydides, Luke was interested in the meaning of things, and would tell his orderly account in such a way as to convey truth.

This eavesdropper on debates about the travel narrative of Luke's Gospel wonders why more has not been made of the fact that Luke and Acts are full of journeys, which are hardly confined to the Gospel's central section. It is understandable why this should be so. All of the gospels record travels, but Luke's intention to record an orderly account of Jesus's life as an itinerant preacher and healer who traveled about to tell his message of God's kingdom, and then of the spread of the Good News from Jerusalem to Damascus, Antioch and eventually to Rome, was bound to involve him telling travel narratives. As he puts it, "You will be my witnesses in Jerusalem, in all Judea and Samaria, and to the ends of the earth" (Acts 1:8). Luke tells of travels, because his story demands that he does.

But there is more to Luke's emphasis upon journeys than the obvious point that he was describing a movement that began in a far-flung corner of the Roman Empire and very soon reached its capital city. Indeed, the very fact that he tells it the way he does shows how his usage of the journey motif is redolent with sacred meaning. The gospel starts in Jerusalem, the center of Jewish religion, with Zechariah praying in the Temple, and it ends there, with the disciples returning to the city after the ascension of Jesus, where they were continually in the Temple, praising God. This gospel for the Gentiles, by emphasizing the central importance of Jerusalem and especially the Temple, recognizes that the story of salvation is from the Jews. When Jesus sets his face towards Jerusalem and takes the best part of ten chapters to get there, this is surely Luke's powerful, dramatic way of having Jesus journey towards a place that focuses human understandings and aspirations about the significance of holiness and true religion, but also illustrates human failures to live out of and share divine grace.

In Luke's second volume, the Good News moves, not towards Jerusalem, but outwards from it, and ends with his hero Paul in Rome, awaiting the outcome of his appeal to Caesar. It is difficult to believe that Luke did not know how Paul's life ended; so, it is natural to speculate about why he does

---

4. Robertson, "Passion Journey," 54–55.

not record it. One reason could be that, assuming the truth of the tradition that Paul died as a result of the Neronian persecutions in the mid-60s, Luke wanted to play down imperial oppression of Christians and any suggestion that they were a group of antisocial troublemakers. But the text gives us another reason why Paul's death is not the climax of Luke's message. Acts ends rather with the mystery of the Jewish rejection of Jesus as messiah and with Paul's certainty that the Gentiles will listen to the news of God's salvation, even if Jews won't (28:28). This is, of course, a theme that Paul takes up in his own writings, especially Romans 9–11, with greater rigor if less clarity than Luke. (Luke's Paul has sometimes been presented as a different sort of person than Paul's own writings reveal, though my own reading suggests that Luke simplifies his teaching, not always helpfully, rather than completely changes it.) By the end of Luke-Acts, Jerusalem's holiness is seen to be compromised not only by its violent treatment of God's messengers (Luke 13:34–35) but also by its exclusive interpretation of holiness. The city of Rome, the imperial capital, symbolizes the fact that God's salvation reaches out beyond Jews, to include everyone.

I propose to point out some of the many examples of journeys in Luke's gospel and Acts. Then I will ask why he uses the journey motif. I will examine some of his journey stories, to ask what he is telling us through them. Finally, I will look at some of the wider implications of travels in Luke-Acts.

The Gospel of Luke's opening stories about Jesus's birth and childhood are full of journeys. Indeed, after its introductory preface to Theophilus, it begins with an angelic appearance to a man who had just made a significant journey. During the Second Temple period, the twenty-four priestly divisions served in the Jerusalem Temple on a rotation system. Priests would travel to Jerusalem from their homes elsewhere in Judea, and then return after their period of service. So, Zechariah had journeyed from his home in "a city of Judah" (1:39–40) to fulfill his priestly obligations in Jerusalem. Whilst there, he hears from an angel about the gift of a son. Shortly after, his wife Elizabeth's relative Mary likewise has an angelic visitor, also telling her of the birth of a son. She journeys to the house of Zechariah and Elizabeth to tell them of her news, and returns to her home after about three months. Jesus is born on a journey from Nazareth to Bethlehem, and shepherds travel from their fields to see the newborn child. His parents take him to Jerusalem for what Luke describes as their purification (2:22: the evangelist seems to have conflated two birth rituals: the purification of the mother, as required by Leviticus 12, and the presentation of the firstborn son, done by both parents in accord with Exodus 13). Jesus's parents journeyed to Jerusalem every year for the feast of the Passover. When Jesus was twelve years old, he went with them. After Mary and Joseph set out for home, they had to return to Jerusalem to look for him, and found him in the Temple, impressing the teachers with his understanding of religious matters (2:41–52).

The journey motif in Luke's gospel continues after Jesus begins his ministry. The parables of the Good Samaritan and the Prodigal Son, arguably the two best-known stories of Jesus, are found only in Luke's gospel; they are about journeys. The man set upon by thieves on a journey from Jerusalem to Jericho finds his true neighbor to be the despised Samaritan, not the priest and Levite from whom he could have hoped for or even expected compassion and help (10:25–37). Tellingly, the story is told to a scholar of religious law who has a long way to go in order to understand true neighborliness if the best response he can make to the parable is that "the one who showed him mercy" was a neighbor to the one who fell into the hands of the robbers. This unwillingness to use the word "Samaritan" in the context of performing a *mitzvah* reminds the reader of the angry, dismissive, and unseeing rejoinder of the elder son to his father: "this son of yours," in the parable of the Prodigal Son. In that same parable, the younger son travels far away from his father's love and then journeys back to it (15:11–32). Another story about (rather than told by) Jesus, also found only in Luke, is the resurrection account of the journey to Emmaus (24:13–35). In this exquisite story, a stranger walks with two disciples of Jesus from Jerusalem to Emmaus, a journey of about seven miles, and, when he breaks bread with them, they discover him to have been Jesus.

In Acts, the journeys continue, especially Paul's travels that plant Christian faith in various urban centers of the Roman Empire. Paul's own transformative encounter with the risen Lord, the original road-to-Damascus experience (Acts 9:1–9), happens on a journey which he had undertaken to find and arrest followers of Jesus and bring them back bound to Jerusalem. That story is preceded by the meeting of Philip and the Ethiopian eunuch (Acts 8:26–40). Philip had been told by an angel to travel along the desert road from Jerusalem to Gaza. The eunuch had made a journey to Jerusalem, to worship there, and was on his way back to Ethiopia. Paul's visit to Damascus is followed by Peter's journeys "here and there among them all" (9:32), which culminates in his initially reluctant encounter with the God-fearer Cornelius (10:1—11:18). Peter's journey from Joppa to Caesarea to see that centurion, a distance of about thirty-six miles, was also his voyage into understanding that "God shows no partiality, but that in every nation anyone who fears him and does what is right is acceptable to him" (Acts 10:34).

This by no means exhaustive list of journeying in Luke and Acts compels us to ask: why so many references to traveling, and to what end? If the reader is to search for a clue to the meaning of all these journeys, it is found in Luke's interpretative comment about Mary at the end of his stories about Jesus's birth and childhood: "and his mother kept all these things in her heart" (2:51). This is surely the Evangelist's way of telling his audience to ponder the meaning of these things. Journeys take you out of the usual and the taken for granted. They can offer opportunities to look at ordinary things in new and extraordinary ways. They can also offer new, potentially transformative experiences that open our hearts to see things differently so that we are forever changed.

The Ethiopian eunuch met Philip on the way back from the sort of travel that many religious people would call a pilgrimage: he went reverently to a holy place in order to worship God. Whilst not all travelers in Luke-Acts are intentionally worshipful, many of them are surprised, *ad ambulandum*, by an unexpected insight into the presence of God: a journey becomes, unexpectedly, a pilgrimage, an encounter with God's grace. Philip was on a journey too no less than the Ethiopian, and the reader is left to infer that he may not have expected to find a foreigner and a eunuch to be an inquirer into godly things: Luke achieves some of his best effects by his characteristic reticence and discretion (virtues much appreciated by this Englishman in exile in the United States), leaving the reader to discern truth and meaning rather than having all of it spelled out for them, just as the actors on his journeys have to do.

As an example of Luke's subtlety, we can turn to his account of the healing of the centurion's servant (7:1–10), which is somewhat different from an analogous story in Matthew (Matt 8:5–10). In both accounts, Jesus is amazed at the centurion's faith, which is his ability to recognize authority when he sees it. The centurion has the power to command any of his eighty or more soldiers to do as he tells them. He understands then that Jesus has the authority to heal, and asks him to do so.

In Matthew, the centurion comes to see Jesus. He does the talking, not the synagogue elders and his friends, and he refers to the boy twice, both times as ὁ παῖς μου, which could mean "my servant" or "my son." If we did not read this passage influenced by our knowledge of Luke's account of the centurion's servant, we would likely conclude that the centurion is distraught over his son's painful illness. In explaining to Jesus that he can recognize authority when he sees it, because of his own ability to tell soldiers and slaves what to do, the reader should not be misled into seeing the παῖς as a slave. Matthew uses a different phrase there: τῷ δούλῳ μου ("to my slave"), indicating that the centurion is not talking about his παῖς.

In Luke's account, the young man cannot be the centurion's son, because, with one telling exception, he is referred to as δοῦλος ("servant" or "slave"). The soldier sends elders of the Jews to Jesus, asking him to come and heal the slave. They inform Jesus that he loves the Jewish nation and has built a synagogue. He seems to be a God-fearer, a man rather like Cornelius in the book of Acts (10—11:18), one of a significant number of people in the Roman Empire who admired Judaism's ethical monotheism and, to some extent, allowed themselves to be influenced by it. Jesus sets off and travels a distance with the elders, until he is "not far from the house." There, they encounter some of the centurion's friends, who convey to Jesus what, in Matthew's gospel, the centurion tells him himself. The friends tell of the centurion's sense of unworthiness to have Jesus come under his roof; hence, the centurion did not presume to come to Jesus himself. Intriguingly and by contrast, the elders had told Jesus he was worthy of his help. The centurion's self-deprecation is surely a measure of his respect for a man who as an authority even greater than his own, to whom he comes as a suppliant. He knows that Jesus has only to say the word, and his servant will be healed, for he recognizes power: he is under authority himself, and has people under him to whom he can give orders in the confidence that he will be obeyed. Jesus marvels at him, turns to the crowd, and says, "I tell you, not even in Israel have I found such faith." And when those who had been sent by the centurion (therefore, not Jesus, which underlines that he and the centurion never meet) return to the house, they find the servant well.

Jesus does the traveling in Luke's story, not the soldier, because it is he who learns from the centurion's faith in him. What the centurion knew of Jesus, he had already discerned before this story begins. Given the cultural assumptions of Jesus's society and day, few Jews would expect to find such a clear-eyed, urgent understanding of divine authority in a Gentile, even if he were a God-fearer; especially, perhaps, when that Gentile was a powerful agent of empire. Jesus had not realized that he could be taken seriously by the centurion, for who he was and what he could do. Jesus's sense of wonder is not (as Matthew emphasizes) that Jews, his own coreligionists, have failed to put their faith in him. It is, rather, that a Gentile, a man feared and loathed by many Jews because of his job, can get the point with unnerving accuracy. Jesus has learned something from his encounter at one remove with the centurion. Perhaps the fact that Jesus and the centurion do not actually meet is a way of Luke's hinting to his readers that the implications of this story will become much more explicit in Acts, with its message of taking the good news of Jesus to the Gentiles.

The story may imply another learning moment for Jesus, even more difficult for some Christians to accept than Jesus's willingness to do business with a foreign soldier. Why did the centurion make a big deal out of this dying boy, his slave? For boy, or young man, he was. Luke's care and subtlety in telling a story is wonderfully illustrated by the fact that throughout his account, the boy is referred to as δοῦλος, except on the one occasion when the friends record the centurion's words; he uses παῖς. In fact, he says: ἀλλὰ εἰπὲ λόγῳ καὶ ἰαθήτω ὁ παῖς μου ("but say a word, and let my boy be healed"). Luke has earlier taken care to tell us that the dying slave is dear to the centurion (the Greek word translated "dear" is ἔντιμος and often indicates profound intimacy). In some Greek authors, the word παῖς was used to denote a boy who was the adolescent lover of an older man. Could that be the case here? We can't be sure. Nothing is said in the gospel of the precise nature of the relationship between the boy and the centurion. But, maybe it doesn't need to be. Slaves were easily replaceable. Why was this young man so important to the soldier? Was the centurion an especially nice man who took an interest in all those who worked for him? It seems unlikely. However good a master and a man he was, he was above all a soldier, used to men dying, and mostly young men dying, painfully, in battle. It seems odd that he should favor one young man out of many. Unless he loved him. Moreover, the fact that Luke pairs the narrative with the story of the healing of the widow's son, who was not just at the point of death but had actually died (7:11–17), suggests that "these two stories, then, share a common focus on the predicament of the person who faces the death of a loved one."[5] The widow may face destitution at the loss of her only son, whilst the centurion's economic status remains unchanged, but grief and love and a desolating sense of loss are about more than survival.

Would Jesus have healed the boy if he knew that he was sleeping with the enemy? Some Greeks thought it was a rite of passage for a young man to be mentored by an older man, even sexually; Romans could be even more liberated about human sexuality, though they might be taken aback by a soldier who allowed such a relationship to become too affectionate for conventional lust to be overtaken by overwhelming love and a desperate sense of impending loss. Whatever Greeks and Romans allowed and did, Jews had an aversion to any form of same-sex physical relationship. And Jesus was a Jew. He accepted most of the customs and conventions of his people. But not all of them. In particular, his attitude towards those regarded as outside the pale by polite society—women alone in public space, tax collectors, and others—was often generous and warm and knowing and understanding.

Jesus might have healed the soldier's boy because the centurion was subtly calling him out on the different sources of their authority. The centurion, ironically, as a soldier in command of many military men accustomed to violence, was tuned in to Jesus's commitment to the power of God's compassion. The centurion was, in effect, saying to Jesus: "My power is the power of Caesar's legions that dominate the world through force. Your

---

5. Carey, "Between Text and Sermon," 200.

power is the power of love, which I know to be different than my source of power. I don't believe that you'll ignore my love for the boy, nor your God's love for all that he's made." Faced with the centurion's insight, Jesus heals the boy, with no questions asked about the centurion's status as an agent of the colonial power; or even about his private life, though Jesus must have had his suspicions.

The gospels are full of irony, of conventional expectations about God's attitudes and actions overturned by the universality of his love. Luke's account of the healing of the centurion's boy is an especially astute example of how Jesus himself, as well as Luke's hearers, can be surprised by where faith is found on life's pilgrimage of grace. The centurion stays at home, having already got the point about divine grace. Elsewhere, stay-at-homes can completely miss the point, as we shall see later when we encounter the elder brother in the story of the Prodigal Son (15:11–32).

The healing of the centurion's boy and the parable of the Prodigal Son are about, *inter alia*, how people perceive (or don't) and then receive God's healing love. The story of the two disciples walking to Emmaus (24:13–35) on the day of resurrection is about that too, but is also about the resources humans have for grasping such grace. It is their day of resurrection too. They have been blind to Jesus and how God is at work in him. Jesus walks unrecognized with them, listens to their disappointment at how things had turned out, and explains to them that, as the one to redeem Israel, the Messiah had to suffer. When they reach Emmaus, they ask him to stay with them. "When he was at the table with them, he took bread, blessed and broke it, and gave it to them. Then their eyes were opened, and they recognized him; and he vanished from their sight" (24:30–31).

On this journey, the two disciples move towards a profounder knowledge (arguably towards the truth and away from false notions they had about Jesus's political aspirations to free Israel from Roman rule, which they and others had foisted upon him). They begin to come to terms with the idea of a suffering messiah, which Christians have long taken for granted, but which was a scandal to much first-century Jewish belief: "Beginning with Moses and all the prophets, he interpreted to them the things about himself in all the Scriptures" (24:27). Among the resources, then, for Christian discipleship are the Scriptures, interpreted to find their deepest meaning in the sufferings and resurrection of the Messiah. But it is when Jesus breaks bread that they finally recognize him, and this is surely Luke's way of indicating that it is in the Eucharist that Christians most clearly recognize and encounter the power of the suffering Messiah. For Jesus had, of course, broken bread and given it to disciples at the Last Supper before his arrest and crucifixion (22:19).[6]

Only one of the two disciples who walked with Jesus is named: Cleopas. Is this Luke's device to draw those who heard his gospel into the story by inviting them to participate in this journey of discovery as the second disciple, rather like a Victorian novelist's appealing to his or her "Dear Reader"? If so, then we too are encouraged to walk with Jesus, to understand that he had to suffer, and to recognize the Lord in the breaking of the bread.

Another example of Luke's concern for rituals that affirm and sustain the Christian way can be found at the end of his account of the story of the meeting of Philip and the Ethiopian eunuch on the road from Jerusalem to Gaza. Just as Jesus had explained to Cleopas and the unnamed disciple that the Messiah must suffer, using the Scriptures to do so, Philip likewise counsels the eunuch. The story ends with the eunuch's asking to be baptized and, when this is done, he goes on his way rejoicing (Acts 8:26–40). An echo of the Gospel account of the walk to Emmaus in this story is surely deliberate, as is the contrast of Eucharist and Baptism. After the resurrection, as the Good News spread into the Mediterranean world and wider, the story of Jesus's suffering had the power to convert people, for which Baptism is the appropriate sacramental response.

Right after this story, Luke begins to use the word "way" (which would remind his hearers of the exodus from Egypt, when God's people wandered in the wilderness) in Acts (9:2; 16:17; 18:25, 26; 19:9, 23; 22:4; 24:14, 22) to refer to the religion of the early Christians. *Way*, of course, implies a journey, a path to be followed, with the resources that are needed for it. It would also suggest to Luke's readers that they are going "from a corruptible to an

---

6. Some scholars deny eucharistic overtones in Luke's gospel. For example, Joel Green contends that the evidence for eucharistic practice is patchy in the earliest period of the church's history, and that the point of the Emmaus story is to affirm that Jesus is alive (Green, *Gospel of Luke*, 842–43 and nn. 7–8; cf. 851 nn. 42–43). To be sure, early evidence for both eucharistic and baptismal practices is varied, reflecting the fact that they would likely have taken many different forms place to place. (Moreover, John's story of Jesus washing his disciples' feet [13:1–11] may suggest that other important ritual practices were commonly held among some early Christians, which later took a less important role in Christian life, or even died out). Nevertheless, eucharistic and baptismal practices began early among followers of Jesus. For Paul, both these practices connect the believer with the death and resurrection of Jesus (e.g., Rom 6:1–4, 1 Cor 11:23–32), and face him or her with the grave judgment of God should s/he abuse them. Characteristically, Luke's references to baptismal and eucharistic practices come in the form, not of teaching (as with Paul), but of stories. His accounts of the feeding of the five thousand (9:12–17), the Last Supper, and the road to Emmaus would have had eucharistic overtones to early Christians who heard them, just as his story of the meeting of Philip with the Ethiopian official (which will shortly be discussed) is overtly about baptism.

incorruptible crown; where no disturbance can be, no disturbance in the world."[7] This way of suffering had been prefigured in Luke's account of the transfiguration of Jesus: "Suddenly they [Peter, John and James] saw two men, Moses and Elijah, talking to him. They appeared in glory and were speaking of his departure, which he was about to accomplish at Jerusalem" (9:30–31).[8]

Luke goes back further in time than Moses in order to get across his message of God's universal care. His genealogy takes us back to Adam, the Son of God (3:38), whereas Matthew starts his with Abraham (Matt 1:1): Matthew sees Abraham and David as significant figures in the Jewish experience of God. For Luke, Abraham is a momentous person, but for rather different reasons than for Matthew. Abraham had faith in God and journeyed to a land promised to his descendants (Gen 12:1–3). In Luke's gospel, Zacchaeus begins a journey back to God in faith and repentance, so Jesus says that "he too is a son of Abraham" (19:9). In the parable of Dives and Lazarus (16:19–31), the rich man, unlike Zacchaeus, has left it too late to make such a journey, and not even father Abraham can help him make it.

Luke's teaching of the suffering Messiah in the stories of the journey to Emmaus and Philip and the Ethiopian eunuch does not have any propitiatory or expiatory element. Philip refers to Isa 53:7–8 but does not take the opportunity to quote directly vv. 4 and 5: "Surely he has borne our infirmities . . . ." This has led many New Testament theologians to fault Luke for having an inadequate doctrine of the atonement, or for not having one at all. Unsurprisingly, this widely held position has led other scholars to offer a contrary one, locating atoning or expiatory material in Luke-Acts, though these attempts mostly seem strained and far-fetched.[9] To some extent, this debate shows how many theologians, including New Testament theologians, are inadequate historians. The overwhelming influence of Paul's interpretations of the death of Jesus has persuaded many theologians (at least of the Western church) either that there is no other quality show in town (besides, perhaps, the Johannine one), or even that any other presentation of the drama of salvation is inadequate or just plain wrong.

Paul was one of Luke's heroes, but more for his zeal as an apostle to the Gentiles and as a church planter than for the intricacies of his Christology. Luke's most straightforward use of atonement language is in Acts 20:28:

---

7. The words are those of King Charles I, at his execution on January 30, 1649.

8. Philip is an Elijah-type figure, traveling the desert road, and being caught up by the Lord just at the point before Luke tells the story of Paul's Damascus-road experience. Philip could be claimed to be the forerunner of Paul, Luke's chief apostle to the Gentiles.

9. See, e.g., Carpinelli, "'Do This as My Memorial,'" 74–91.

"Keep watch over yourselves and over all the flock, of which the Holy Spirit has made you overseers, to shepherd the church of God that he obtained with the blood of his own Son." Revealingly, this verse forms part of a speech by Paul. This suggests that Luke was well able to offer a summary of Paul's theology but that he obtained his own theological effects by different means.

Ever since Hans Conzelmann argued that Luke has no clear theology of atonement,[10] scholars have offered a variety of different strategies to account for this. There has been a consensus that Luke recognizes the importance of Jesus's death but that he stresses the exalted glorified Lord Jesus more than other New Testament writers. Otherwise, many different views have been offered about how Luke presents the death of Jesus. For example, Howard Marshall is one of those scholars who have detected a servant soteriology in Luke, finding echoes of Isa 53:11 in verses like Acts 3:14, 7:52 and 22:14.[11] It may be that, for all the important work that such scholars have done, they have missed the point of letting Luke have his own voice in making sense of the meaning of Jesus, by implicitly or sometimes explicitly favoring a particular reading of Paul's theology of Jesus's death and resurrection.

In fact, any reading of Luke's Christology as minimalist and inconsequential does not do justice to his intention or to his artistry. His theology is carefully crafted, elusive, and, despite his frustration with Jews' rejection of Jesus, for the most part inclusive. As a Gentile Christian, he was less inclined than Jewish Christians to assess Jesus by Jewish law, or by any rules and dogmas. His subtle and wide-ranging use of a journey motif encourages us, rather, to map out our lives and experiences onto the life of Jesus, whom we encounter in the sacraments and in all sorts of unexpected meetings and to unforeseen ends, and to reckon that as we learn from him, our lives may eventually achieve a kind of *imitatio Christi*. A masterly storyteller, Luke achieves his effects by a restraint that draws his audience into the Christian story, which is a pilgrimage of grace.

Let the parable of the Prodigal Son (15:11–32) make this point for me. Some scholars and pastors work hard to find elements of atonement in the story. A particularly interesting attempt was mounted by Kenneth Bailey and, at the beginning of his article, he explains why he felt it necessary to make it:

> I was stunned! It was 1958 in Jerusalem. A British scholar and churchman, Dr. Kenneth Cragg, was lecturing on the Muslim-Christian debates of the Middle Ages. He had just pointed out that the Muslim scholars of the period loved to quote the parable

---

10. Conzelmann, *Theology of St. Luke*, 200–201.
11. Marshall, *Luke: Historian & Theologian*, 173.

of the Prodigal Son as evidence against Christians. The reason was that, in the story, a son who leaves his father (God), goes into a far country, gets into trouble, decides to return home, is on his arrival welcomed, and his return is celebrated. He needs no incarnation and no atonement, no cross, and no salvation. There is no mediator between the two of them. He simply returns home and his father accepts him. Ergo: Jesus is a good Muslim.[12]

Any Muslim who reacts that the son simply returns home and the father accepts him cannot have paid close attention to the text. After all, the story hardly accords with concepts of honor prevalent in many Muslim cultures, past and present. More important, Protestant Christians, and some Catholics, have been too eager to hammer out Christian-Muslim encounters entirely on the anvil of atonement theology. If deeper resources from both religions were drawn from, especially the mystics and their witness to divine love, dialogue about this parable and other subjects might be more fruitful and less trivial.

There are a number of problems with locating atonement theology in this story. The younger son doesn't show any real signs of repentance. He comes to his senses as a penniless Jewish boy amid pigs, realizes that he has nowhere else to go except back home, and makes a realistic choice about what he must do. This theme of getting real about painful situations and working them to best advantage is common enough in Luke, and is found most shockingly in the parable of the Unjust Steward (16:1–9). Indeed, the younger son's chutzpah is crucial to the story and shows Luke's magnificent artistry in telling a tale. At the end of the story, the elder brother is, as yet, in denial about his own shameful treatment of his father, even though he was as culpable as his feckless brother in taking the property that the father divided between them, when such a division should only happen after the father's death. He stayed at home, simmering with resentment, where he learned little of importance about life and its moments of grace.

The younger brother may not have learned as much from his experiences as he could have. But his cold calculation was at least the beginning of realizing the plight he was in, and to be met upon his return by love when he had expected, at the best, only cold duty, sufferance and charity, could be his spur to deeper thinking and self-evaluation. If the younger son is the flighty teenager, the elder one is the sulky sort, refusing to greet the party guests with his father, which it was his duty to do, and jealous of the generosity shown to his brother, whom, as we have seen, he can only bring himself to call "this son of yours." He has a greater distance to go than his brother has

---

12. Bailey, "Pursuing Father," 1–4.

in understanding the need for and certainty of grace. The story ends with the implicit question, what next for them? Will they be able to respond to the father's extraordinary patience and love, and, if so, how? Luke's masterly reticence provides a far more adroit and thought-provoking culmination to the parable than if he had tied all the loose ends together and provided a happily-ever-after ending.

The father's love is costly, to be sure, as most parents with teenagers will readily see. But it is not adequately seen through the language of atonement. A better case can be made that in this story Luke is suggesting that the power of suffering love is always available on the journey of life, persuading people to change their lives and to live righteously. Tellingly, Luke has Jesus say, "Whoever wants to be my disciple must deny themselves and take up their cross daily and follow me" (Luke 9:23). This verse's parallels in Mark 8:34 and Matt 16:24 omit "daily." For Luke, the cross is a symbol for everyday life, illustrating the deepest possibilities about how divine love and forgiveness constantly engage with human need. Sacrifice is exemplary rather than atoning. The cross is an extraordinary example of the power of love to persuade, not coerce. The resurrection offers us the opportunity, with Cleopas and countless others, to tread the way of grace. Such an interpretation of the suffering Messiah may lack the theological power of Paul's take, but it is also much less likely to be turned into unjust and immoral theories that, ironically, make God into a capricious, unloving and unreasonable tyrant. Luke's story about Jesus and stories by Jesus have their own power to move and change us, if we let them, on life's pilgrimage of grace.

BIBLIOGRAPHY

Bailey, Kenneth E. "The Pursuing Father." *CT* 42/12 (1998) 1–4.
Carey, Greg. "Between Text and Sermon: Luke 7:1–10." *Int* 67 (2013) 200.
Carpinelli, F. G. "'Do This as My Memorial' (Luke 22:19): Lucan Soteriology of Atonement." *CBQ* 61 (1999) 74–91.
Conzelmann, Hans. *The Theology of St. Luke*. Translated by Geoffrey Buswell. New York: Harper, 1960.
Evans, C. F. "The Central Section of St. Luke's Gospel." In *Studies in the Gospels: Essays in Memory of R. H. Lightfoot*, edited by D. E. Nineham, 37–53. Oxford: Blackwell, 1955.
Fitzmyer, Joseph A. *The Gospel according to Luke*. Vol. 2, *Luke X–XXIV*. Anchor Bible 28A. Garden City, NY: Doubleday, 1985.
Green, Joel B. *The Gospel of Luke*. NICNT. Grand Rapids: Eerdmans, 1997.
Marshall, I. Howard. *Luke: Historian & Theologian*. New Testament Profiles. Downers Grove, IL: InterVarsity, 1998.
Robertson, J. A. "The Passion Journey." *Expos* 8th ser. 17 (1919) 54–55.

Part 3

Theology

6

On Systems, Circles, and Centers
Christianity as a Christocentric "System"

—Richard Bauckham

JOHN BOWKER ON SYSTEMS AND CIRCLES

From an early stage in his long and fruitful study of religion and the religions, John Bowker has made use of information theory and systems analysis, which can be applied both to the biological world and to human culture.[1] Like many other organized structures in human society, religions

> are systems of information process. They are contexts in which information flow, and in this case primarily religious information, is intended to occur. Each religion is a system—or more often a complex of subsystems—in which fundamental resources of information are designated and are linked to goals which lives may attain (usually lives informed from those resources).[2]

Or, as he put it on another occasion, "religions are elaborately organized systems, extremely well-tested and adapted through time, for the coding,

---

1. Bowker, *Sense of God*, 86–115; Bowker, *Religious Imagination*, 4–30; Bowker, "Religions as Systems"; and frequently in later books.
2. Bowker, "Religions as Systems," 166.

protection, and transmission of the most highly valued human information."[3] Lest *information* be understood in too exclusively verbal a sense, he points out that information process does not necessarily occur in verbal forms, but may also include art, architecture, ritual, personnel, institutional structures, and so on.

The key point is that religions need to be highly organized systems if they are to preserve and to transmit the information that is believed to be of decisive, even salvific importance to human life. Information flow that is more than trivial is never left to chance:

> [I]nformation (whether verbal or non-verbal) does not slop around in the universe in a random or arbitrary manner. It is channelled and protected, coded and organized; and precisely for that reason the construction of complex organisms and highly complicated behaviour is possible. At the social and cultural level, information is not left to chance, either.[4]

Contemporary mistrust of systems as such is therefore misplaced, though it is certainly important to be on our guard against abuses of systems.[5]

A feature of systems about which Bowker has much to say, especially in his more recent work, and on which we shall focus in this essay, are boundaries. Systems must have boundaries, but contemporary suspicion of systems has a lot to do with the sense that boundaries are restrictive. When, as in the modern period, a particular religious system is no longer the context for the transmission of all the information that is important for life, then a religious system may seem to be excluding other sources of valuable information. Instead of providing a comprehensive universe of meaning, in the context of what Bowker calls "the extremely wide practice and acceptance of multiple resourcefulness,"[6] a particular religious system may seem narrow-minded, restricting understanding or even in conflict with other kinds or sources of knowledge.

Bowker frequently stresses that systems require boundaries:

> The maintenance and continuity of a system demands some sense of a boundary—some way of marking what the system is, who belongs to it and who does not, who controls it and makes

---

3. Bowker, *Is God a Virus?*, 135.
4. Bowker, "Religions as Systems," 167.
5. Ibid., 159–60.
6. Ibid., 176.

decisions within it, how the system is related to its environment (to whatever lies outside the boundary).[7]

Thus religions, as systems, must necessarily have ways of maintaining their boundaries,[8] though this may be done in a wide variety of different ways—"by ritual, creed, birth, behaviours, subscription, law, compulsion, consent."[9] Boundaries may be more or less strong:

> The boundaries can be extremely strong, resulting in high-definition systems, or they can be almost self-destructively weak, resulting in low-definition systems. A high-definition system, like Vatican Catholicism, usually regards a low-definition system, like Anglicanism, with an incomprehension amounting to contempt.... Either is viable, and they result in very different styles of life, which are subject to different kinds of threat and vulnerability.[10]

In the light of contemporary disputes in Anglicanism, we may note that this example also shows that, within a system, there can be disputes about what its boundaries should be and how strong they should be.

It is important to note, in view of the contemporary suspicion of systems that we have already noticed, that boundaries do not necessarily oppress but can be seen to

> *enable* creativity and freedom. In a strongly bounded system, where individuals know where they are and what counts as appropriate or inappropriate behaviour, they can get on with the business of living, without being preoccupied with the foundations of what they are doing. It is in this way that strongly bounded systems may produce, not only mindless conformity (which sometimes happen) but, at the other extreme, powerful and creative explorations of the implications of the system in art, music, iconography, architecture, self-sacrificing lives and the like.[11]

A religion transmits understandings and practices that its adherents regard as supremely important in life, a way of salvation, and for which, therefore, they may even be prepared to die. This is what makes the maintenance of boundaries, by which the religion's continuity of identity is ensured,

7. Ibid., 161; cf. Bowker, *Is God a Virus?*, 151, 156.
8. Bowker, *Is God a Virus?*, 140.
9. Ibid., 170. Elsewhere he also refers to the importance of Scriptures.
10. Ibid.
11. Bowker, "Religions as Systems," 182; cf. Bowker, *Sacred Neuron*, 144–45.

also of great importance. A religion with no boundaries would quickly dissolve. Boundaries, of course, mark the differences between religions, and warn us, were we tempted to doubt it, that religions really are different, as Bowker often insists.[12] A religion's boundary protects from dissolution a whole tradition, tried and tested, of attaining an ultimate goal of human life. It is not surprising that even the many subsystems of Christianity, despite greater appreciation of their commonality and much in the way of mutual enrichment, seem stubbornly unwilling to remove the boundaries. In many such cases, boundaries no longer separate, but their role of maintaining a much-valued tradition persists. A distinction, of course, must be made between maintaining a system as a tried and tested way towards the Christian goal of life and maintaining it for its own sake or for reasons extraneous to that goal.[13]

Religious boundaries doubtless have something to do with the issue of religious conflict, which has become a matter of pressing contemporary concern (as well as a reason now not infrequently given for considering all religion a bad thing). By his own testimony, John Bowker has "spent a lifetime trying to understand why it is that religious people hate each other so much, and why it is that religions are a real threat to the future of human life as we know it."[14] Bowker has no doubt (and history supplies much evidence) that religions can coexist peacefully, even in very close relationships. He maintains this is possible "provided the boundaries are reasonably secure."[15] It is when the stability of existing boundaries seems under pressure, and the identity and continuity of the religion therefore seems threatened, that the potential for both fundamentalist strategies and religious conflict arises.[16]

In one of his more recent works,[17] Bowker addresses the problem of religious conflict by way of the nature of religious systems as "closed systems," for which he uses the image of the "closed circle." It is interesting to note that in a much earlier discussion he referred to religions as "open systems," in the sense that they interact with their environment, allowing information flow across their boundaries, while also maintaining their boundaries.[18] In returning to this topic, he relates the issue to what are usually called a

---

12. E.g., Bowker, *Is God a Virus?*, 164–67.

13. Cf. Bowker, *Sacred Neuron*, 145–46.

14. Bowker, *Is God a Virus?*, 122–23. The "threat" refers to weapons of mass destruction being used for religious ends (124).

15. Ibid., 150.

16. Ibid., 175.

17. Bowker, *Sacred Neuron*, especially chapters 5–6.

18. Bowker, *Religious Imagination*, 9.

"coherence theory of truth" and a "correspondence theory of truth," but which he points out are not really theories of truth so much as of epistemic justification.[19] Every religion system justifies its beliefs and actions by the standard of coherence within the system as a whole and, especially, in religions claiming to be derived from revelation, coherence with that religion's scripture.[20] Coherence is unavoidably the major criterion, since the central claims of a religion cannot be verified empirically (by correspondence with independently accessible reality). Religions therefore seem to be inescapably "closed systems of internal coherence." They rely on coherence for justification of what they say and do, but make a disastrous error when they suppose that "justification is the same thing as absolute truth."[21] This makes them dangerous.

The criterion of coherence has to be the major one by which a religion tests and validates claims to truth. However, if religions are genuinely concerned with truth, Bowker maintains, they cannot remain completely closed circles, but must be open to the many facets of human knowledge outside their own systems.[22] An openness of religious systems to each other, as well as to other resources of knowledge and understanding, is implied, if not explicitly stated, in this argument. This is not at all to abandon the necessity of boundaries. Circles must have circumferences. The question is whether religions must be merely defensive of their circumferences or can treat them as permeable means of communication.[23] At work here is Bowker's epistemological conviction that everything we say is "provisional, corrigible and often wrong."[24] Religions cannot claim absolute truth but to be on the way to truth, which lies beyond any system. (This view, which is rooted in the apophatic tradition, should not be confused with the view that all religions are ways to the same goal, however differently they may appear to define it. Bowker strongly rejects this view in his argument against John Hick.[25])

This approach suggests that in attempting to transform relationships between and within religions from hostility to peace and truth, we need an "analysis of the kind of circle that each system or subsystem is, and the

---

19. Bowker, *Sacred Neuron*, 120–25
20. Ibid., 123, 127.
21. Ibid., 127.
22. Ibid., 130–33.
23. Ibid., 146.
24. Ibid., 126. Cf. Bowker, *Sense of God*, 112–14; *God*, 16–17, 248–51.
25. Bowker, "Christianity and Non-Christian Religions." See also Bowker, *Is God a Virus?*, ch. 17.

extent to which it will or will not move from coherence dependent on closure to the truth beyond itself."[26] What follows is a small contribution to such an analysis of the Christian tradition, made from the perspective of a New Testament scholar and Christian theologian. I deliberately begin in a difficult place.

JESUS ON DIVISION AND BOUNDARIES

For or Against?

There are two sayings of Jesus that appear to be flatly contradictory. In one case, Jesus says, "Whoever is not with me is against me" (Matt 12:30; Luke 11:23). In the other he says, "Whoever is not against us is for us" (Mark 9:40; cf. Luke 9:50). If we read these sayings in terms of boundaries, they give two rather different impressions of how Jesus distinguished between followers and outsiders. In a certain kind of interpretation of the Gospels, the difference would be explained as reflecting different early Christian communities with different attitudes to boundaries.

It is better to start with the recognition that these are proverbial sayings. Proverbs are often cast in very general terms but actually only apply in suitable contexts that users of the proverbs recognize. People who use English proverbs might cite "Too many cooks spoil the broth" in one situation, but "Many hands make light work" in another. Formally the two proverbs seem contradictory, but users of them intuitively know that each is valid only in appropriate circumstances, different in each case. The biblical book of Proverbs places side by side two proverbs that are in direct verbal contradiction, just as the two sayings of Jesus are, in order to make the point that one needs the wisdom to know how to use proverbs appropriate to different contexts (Prov 26:4–5; cf. 7, 9). Jesus, whose teaching style was that of a teacher of radical wisdom, was a master of the appropriate use of proverb-like sayings, whether of his own coining or, as probably in this case, already existing. We should read them for their rhetorical force in the kinds of contexts to which the Gospels show them to be appropriate.

In Luke 11:23, the saying "Whoever is not with me is against me, and whoever does not gather with me scatters," concludes Jesus's response to those who have accused him of casting out demons by the power of Beelzebul (11:14–23). Jesus portrays himself as engaged in a campaign against the forces of evil. His exorcisms indicate the overthrow of Satan and the coming of the kingdom of God. In this war against evil there can be no neutral

---

26. Bowker, *Sacred Neuron*, 146.

ground. To take Jesus's side is to participate in his work of gathering the lost sheep of Israel; not to take his side is to aid and abet the forces of evil in their work of scattering Israel. The proverb thus functions to challenge people to decision in a situation in which there are only two options. In this respect, it resembles Jesus's saying "You cannot serve God and Mammon" (Matt 6:24; Luke 16:13), and Elijah's demand that the people stop dithering and decide either for YHWH or for Baal (1 Kgs 18:21).

In Mark 9:40, the saying "Whoever is not against us is with us," is addressed to Jesus's disciple John. Since John, as one of the Twelve, is unequivocally on Jesus's side in his campaign against evil, the plural "us" is appropriate, by contrast with "me" in Luke 11:23 and Matt 12:30.[27] Significantly, the context again concerns exorcisms, actions in which the battle with Satan is dramatically evident and which were important for Jesus as signs of the coming of God's kingdom (Matt 12:28; Luke 11:20). John has reported that he and other disciples had come across a man performing exorcisms in the name of Jesus. They tried to stop him "because he was not following us" (Mark 9:38). John may well have thought that they were acting in line with Jesus's own demands for discipleship, but, no doubt to his surprise, Jesus does not endorse their action: "Do not stop him," says Jesus, "for no one who does a deed of power in my name will be able soon afterward to speak evil of me" (9:39). We should recall that in the Beelzebul debate, those who are on the wrong side in the struggle with evil are those who attribute Jesus's own exorcisms to the power of the devil. Here it is clear that the exorcist is not going to speak evil of Jesus in that way, since he is performing his own exorcisms by appealing to Jesus's power to cast out demons. By using Jesus's name he has put himself on Jesus's side in the struggle, just as Jesus's disciples had.

John has taken it on himself to police the boundaries of Jesus's fledgling movement. Jesus, however, is unconcerned with boundaries in this sense. In the context of struggle against evil that exorcisms represent, what matters is being on Jesus's side. In the context, the saying "Whoever is not against us is with us," cannot refer to someone who is indifferent to Jesus or has never heard of him. It does not envisage the mere neutrality that the saying in Luke 11:23 and Matt 12:30 rules out. Rather, Jesus uses the proverb here as an epigrammatic summing up of what he has said in v. 39. To be "not against" Jesus is equivalent to not speaking evil of Jesus, not taking Satan's side against Jesus and his mission to overcome evil. Someone who

---

27. In Luke 9:50, the parallel to Mark 9:40, there are several textual variants, and it is hard to tell whether "us" or "you" is original.

exorcizes in Jesus's name must be in this category, and therefore "with us," even though he has not joined the group of Jesus's followers.

In neither of these passages does Jesus have in view people outside the context of his ministry. The point is that when Jesus appears, heralding the arrival of God's kingdom and enacting God's victory over evil, there are only two options. One may attribute Jesus's power to the forces of evil, thus completely and disastrously misreading the situation. Or one may take Jesus's side, which is that of God's rule. Neutrality is not an option, given the critical nature of the situation Jesus has created by acting with the power of God's coming rule. Ignoring Jesus is not an option since his acts and his message demand a response. In this situation Jesus uses the proverb in the form "Whoever is not with me is against me" as a challenge to decision. He uses the reverse form, "Whoever is not against us is with us," to dissuade his disciples from drawing an irrelevant boundary, one that does not correspond to the distinction between the opposing battle lines drawn up by Jesus and Satan.

In neither case is Jesus in the least concerned with defining boundaries to his movement in order to maintain its identity. He is engaged in a personal mission from God that has eschatological urgency, and the only distinction that concerns him in these passages is between those who join his mission and those who oppose it.

Jesus Came to Divide

> Do not think that I have come to bring peace to the earth; I have not come to bring peace, but a sword. For I have come to set a man against his father, and a daughter against her mother, and a daughter-in-law against her mother-in-law; and one's foes will be members of one's own household. (Matt 10:34–36)

The image of the sword here has occasionally been used to support the view that Jesus intended armed revolution against Rome. But this would not fit well with the depiction of divisions within families that follows. Luke's version of the saying stresses "division" in families (Luke 12:51–53), whereas Matthew's, borrowing from Micah 7:6, speaks of enmity between family members; but the general sense is similar.

While the saying does not envisage literal warfare, it is certainly designed to shock. Like Mark 2:17b, which deploys the same rhetorical form ("I have come not to call the righteous, but sinners"), the saying defines Jesus's mission in a way that contradicts reasonable expectations. In this case. he seems to be saying that he has come with the deliberate intention of frustrating hopes of peace and setting people at odds with each other. Family relationships are instanced because it is in these that division generally causes the most grief and hurt. Of course, the saying displays Jesus's habit of pedagogic hyperbole, making one point at the expense of others that he makes elsewhere. It gives no hint of why Jesus's coming will prove so divisive, insisting merely that it undoubtedly will. But from the rest of Jesus's teaching it seems clear that what divides people so seriously is Jesus's demand for completely unreserved allegiance to himself and his mission (cf. Matt 10:37–38; Luke 12:57–62; 14:26–33). This is the form that devotion to God's will must take in the context of Jesus's coming to inaugurate God's kingdom.

The Divisive Jesus of John

These Synoptic sayings of Jesus, in which Jesus divides people into those who take his side against the forces of evil and those who oppose him, provide Synoptic parallels to the so-called dualism of the Gospel of John. This gospel makes prominent use of the theme of light and darkness, representing opposed forces, and also of the contrast between God and "the world." Recent interpretation of the Gospel of John has focused on the supposed situation of the "Johannine community" as responsible for this dualism. This community that supposedly produced the gospel is thought to have been a highly sectarian group with strong boundaries between itself and a Jewish community from which it has painfully broken.

Probably most early Christian communities were quite sharply demarcated from their social environments because their central beliefs and some of their characteristic practices were markedly distinctive. Recurrently, at least, they faced hostility from influential groups or authorities in their social and political contexts; and this is doubtless reflected in those passages of John's gospel that portray the disciples, after Jesus's departure from the world, facing opposition and violence (15:18—16:4), just as it is similarly reflected in comparable passages in the Synoptic Gospels (Matt 10:16–25; Mark 13:9–13; Luke 21:12–19).

What is really more significant is that the Gospel of John portrays Jesus as a divisive figure in much the same way as the Synoptic sayings we have discussed do, and uses its two major types of dualism (light and darkness, God and the world) to develop this. The dualisms represent the divisive effect of Jesus, who comes into the world to save it and to overcome evil, but inevitably thereby also divides it. By coming as light into the darkness of the world, Jesus creates a new situation in which people must either live in the light and walk by it, or stay in the darkness (see 3:19–21; 8:12; 12:35–36, 46). The contrast of light and darkness functions, in Rudolf Bultmann's phrase, as a "dualism of decision."[28] It puts before people the challenge of the new situation created by Jesus, making clear that in this concrete context there are only two options.

The contrast between God and "the world" (when this term is not a merely neutral term for God's creation) functions rather differently—as a "dualism of opposition." It depicts the opposition to Jesus, his mission, and his disciples that his coming provokes. In the situation in which people must be for or against, "the world" has decided against Jesus, and a protracted conflict ensues (see 8:23; 15:18–19; 16:20).[29]

Though the idiom is very different, the dynamics of decision and opposition are closely comparable with those implied by the Synoptic sayings that pose the stark alternative of being "with" Jesus or "against" him, and which represent the effect of Jesus's mission as the most painful kind of division and conflict.

Hard Questions about Hard Sayings

While the problematic nature of Johannine "dualism" has been widely discussed in recent studies, the divisive Jesus of the Synoptics is less often felt to be problematic. But in the context of our current sensitivity to issues of religious hatred and conflict, might not the Synoptic sayings we have discussed be at risk of inciting such conflict by the way they polarize Jesus and his opponents and even demonize the latter? One way of meeting this challenge would be to recall that Jesus was a teacher of radical wisdom. He frequently deploys an epigrammatic, proverb-like style of teaching that makes its point by hyperbole and stark contrasts. Sayings of this kind are more situation-specific than their words alone might suggest. They do not attempt to say everything at once, but make the point they make with such force as to appear to contradict other sayings that treat a different point with the same hard-hitting exclusivity. Knowing when such a saying applies and when a different one applies requires wisdom.

Those who take the teaching of Jesus in the Gospels seriously must therefore learn from Jesus the wisdom that applying his wisdom sayings requires. This comes from attending to the whole scope of his teaching, not

---

28. Bultmann, *Theology*, 23.

29. I have discussed the dualisms of John's gospel in Bauckham, *Gospel of Glory*, ch. 6.

ignoring the difficult or surprising sayings or those that may even seem bizarre, and not achieving hasty harmony by ignoring the sayings that challenge it. To understand how the Jesus who divides can also be the Jesus who commends reconciliation (Matt 5:23–26) and love for enemies (Matt 5:43–47; Luke 5:27–28, 32–33), and who declares the peacemakers blessed (Matt 5:9) will be to enter more fully into "the mind of Christ."

Jesus and Boundaries

Recent studies of Jesus tend to stress an "inclusive" Jesus rather than a "divisive" Jesus, and there is no doubt that the former is generally more appealing in the contemporary world. Indeed, it is clear from the Synoptic traditions that Jesus, in his practice of the kingdom of God, gave priority to people who were, in a variety of different ways, marginalized in society: the sick, the disabled, the destitute, the tax collectors, and those commonly denigrated as "sinners." By healing and forgiveness and by simply associating with such people and sharing meals with them, Jesus included them in God's coming kingdom. But this policy was controversial and itself divisive. It made some people very critical of Jesus (Matt 11:19; Luke 7:34). So, Jesus's very "inclusiveness" was a factor in obliging people to take up positions for or against him and his mission.

Jesus, of course, was not founding a religion or defining its boundaries. He understood himself to have a mission from God to God's people Israel, who were defined already by their exclusive worship of this God, YHWH, and their obedience to his law, the Torah. Jesus did not question these boundaries as such, though he took a distinctive approach in the ongoing debate about how the Torah should be interpreted and obeyed. His own movement was not a religion or even a new sect within Judaism. It was a movement for the renewal of Israel, open to the inclusion of all Israel, even as it proved divisive.

In fact, Jesus's "inclusiveness" related to the seriousness with which he took the identity of God's people Israel and his mission to include *all* Israel, especially the marginalized people, who were in danger of being excluded, in the renewed people of God. These people too were daughters and sons of Abraham (Luke 13:16; 19:9). Jesus also travelled around the geographical boundaries of the land of Israel in order to reach Jewish communities that were literally on the margins of the Jewish people in the land.

Jesus evidently accepted that the boundary between God's people and the Gentiles was, as all Jews agreed, marked by worship of YHWH alone and obedience to the Torah. Moreover, he accepted this ethnoreligious boundary as the limit of his own mission, declaring that he was sent only to "the lost sheep of the house of Israel" (Matt 15:24). But this did not mean excluding Gentiles from the kingdom of God. Jesus must have expected, as the prophets had predicted, that the renewal of Israel would lead to the conversion of the nations to the worship of YHWH. Israel had priority—for the sake of the other nations. Thus the Gospels present the few occasions on which Jesus extended his ministry to Gentiles as exceptions that anticipated a mission to the Gentiles still to come. While accepting the boundary, he treated it as permeable (Matt 8:5–13; 15:21–28; Mark 7:24–30; Luke 7:1–10).

In the longer term, as Jesus's own movement developed into the early Christian movement, it was the inclusion of Gentiles that would raise the issue of boundaries. Like Jesus's own movement, the earliest Christian movement lived within the boundaries of Judaism, evidently without question. But with Gentile converts came the question whether they too must live within Judaism's boundaries. In the event a distinction was made between exclusive worship of YHWH, to which Gentile Christians must adhere, and the Torah, which, since they were Christian *Gentiles*, not Christian *Jews*, they need not observe in its entirety.

As Christianity became a "religion,"[30] no longer a movement within the boundaries of Israel, inevitably it acquired boundaries of its own. In John Bowker's terms, it became a "system" that could not have survived, let alone flourished as it has done, without boundaries. All the same, we may not understand Christianity adequately unless we reckon with the extent to which it retains features of the movement Jesus led, partly owing to the centrality of the Gospels in Christianity. Movements of renewal and revitalization within Christianity, requiring radical discipleship for the sake of the kingdom and prioritizing the marginal, are one result of this, often proving divisive in just the way that Jesus did.

CHRISTIANITY AS A CHRISTOCENTRIC RELIGIOUS SYSTEM

The identity of Jesus's movement during his earthly ministry depended entirely on Jesus himself, as the one who embodied God's gracious presence in the kingdom that was arriving. The kingdom was inseparable from Jesus himself. As we have seen, the only boundary to Jesus's movement was formed by the division between those who aligned themselves with him

---

30. It has often been pointed out that the modern concept of a religion did not exist in the ancient world, but Judaism and Christianity came closest to being what we call religions.

and those who opposed him. This centrality of Jesus to his kingdom-of-God movement is the deepest root of the Christocentricity that came to define both the identity of Christianity and the boundary it required as it became something more like a religious "system."

Christianity's Christocentricity is certainly more than a continuation of the centrality of the earthly Jesus to his movement during his ministry. Its focus is not merely the earthly Jesus, but the divine Son of God in his entire narrative identity: incarnate, crucified, risen, exalted, and coming. But the life and teaching of the earthly Jesus have colored the Christocentricity of Christianity in at least two significant ways. The first is the way that Christian faith and life have so often, in the Christian tradition, been understood and practised as personal allegiance to Jesus. Being a Christian involves a personal bond of friendship, service, and commitment, such as Jesus's disciples in his lifetime had with him. The second is the way that the Christian focus on Jesus relates to the kingdom of God. Just as, in the Gospels, the kingdom that Jesus preached and practiced is inseparable from him, so he is inseparable from the kingdom of God. Thus when Christian faith is faithful to the Jesus of the Gospels, it is also orientated to the kingdom. To be a Christian is not only to believe in Jesus for personal salvation or to be incorporated in his church, but also to follow Jesus as a disciple on the way to the kingdom in company with other disciples. This is in part what gives the Christocentricity of Christianity its missional and eschatological direction. The kingdom is more than the church and, unlike the church, knows no boundaries short of God's whole creation. Thus Jesus himself always points and leads his people beyond itself.

When John Bowker portrays religions as (more or less) "closed circles," he has in mind the fact that a circle has a circumference, but he does not develop the image in such a way as to bring the center of the circle into view. Yet a circle must have both a center and a circumference. Only from the perspective of the center can the circumference be drawn. Applying the image of the circle in this way, we might say that the kind of center a religion has will affect, if not determine, the kind of circumference it has. It may be that the identity of a religion depends less on drawing strong boundaries than on having a strong center. At any rate, I would suggest this in the case of Christianity.

Christocentricity is not, of course, an alternative to theocentricity. It is the Christian way of being theocentric. This is why, in the key theological debates and conciliar definitions of the fourth and fifth centuries, getting Christology right was closely connected with getting the Trinity right. The Niceno-Constantinopolitan Creed and the Chalcedonian Definition define the center of Christianity by constructing a doctrine of God that makes

Christology decisive for the Christian understanding of God without, so to speak, limiting God to Christology. They also provide the theological framework for reading the Christian story of the world correctly: as the story of God with the world in which he is truly involved, centrally *as* the human being Jesus, but is not limited to or absorbed into the world. Insofar as these doctrinal definitions of Christian faith have served to define the boundaries of authentic Christian teaching (as very widely they have[31]), the church has sought to get the circumference of the circle right by getting the centre right. Christocentricity sets the boundaries.

If Christocentricity sets the boundaries, then it is also important to think about how Jesus Christ relates to all people and to all things (as the New Testament claims he does and as the Niceno-Constantinopolitan Creed also claims, by echoing the New Testament). The universality of Christ—a topic we have already broached in speaking of the mutual inseparability of Jesus and the kingdom of God—is what should keep the circle of the Christian system open. There is no space here for a full development of this thought, but I can summarize briefly by stating that the universality of Christ should be understood incarnationally, relationally, and eschatologically. If Christocentricity is rooted first in the earthly Jesus and subsequently in his cross, resurrection, and exaltation, then the universality of Christ cannot be understood merely as the relationship of the preincarnate Logos to all things, but must be understood as that of Jesus Christ, the Jesus of the Gospels. But, second, the universality of Jesus Christ must be understood relationally; that is, he is not, so to speak, in himself the sum of everything, but comes to his universal identity through actually relating to all people and all things. What it means for Jesus Christ to be the decisive center of God's purposes for the whole creation can only be sketched in a preliminary way in advance of his actual achievement of his universal relationship to all things. Third, therefore, the full achievement of his relationship to all things awaits his coming and that of the kingdom of God with him.

If Jesus Christ has this kind of universality, then what he means for the world cannot be confined to the boundaries of the Christian religious system, essential though that is for its witness to his identity, but must come to further light in relationship to truth wherever it is to be found. If he has that sort of universality, then the full significance of all human knowledge, wisdom, and insight will come to light in relation to him; but also, conversely, his own universal identity as Lord and Savior of all will come to light only in relation to all human knowledge, wisdom and insight. Both sides

---

31. I do not intend to ignore the non-Chalcedonian churches of the East, whose critiques of Chalcedon should bear on the way other Christians interpret Chalcedon.

of this claim anticipate the eschatological revelation to come, which alone will bring the full and final truth of all things in this world to light. Here and now our attempts to see all things in the light of Jesus Christ and Jesus Christ in the light of all things are provisional and corrigible. They remain open to truth wherever it may be found.

While this understanding of the universality of Christ opens, in principle, the Christian circle of religious understanding to truth wherever it is to be found, a criterion of coherence is certainly essential—coherence with what Christians claim to know of Jesus Christ from Scripture and tradition. However, judgments of coherence are not always easy to make. Those judgments themselves may be provisional and corrigible, at least in the light of later developments, as the history of Christian theology amply demonstrates. In relation to other religions, for example, we may need to continue to live with tensions and unresolved issues. We should certainly not feel obliged to choose between the options of exclusivism, inclusivism, and pluralism (even with the addition of John Bowker's proposed fourth option), since there could very well be some truth in all of them. They tempt us to make all too generalized judgments about religions in advance of actually trying to understand them, ignoring the fact that understanding religions other than one's own is always difficult and never conclusive.

I have argued that it is its Christocentricity that sets Christianity's boundary most authentically and importantly, though I am not suggesting that other factors in defining the boundary may not have a place. But it is holding to its strong center that maintains Christianity's identity. It is this center that requires the boundary to be, not only maintained, but also transcended, in discipleship and mission, on the way to the kingdom of God. It is a center that permits and even requires critical openness to truth wherever it is to be found. It is a center that requires us to seek peace, but not without the knowledge that the peace we seek may itself be divisive.

BIBLIOGRAPHY

Bauckham, Richard. *Gospel of Glory: Major Themes in Johannine Theology.* Grand Rapids: Baker Academic, 2015.
Bowker, John. *The Sense of God: Sociological, Anthropological and Psychological Approaches to the Origin of the Sense of God.* Oxford: Clarendon, 1973.
———. *The Religious Imagination and the Sense of God.* Oxford: Clarendon, 1978.
———. "Religions as Systems." In *Believing in the Church: The Corporate Nature of Faith: A Report by the Doctrine Commission of the Church of England,* 159–89. London: SPCK, 1981. Reprinted in *Licensed Insanities,* 112–43, 152–54.
———. *Licensed Insanities: Religion and Belief in God in the Contemporary World.* London: Darton, Longman & Todd, 1987.

———. "Christianity and Non-Christian Religions: A Neo-Darwinian Revolution." *God, Truth and Reality: Essays in Honour of John Hick*, edited by Arvind Sharma, 87–97. New York: St Martin's, 1993.

———. *Is God a Virus? Genes, Culture and Religion*. Gresham Lectures 1992–93. London: SPCK, 1995.

———. *God: A Brief History*. London: DK, 2002.

———. *The Sacred Neuron: Extraordinary New Discoveries Linking Science and Religion*. London: Tauris, 2007.

Bultmann, Rudolf. *Theology of the New Testament*. Vol. 2. Translated by Kendrick Grobel. London: SCM, 1955.

7

"In Persona Christi"
Who, or Where, is Christ at the Altar?

—SARAH COAKLEY

INTRODUCTION

AMONG THE MANY REMARKABLE interdisciplinary gifts that John Bowker has manifested in a lifetime of research and writing on matters of religion is a palpable instinct (perhaps too rarely remarked upon by those who admire his work) for what one might call the logic of ritual enactment.[1] In Bowker's case, this sensitivity has of course been fed not only by his extensive knowledge of the anthropology, sociology, and psychology of religion; his acquaintance with a dazzling array of religious texts and practices; and his forays into religion and neuroscience, but perhaps most especially by his own prayerful commitment, as an Anglican priest, to the regular celebration of the liturgy of the Christian eucharist. What I offer him by way of *Gratulierung* and thanks in the following is a set of theological musings on a ritual matter—the status of a woman priest at the eucharistic altar—which has of course become newly, indeed paroxysmically, divisive in the churches in recent years.

---

1. I first became aware of Bowker's interdisciplinary range in his remarkable Wilde Lectures: Bowker, *Sense of God*.

Clearly a great deal hangs on this question theologically and ecumenically, and especially for the Church of England as it attempts to go forward positively in its relations to Roman Catholicism and Eastern Orthodoxy. As will be intimated in short compass below, a great deal of theological controversy within Roman Catholicism has been devoted to this matter without clear resolution, and with ongoing negative implications for Christianity under "secular" critique. Yet, as I shall also go on to argue (somewhat in the spirit, I trust, of John Bowker's own distinctive religious insights), this is a topic in which merely propositional approaches to theology quickly reach their limits. What is required of the astute commentator is a certain subliminal awareness of the power of the bodily movements of liturgy, of ritual's capacity to evoke and transform unconscious forces, and—not least—of the relationship between these factors and associations of desire and gender.

The heart of what I aim to explore here is that the eucharist is indeed the locus of potentially powerful evocations and transformations of human desire. Such a proposal might immediately meet an objection, especially from a Protestant perspective, that the elucidation of the category "desire" has, *prima facie*, little obviously to do with Jesus's initial institution of the eucharist (in Mark 14:22–25 and parallels), or with the immediate implications of Paul's account of its significance in 1 Cor 11:23–26.[2] However, any repression of the category of desire in relation to the eucharist would emphatically not be the view of the Roman magisterium, whose insistence on a *nuptial* vision of the eucharist (founded in Eph 5:25–33 and in the tradition of the Song of Songs, and perceived fundamentally as Christ loving the church) forms now the crucial fulcrum of the Roman Catholic rejection of the ordination of women. For Rome therefore of late, questions of eroticism and gender have become the *more* central—not the more peripheral—to the official theology of the eucharist. Rather than sanitizing the issue from the outset, I propose to walk boldly, first, into the fanned flames of ecumenical debate that this question of women priests enshrines. Whereas the usual feminist (and predominantly Protestant) *riposte* to Rome on women's orders has been to de-sexualize the eucharist, to stress "commensality" over sacrifice, and to declare eroticism and gender irrelevant to eucharistic celebration, I shall here take the opposite tack. Starting from this hotly contested base, I shall seek in this short paper to provide a new response to the issue of what it is for the priest or minister to act *in persona Christi*. True to my focus on the category of desire, I shall argue that Rome and the Orthodox are entirely right to seek the Christic clue to eroticism and gender in the

---

2. However, not to be overlooked in this context are the evocative words recorded by Luke of Jesus to his disciples at the Last Supper (Luke 22:15): "I have eagerly desired [lit., 'with desire I have desired'] to eat this Passover with you before I suffer."

eucharist; but that Rome's particular attempt to debar women from the altar and to "freeze" the gender binary back into mandated roles finally fails in its very articulation.

In order to sustain this thesis, I shall turn first to the contemporary Roman treatment of the classical Thomistic theme of the priest's role as *"in persona Christi."* What I shall trace briefly here is the particular way that the 1976 magisterial document *Inter Insigniores* interprets Thomas on this topic, and—more crucially—how it is forced at points to depart from Thomas. Then I shall note how one conservative defender of the Roman position (Sara Butler), and one liberal Catholic detractor (Dennis Ferrara), have extended—and bifurcated—the debate on the reading of Thomas; and how—hovering behind and between these readings—lies the now-massive influence of Hans Urs von Balthasar, with his significantly greater emphasis than these other writers on the *Marian* role of the priest. This Marian priestly theme is one strangely suppressed in *Inter Insigniores,* but entirely congruent with late-medieval sensibilities, and indeed with Thomas's own insistence that the priest is *medius* between divinity and humanity—*in persona Christi* but no less *in persona Ecclesiae,* for whom Mary is the ultimate prototype. But once this *duality* of the priest's role is recaptured, I shall argue, the central argument of both the magisterium and of von Balthasar himself begins to unravel. Finally, and in the light of this exposition, I shall state my own view: that precisely in the light of the Christ/church nuptial model of the eucharist, a fixed gender binary becomes impossible. For in fact the priest is in an inherently complex gender role as representative of *both* Christ and church, strategically summoning the stereotypical gender associations of each, but always destabilizing the attempt to be "held" in one or the other. Thus, a significant part of the undeniably "erotic" tug of the priest's position at the altar lies in this very destabilization: a gesturing towards a *divine* "order" of union and communion beyond any tidy human attempts at gender characterization and binary division.

INTER INSIGNIORES (1976) AND THE USE OF THOMAS AQUINAS'S THEME OF *"IN PERSONA CHRISTI"*

But this is by way of forecast. Let me now begin with *Inter Insigniores.* The document starts—positively—with an acknowledgement of the changed and improved status of woman in the modern world, and a valorization of the theological leadership of certain women religious in the history of the Church (Saint Catherine of Siena and Saint Teresa of Avila, *par excellence,* as "doctors" of the Church); but it immediately presents the issue of the ordination of women as an "ecumenical problem."[3] There are in fact two major prongs to the argument against the ordination of women presented in this document. The first is simply the argument from tradition: Jesus and the early church did not ordain women, it says (barring what it sees as some gnostic aberrations in the second century), and the unchanging tradition is therefore against it. The second prong of the argument, however, is the one that interests us here and on which much weight is made to hang. Citing Thomas Aquinas, first from the *Summa* and then from the commentary on the *Sentences*, the crucial argument of the priest's status "*in persona Christi*" is invoked. A woman cannot be a priest, it is said, because in the eucharist the priest acts "not only by the power conferred by Christ in ordination," but "*in persona Christi*, taking the *role* of Christ, to the point of being his very *image*, when he pronounces the words of consecration."[4] But what exactly does this mean? *Inter Insigniores* does not mention that this matter remains somewhat elusive in the *Summa* treatment at this point, in which Thomas does not expatiate on the impediment of gender, although he considers a whole range of other possible difficulties, such as senility or living in sin or blindness or leprosy-infested limbs. But in the *Sentence* commentary, to which *Inter Insigniores* next appeals, Thomas ostensibly fills in a gap here: "Sacramental signs," he says, "represent what they signify by *natural resemblance*";[5] and *Inter Insigniores*—by a certain sleight of hand—uses this principle to drive home its point of the necessity of male priesthood. However, it actually tacitly departs from Thomas's own line of argument in three significant ways.

First, *Inter Insigniores* does not argue, as Thomas does in *In IV Sent.*, that what clinches the argument against the ordination of women is (a) a scriptural warrant against female teaching authority over men (1 Tim 2:12), and (b) the supposed inherent inferiority of woman as "in the state of subjection" (based on an Aristotelian biology of sex and reproduction, now defunct). These particular appeals are seemingly now an embarrassment to the magisterium, and are passed over. Second, *Inter Insigniores* signally fails to mention, as Thomas does not fail so to do, (a) that "the power of Orders is founded in the soul," which would apparently make sex indifferent to the reception of orders, and (b) that the office of prophecy has been exercised by women to great effect in the tradition, and that—ostensibly—the "office

---

3. Congregation for the Doctrine of the Faith, *Inter Insigniores*, 23.

4. Ibid., 41 (my emphasis), citing *ST* III. 83, art. 1, ad 3: "the priest . . . enacts the image of Christ."

5. Ibid., 43, citing *In IV Sent.*, dist. 25, q. 2, quaestiuncula 1 ad 4 (my emphasis).

of prophet is greater than the office of priest," which should surely affect our approach to female ordination. Both these points are honestly raised by Thomas, and then trumped by his Aristotelian biological argument; but since *Inter Insigniores* has now tacitly abandoned that biological line of approach, these other points arguably still have to be faced. Third, then, *Inter Insigniores* has to fill in the gap left by the embarrassing and now-defunct biological argument in new ways (and this it does with great haste and stealth, in one short paragraph).[6] It argues, in fact, that the "natural resemblance" that must adhere between Christ and the priest is not now based in supposed greater male authority and superiority, but rather in physiological resemblance; and that without this resemblance, *qua* male, it would be "difficult" (not, note, impossible) "to see in the minister the image of Christ." It then adds, quickly, "For Christ himself was, *and remains*, a man."[7]

Now neither of these last points, as far as I know, is ever wielded by Thomas himself against the ordination of women; and the question of Christ's genital maleness, *qua* risen body, might well continue to be a matter of dispute between Eastern and Western Christian traditions: the insistence on it is a *novum* and might, on one understanding, appear to compromise the soteriological principle that "the unassumed is the unhealed" where women's salvation is concerned. Be that as it may, the crucial dimensions of the Thomistic appeal in the magisterial document have now been dissected. But what we should also note, finally, is that *Inter Insigniores* then goes on, in clear distinction from the Thomistic appeal, to expand at some length the nuptial theme of Ephesians 5 beloved both of Hans Urs von Balthasar and of the then-pope (John Paul II); and it is this which purportedly, and finally, clinches the argument. Now, as Kari Børresen demonstrated long ago, in her classic feminist account of Augustine and Thomas on the status of women, Thomas himself interestingly makes little of, indeed generally eschews discussion of the marriage metaphor for Christ and the church, although it had been dear to Augustine;[8] and so this appeal plays no part in his argument on women's supposed incapacity for ordination. Not so *Inter Insigniores*. It is actually the supposed "deep" mystery of sexual "difference,"[9] as enunciated in the eucharist, and in no way "suppressed in the glorified state,"[10] that here renders a female *unable* to be a priest. The priest, *qua*

---

6. Ibid., 43.
7. Ibid. (my emphasis).
8. Børresen, *Subordination and Equivalence*, 234.
9. Congregation for the Doctrine of the Faith, *Inter Insigniores*, 45.
10. Ibid., 46.

eucharistic, Christic bridegroom, "must be [it is said] . . . a man."[11] There is an ostensibly awkward moment, at the end of this section of the document, when it is admitted that the priest does also act *"in persona Ecclesiae"*—"in the name of the whole Church and in order to represent her"—as well as *"in persona Christi."*[12] But no mention, interestingly, is made of this other posture as inherently "feminine" or "Marian"—even though the logic of the nuptial argument implicitly demands it—and the immediate conclusion is drawn that "it is true that the priest represents the Church, which is the body of Christ. But if he does so, it is precisely because he *first* represents Christ himself, who is the head and shepherd of the Church."[13] No argument is given for this final move, although—as we shall shortly see—much hangs on it.

DISPUTING THE THOMISTIC READING: DENNIS FERRARA AND SARA BUTLER

Unsurprisingly, the appeal to Thomas in *Inter Insigniores* did not go long unchallenged within the Roman Catholic world of scholarship. A significant dispute ensued, mostly in the pages of the journal *Theological Studies* between Dennis Ferrara and Sara Butler;[14] but the Benedictine scholar Guy Mansini later added his further corrections to Ferrara in *The Thomist*.[15] Not all the details of this complicated exegetical debate need detain us here, for we have already sketched some of the ways that *Inter Insigniore*s significantly departs from Thomas's own intentions. The crucial dividing issue for our own purposes lies in Ferrara's well-intentioned, but ultimately misleading, attempt to read Thomas on *in persona Christi* "apophatically," as he puts it, rather than "representationally." What is evidently motivating him here (and is worthy of note, because it is a classic "liberal" ploy that I explicitly wish to eschew in my own argument) is a desire to make eroticism and gender entirely *irrelevant* to the matter of priesthood. Thus, according to Ferrara, Thomas does not intend by speaking of the priest acting *"in persona Christi"* a personal, let alone, gendered, "representation" of Christ. Rather, says Ferrara, he is inviting the priest merely to "quote" Christ, and so to "give

11. Ibid., 45.
12. Ibid., 47.
13. Ibid. (my emphasis).
14. See Ferrara, "Representation or Self-Effacement?"; Ferrara, "Ordination of Women"; Butler, "*Quaestio Disputata*"; Ferrara, "Reply to Sara Butler"; and Ferrara, "*In Persona Christi*."
15. Mansini, "Representation and Agency."

way visibly to the *persona* of Christ."[16] On this (so-called) apophatic reading of the elusive *in persona Christi* theme, Ferrara can claim that gender has nothing to do with priesthood, once Thomas's erroneous Aristotelian biology is jettisoned.

To this argument Butler rightly replies, in my view (and some of her points are echoed in the later article by Mansini) that Ferrara on this particular issue of *in persona Christi* has utterly misconstrued Thomas—or rather, flattened the elusive subtlety of his position. Thomas intends the priest to be both *sign* and *instrument* in the sacrament of the altar: it is therefore not enough for the priest simply to "quote" Christ in order to consecrate the elements. If that were all that was involved, there would be a mere memorial, but not a *bona fide* "sacramental representation." Thomas argues in the *Sentence* commentary, points out Butler, that Christ uses not just the words, but the minister too, as "instruments" in the form of the sacrament (*In* IV *Sent.* d. 8, q. 2, a. 3, sol. 9); and thus it must be that the *person* of the priest "gives sacramental visibility to Christ whose minister and instrument he is."[17] Were this not so, there would be no reason for Thomas to reject the ordination of women at all. Ferrara's "apophatic" reading of Thomas therefore abstracts—gnostically we might say—from the essential bodiliness of the sacramental representation; and this is an ironic position to arrive at given that Ferrara wishes to make a *feminist* commitment to the ordination of women. But Butler is surely right to insist that Thomas intends the minister neither to be physically insignificant nor merely to "play act" Christ: as she puts it, the sacramental mode of representation in Thomas is "*sui generis*,"[18] and that is doubtless why it is so hard to describe or encapsulate clearly. It is neither a complete self-effacement nor yet a *dramatic* representation. Both those analogues are misleading.

There are two remaining points, however, on which Butler has to admit a certain defeat where the limits of Thomas's argument are concerned. One issue finds her in agreement with *Inter Insigniores*, the other in implicit criticism of it. Like the authors of *Inter Insigniores*, first, she has to acknowledge her modern disavowal of the faulty biological argument that finally undergirds Thomas's rejection of the ordination of women; women are *not* naturally subordinate to men, and this means, she admits, that some different—and, as she puts it, "complementary"—view of the sexes[19] will have to be brought in to sustain the magisterial rejection of women's ordina-

---

16. Ferrara, "Representation or Self-Effacement?," 213.
17. Butler, "*Quaestio Disputata*," 73.
18. Ibid., 74.
19. Ibid., 80.

tion. (Butler does not acknowledge at this juncture in her argument that the modern rendition of the sexes as "complementary" or "opposite" is a particular invention of the Romantic era—but to this point I shall shortly return in discussing von Balthasar.) Second, Butler helpfully clarifies that there is an apparent sleight of hand in *Inter Insigniores* in suggesting—albeit briefly—that it is Thomas who makes the argument for the necessary likeness to Christ in the priest's male *body* or *visage*. On the contrary, notes Butler, the fittingness of the male representation in Thomas resides in the man's supposed natural superiority (back to the faulty biology again), not in his physiological impression; it is in fact a strand in Bonaventure's sacramental theology that is being drawn upon here, she rightly points out, not Thomas's; and it is this that is needed to fill the gap in the argument as to the relevance of the "male sex to the signification of Christ the Mediator, who became incarnate as a male."[20] It is Bonaventure, then, who—in commenting on the same point in the *Sentences* that Thomas also responds to—insists that only a man can "signify" the Mediator, not because the male is superior, but simply because Christ *was* a man: "quoniam mediator solum in virili sexu fuit et per virilem sexum potest significari" (*In IV Sent.* d. 25, a 2, q. 1 concl.). But where does all this leave us? Let me gather the strands of the argument so far so that we can see where we are going.

What the complex technical debate over Thomas's account of *in persona Christi* shows us, it seems to me, is three things. First, there is something irreducible about the *bodiliness* of the priest's representational function at the altar—and not just of the recitation of words—that cannot be magicked away; but the question of how that bodiliness relates to Christ as a *man* remains obscure once Thomas's Aristotelian biology is questioned. Second, if Thomas's faulty gender theory is to be replaced by a Romantic view of the so-called complementarity of the sexes—as Butler proposes—then this has to be made explicit. It is here that we shall find von Balthasar's example peculiarly revealing; but at the same time it must be acknowledged, as *Inter Insigniores* does not acknowledge, that the notion of woman as the "opposite sex"—as Thomas Lacqueur and others have controversially explored of late[21]—was a product of a particular period of Western medical and cultural history, precisely replacing the "subordinate sameness" theory that Thomas Aquinas and the whole Aristotelian tradition had long taken for granted. It is in no way obviously mandated by Bible or earlier Christian tradition. Third, when *Inter Insigniores* covertly slides away from Thomas to invoke a Bonaventuran principle of necessarily male representation at the altar, the

20. Ibid., 67.
21. See esp. Lacqueur, *Making Sex.*

issue of the priest's representation of the *laity* becomes obscured. Yet, as Thomas himself rightly insists, it must be that the priest is representative *both* of Christ and of the people.

In the remainder of this paper, I shall now make a brief analysis of the telling gender arguments of von Balthasar—which themselves lap at the edges of *Inter Insigniores*, given von Balthasar's role as an official commentator on the document—and are, I believe, credible extensions and clarifications of the official Roman position. All three of the issues just highlighted come explicitly to the fore in von Balthasar's treatment; but all three—as I shall argue—reach a certain point of logical crisis. From our treatment of von Balthasar we shall then be able to conclude with a reading of the *in persona Christi* theme that chooses neither the "apophatic" route of Ferrara nor the Bonaventuran argument of Butler. Instead, I shall plot a third way through the dilemma and argue that the very nature of the priest's role *destabilizes* the fixed gender binary: precisely the bodily and gendered significance of priesthood, and especially the nuptial and erotic overtones of the eucharist, make the "freezing" of the gender binary impossible. But first, to von Balthasar.

HANS URS VON BALTHASAR (1905–1988) ON THE EUCHARIST AND GENDER

The extraordinary richness and complexity of Balthasar's theory of gender has of late received increasing attention, both critical and appreciative.[22] To read, say, von Balthasar's short *Mysterium Paschale* (alone), as many in the English-speaking world do, is to miss completely the gender evocations with which his kenotic Trinitarian theology of the cross is larded elsewhere (most notably in his *Theodramatik*).[23] Gender is so profoundly woven into his deepest theological themes (Trinity, Christology, ecclesiology, Mariology), and so surprisingly and counterintuitively in some of its twists and turns, that I cannot possibly do full justice to its entanglement with the issue of priestly status in this brief treatment. I shall simply fasten for these

22. A doctoral dissertation written at the Gregorian in Rome gives an exhaustive, but entirely adulatory, account of von Balthasar's views on gender and the priesthood: Pesarchick, *Trinitarian Foundation*. With this should be compared, amongst a burgeoning secondary literature: Gardner et al., *Balthasar at the End of Modernity*; and the essays by Williams, "Balthasar and the Trinity"; and Crammer, "One Sex or Two?," in Oakes and Moss, *Cambridge Companionå*, 37–50 and 93–112.

23. Compare Balthasar, *Mysterium Pascale*—a text originally written at speed for an encyclopaedia, and strikingly devoid of gender allusions—with Balthasar, *Theo-drama*, esp. vols. 3 (1992) and 4 (1994), which are replete with gender themes.

present purposes on three central points of analysis, which roughly correlate with the three issues for further discussion which I have just raised: together these will provide us with a fulcrum for critical discussion. I shall turn, first, to the central issue of his rejection of the ordination of women, and his ostensible reasons for it; and then, second, to his accompanying Mariology, as the crucial extra focus for his reflection on the church as "feminine"; and then, finally, to the complexity of his gender-theorizing on the Trinity, a place where—I shall argue—the influence on his work of the patristic writer Gregory of Nyssa shines through, with its strong hint of a possibility of gender transformation as a continuing condition of the life of incorporation into God.[24] To anticipate: what I find here is a stern argument for the cosmological *impossibility* of women's priestly sacramental ministry, paradoxically *combined with* the very potential for that argument's undoing. To these three tasks I go briefly in turn, then.

At the heart, first, of Balthasar's explicit rejection of the ordination of women is a key paradox, which simultaneously reveals a capacity for "fluid" thinking about gender *vis-à-vis* men, and yet a means of "fixing" womanhood outside the bounds of priesthood. It is well expressed in the essay he wrote as commentary on the publication of *Inter Insigniores*, titled, "The Uninterrupted Tradition of the Church," and also in a later essay on "Women Priests?" in *New Elucidations*. On the one hand, men and women are "equal," and nowhere is this clearer than in the person of Christ: as Balthasar puts it in the latter essay, "One can say that Christ, inasmuch as he represents the God of the universe in the world, is likewise the origin of both feminine and masculine principles in the church."[25] Yet, this equality does not suppress a "difference" which is even more fundamental: "the Catholic Church is perhaps humanity's last bulwark of genuine appreciation of the *difference* of the sexes," he writes, and of "the extreme oppositeness of their functions."[26] It is actually the "feminine" which for Balthasar is seen as primary for the church, and pedestalized as the "comprehensive feminine, the marian," unsullied and actively "fruitful," "already *superior* to that of the man";[27] and yet it is the man, "consecrated into [his] office" who alone can represent the "specifically masculine function—the transmission of a vital force that originates outside itself and leads beyond itself."[28] As Balthasar

---

24. See von Balthasar, *Presence and Thought*. The original French edition was published in 1988.
25. Von Balthasar, "Women Priests?," 193.
26. Ibid., 195.
27. Ibid., 193, 192.
28. Ibid., 193.

puts it in a much-quoted remark in another essay in the collection *Elucidations*: "What else is his Eucharist but, at a higher level, an endless act of fruitful outpouring of his whole flesh, such as a man can only achieve for a moment with a limited organ of his body?"[29]

So here we confront the essential gender double-think at the heart of Balthasar's system: the priest *must* be physiologically male, although also "feminine" *qua* transmitter of an ecclesial vital force that is more fundamentally that of the "perfect feminine Church."[30] Women, however, are always and *only* "feminine," expressing their "natural fruitfulness" which is "already superior to that of the man,"[31] "equal" but "different," "equal" but *superior* (even), but "equal" and inherently and physiologically incapable of the priesthood. As Balthasar puts it triumphantly in "The Uninterrupted Tradition," alluding to Ephesians 5, "The redemptive mystery 'Christ-Church' is the superabundant fulfillment of the mystery of creation between man and woman .... The natural difference is charged, *as* difference, with a supernatural emphasis." Only this nuptial model can reflect the "decisive light about the real reciprocity between the man and woman."[32] Thus, if a woman aspires to be a priest, she is disordered, breaking the rules of her own primary "fruitfulness."

This central paradox—all are "equal," but men are more equal than women (to adapt a well-known phrase of Orwell)—is reduplicated, second, in the Marian fundament that explicitly sustains it. For whilst the "feminine" here, as Mary, is the *sine qua non* of the church (as Balthasar puts it, "The Church begins with the Yes of the Virgin of Nazareth"[33]), this "feminine" tips over into Petrine "masculinity" *where men are concerned*: "What Peter will receive as 'infallibility' for his office of governing will be a partial share in the total flawlessness of the feminine, marian church," he writes.[34] Thus, a fluidity from and between "femininity" and "masculinity" is the lot of the man, whilst, in contrast, woman is only and solely the "feminine," a conclusion that Balthasar however roundly denies signifies a "precedence" for the man: "Who has precedence in the end? The man bearing office, inasmuch as he represents Christ in and before the community, or the woman, in whom the nature of the church is embodied—so much so that every member of the Church, *even the priest*, must maintain a feminine receptivity to the Lord of

29. Von Balthasar, *Elucidations*, 150.
30. Von Balthasar, "Women Priests?," 193.
31. Ibid., 192.
32. Von Balthasar, "Uninterrupted Tradition," 101.
33. Von Balthasar, "Women Priests?," 192.
34. Ibid., 193.

the Church? This question is completely idle, for the difference ought only to serve the mutual love of all the members in a circulation over which God alone remains sublimely supreme."[35]

If we ask, third and finally, how this (selective, male) potential for gender fluidity finds its counterpart in Balthasar's thought about God-as-Trinity, we confront even more fascinating and labile material. As a careful reading of the *Theodramatik* in particular shows, Balthasar can reapply his theory of "femininity" and "masculinity" at this higher level of theological reflection to arrive at the following conundrum: that the Son is "feminine" in relation to the Father's "masculinity," yet Father *and* Son are "masculine" in jointly spirating the (initially "feminine") Spirit; and yet again that the Father too can be said to be "feminine" in receiving the processions back into himself from the other two.[36] All the persons, in other words, are *both* "masculine" and "feminine" (with the possible exception of the Spirit?); and by extension, it must be again that the Christ/Word/priest who "pours himself out" as seed at the altar is *also* "feminine," receptive, as representing the capacity of the church so to be fructified.

And so we arrive at what I suggest is the internal undoing of Balthasar's own recitation of Romantic gender binaries. For while the woman is fixed normatively as "feminine," both pedestalized and subordinated (though not in rhetoric, as we have seen), the male in contrast has this infinite capacity for reversal and internal reciprocity, just as God's "persons" do in the Trinity. And indeed his priesthood vitally depends on this fluidity. It is possible that an influence on Balthasar from Gregory of Nyssa's fluid theory of gender, so fascinatingly expressed in Gregory's ascetic works and in his commentary on the *Song of Songs*, and alluded to by von Balthasar himself in his own monograph on Gregory, *Presence and Thought*, is here in the ascendancy.[37] Yet it meets, and is stopped short *in the woman's case*, by Balthasar's equally immovable German romanticism, his seeming adulation of the notion of *das ewig Weibliche*. It is an odd, fascinating, and altogether uncomfortable mix, as I hope these brief foci for examination have shown. But it is a mix concocted, however strangely, from two quite different inheritances of the primary symbolism of the nuptial metaphor. For Gregory of Nyssa's treatment of this metaphor (as I have tried to show in my own recent work) precisely *cannot* be constrained into such an immovable binary. For Gregory, gender is always being recast, renegotiated, the closer one gets to intimacy

---

35. Ibid., 197–98.

36. See von Balthasar, *Theo-drama* 3:283 and 5:91.

37. See von Balthasar's own discussion of these themes in Balthasar, *Presence and Thought*, 153–61.

with Christ.[38] Let us now consider finally, then, what this all might mean for our contemporary consideration of gender and eucharistic priestly enactment, and its continuing connection with that erotic metaphor.

THE WOMAN AT THE ALTAR: THE COSMOLOGICAL DISTURBANCE OF THE INCARNATION

I said at the start of this paper that I was set on demonstrating that "the priest is in an inherently complex gender role as representative of *both* Christ and church, strategically summoning the stereotypical gender associations of each, but always destabilizing the attempt to be 'held' in one or the other." Perhaps we are now in a better position, after our interlocutions with Thomas Aquinas, *Inter Insigniores,* and especially with von Balthasar, to argue this more fully in closing. However, I shall need to summon at this point, in addition to the complex historical and textual materials we have already been surveying, certain considerations from ritual and anthropological theory, as well other points of contrast with secular feminist and gender theory. Again, I can gather my argument under three main headings.

First, what the excursus into von Balthasar's thought reveals, surely, is that—once the Thomistic appeal to the inherent inferiority of womanhood is debunked—some developed theory of nuptial reciprocity is required if the argument against women's ordination is to be sustained. But once the crucial role of the priest as *medius* between the divine and the human is fully spelled out—the priest *in persona Christi* precisely because also *in persona Ecclesiae* or *in persona Mariae*—then the implicit gender fluidity of the ministerial role becomes apparent. It is precisely the priest's ritual undertaking—*in persona Christi*—to stand at the boundary of the divine and the human, and indeed *transgressively* to cross it, just as the very act of incarnation also made that transgressive crossing—once for all. Even outside Christianity, anyone familiar with the anthropological literature of ritual will know of a certain parallel *typos*: as Victor Turner put it classically in *The Ritual Process*,[39] the *shaman* or ritual enactor, whose unique job it is to stand on the "limen" between the known and the unknown and to mediate across it, is often credited with "threshold" capacities or traits such as bisexuality, dispossession, or strange humility. Likewise, Catherine Bell's remarkable study, *Ritual Theory, Ritual Practice*, attempts, with the aid of the insights of the cultural theory of Pierre Bourdieu, to explicate how

---

38. For an analysis of these themes in Nyssen, see Coakley, "Eschatological Body," 153–67; and Coakley, *God, Sexuality and the Self*, 281–88.

39. Turner, *Ritual Process*, 95–97.

ritual practice mediates certain cultural "oppositions" in a way that *creates* particular sorts of bodies, bodies that could not be so made simply by taking thought.[40] I do not of course intend, by these allusions to anthropological and ritual theory, to imply that the Christian Eucharist is merely a manifestation of a recurring "structural" type of human ritual; but I do intend to draw attention, beyond the mere words of the Christian rite, to powerful effects that are wrought more subliminally by the physical enactment of it, and in this area anthropologists and psychologists can well provide insight.

And so second, we are surely forced, after what has been revealed in von Balthasar's example and argument, to reconsider the theological *dangers* of the now-fixed West-facing position of most liturgies—both Protestant and Catholic—in the post–Vatican II era in the West. This might be seen as an odd line of argument for a feminist author to take, since it is often presumed—overhastily—that the "antihierarchical" opposition to the Eastern-facing position is precisely what should cohere with a feminist liturgical agenda. But as Kallistos Ware remarks in an important essay on Orthodox attitudes to the ordination of women, the Catholic Western-facing "stuck" position has new dangers of *male* idolatry, and unnecessarily intensifies the facially iconic dimension of the priest's role as being *in persona Christi*;[41] in fact, it emphasizes the *sexed* representation of Christ in a way that (as we now see) even Bonaventure would not have envisaged, given that for him the East-facing celebration would have been normative. The problem may then arise for the congregation *either* of an unconscious male idolatry of the priest's person ("everyone is in love with Fr. X"), *or* of a false—but gnawing—sense of incongruity at the particular appearance of the priest (old, ugly, fat, bespectacled, spotty, etc.). This problem, note, is in no way improved by substituting a woman priest; indeed the symbolic evocations may ultimately be the more theologically worrying if the Eucharist is at the same time perceived, or taught to be, merely a "family" meal: here, we might say, is all the danger of a West-facing "Julia Child" posture, with the woman priest and her female assistants deftly whipping up the Sunday lunch.

My point—to return to Thomas—is that the liturgical circumstances that he could assume as ritual backcloth for his subtle theory of *"in persona Christi"* were those of an East-facing celebration, in which much of the symbolic significance of the rite lay in the priest's movements back and forth across the boundary line between representing Christ and his church. As Uwe Michael Lang has argued in his monograph *Turning towards the Lord*, the long tradition of lining up prayer and eucharistic worship towards

---

40. Bell, *Ritual Theory, Ritual Practice*, esp. ch. 5.
41. Ware, "Man, Woman and the Priesthood of Christ," 47–49.

the East (and so towards Christ's resurrection) is one that is not abandoned without huge symbolic loss.[42] Lang, I need hardly say, does not draw the conclusions that I propose re. women priests and gender theory; but he is fully aware of the labile symbolic significance of the priestly eucharistic movements in an East-facing celebration.

So finally, and third, what *is* the gender theory that I suppose emerges from these accumulated considerations about *in persona Christi*, both textual and liturgical? My precise speculation here is one that I find tends almost always to be misheard as something more familiar, and perhaps more feared; so let me be careful, in closing, to distinguish it from certain brands of secular gender theory that I believe it casts under what we might call "Christic judgment." What I wish to suggest, first, is that the fundamentally "erotic," or "nuptial," nature of the Eucharist might more properly be called "proto-erotic": it is, in fact, the gift of Christ's body to the church by a *desiring* God who longs for our desiring, participatory response. But such desire-in-God, of course, does not in God's case signal *lack*—it is, as the Pseudo-Denys puts it in a memorable passage from the *Divine Names*, IV, that Thomas was later to comment upon, a divine "*ecstasis*" that ceaselessly seeks and yearns for a responsive human "*ecstasis*."[43] If it is an "economy of divine desire" into which we enter in the Eucharist, then, we might rightly say that *this* desire is more fundamental than human gender; the priest, acting *in persona Christi* but no less *in persona Ecclesiae*, and moving between them, cannot be "fixed" in one gender pole or the other in her response to the dictates of this desire (*pace* the masculinist *fiat* in *Inter Insigniores* at this point in the argument). Neither the movements of the rite, nor the theological propulsions of the text, can "freeze" the priestly figure into either pole of the erotic gender play, as von Balthasar too acknowledges.

But it is *not*, note, that the priest—male or female—has obliterated the endless differences in "gender" because, according to some liberal ideology, this is irrelevant to the undertakings of the priesthood; *nor* is s/he performing a form of liberal "androgyny" that leaves Romantic gender stereotypes untouched whilst conjoining them (like "John Wayne and Brigitte Bardot scotch-taped together," as Mary Daly once caustically put it);[44] *nor* again—*à la* the postmodern pragmatist feminism of Judith Butler—is it that the priest is perfomatively conducting a "queer protest" that will condone certain previously banned forms of sexual pleasure;[45] and nor finally, as in certain forms

---

42. Lang, *Turning towards the Lord*, passim.
43. See the discussion of this theme in Coakley, *God, Sexuality and the Self*, 311–17.
44. Daly, "Qualitative Leap," 30.
45. See Butler, *Gender Trouble*. I have given a critical account of Butler's gender

of "third-wave" American feminism (intelligently discussed of late by Astrid Henry) is it that heterosexual binaries have become transgressively *chic* once more precisely amongst those who label themselves as "queer."[46] No: it is none of these successively fashionable forms of secular gender theory, any more than it is the fixed Romantic binary that the magisterium has come to favor; and doubtless this is why this Christic alternative is so hard to "grasp." It is rather that the flow of "divine desire" is what liturgically refuses to allow the human gender binary to settle and "freeze," let alone to be summed up in some triumphant secular ideology. For the fundamental "difference" to be negotiated here is *not* male and female, let alone the Romantic "masculine" and "feminine," but rather the ultimate difference between God and humanity; and this, we might say, only Christ has "negotiated." *This* crossing of difference is indeed a "cosmological disturbance" of unrepeatable status. What happens in the Eucharist, then, happens on the *limen* between the divine and the human, where the miracle of divine enfleshment challenges and undercuts even the most ingenious secular theorizing about the order of this world.

If we are to return in closing, then, to the wider question of "Who, or Where, is Christ at the Altar?," it must be acknowledged that the current fixation on whether the centrally important locus is the priestly *persona* (male or female) is a curious new development in the history of Christian eucharistic theology. If, as I have suggested in contrast, desire for the "body of Christ" brings even gender fixity into uncertainty, what conclusions are to be drawn for the current ecclesiastical ructions on matters of sex and gender? The line of argument I have begun to develop here, in conversation with premodern sources, urges not that this issue is irrelevant, but that the eucharistic enactment of the logic of "divine desire" should in contrast be the *primary* point of reference—the primary "orientation," we might say—both ethical and theological. It is through entering spiritually and ritually into this logic, finally, that one may come to glimpse where, or who, or what "Christ" is, whether evocatively symbolized in the body of the celebrant, or densely present in the host, or located more widely in the gathered

---

theory from a specifically Christian theological perspective in Coakley, "Eschatological Body," 153–67. It may be clear that the view of gender that accompanies (and indeed arises from) the theology of the Eucharist proposed in this essay does not easily fit into *either* side of the theoretical battle lines in current secular gender theory (between the physiological essentialisms of the French feminists, and the pragmatic gender de-stabilizations of American queer theory). That it escapes through the horns of this particular dilemma is arguably a sign of its specifically Christian and incarnational provenance: the transformation of gender is a *divine*—but also an embodied—event, according to this view.

46. See Henry, *Not My Mother's Sister*, passim.

community, or indeed beyond that in the downtrodden of the earth—for those who have eyes to see.[47] The attempt to contain or constrain the glory of the presence of Christ has been but one curious attendant feature of the contemporary resistance to the ordination of women.[48]

BIBLIOGRAPHY

Balthasar, Hans Urs von. *Elucidations*. Translated by John Riches. London: SPCK, 1975.
———. "Women Priests?" In *New Elucidations*, 187–98. Translated by Sister Mary Theresilde Skerry. San Francisco: Ignatius, 1986.
———. *Mysterium Paschale: The Mystery of Easter*. Translated by Aiden Nichols. Edinburgh: T. & T. Clark, 1990.
———. *Presence and Thought: An Essay on the Religious Philosophy of Gregory of Nyssa*. Translated by Mark Sebanc. A Communio Book. San Francisco: Ignatius, 1995.
———. *Theo-drama: Theological Dramatic Theory*. 5 vols. Translated by Graham Harrison. San Francisco: Ignatius, 1988–1998.
———. "The Uninterrupted Tradition of the Church." In *From "Inter Insigniores" to "Ordinatio Sacerdotalis: Documents and Commentaries*," by the Congregation for the Doctrine of the Faith, 99–106. Washington, DC: United States Catholic Conference, 1996.
Bell, Catherine. *Ritual Theory, Ritual Practice*. New York: Oxford University Press, 1992.
Børresen, Kari Elisabeth. *Subordination and Equivalence: The Nature and Role of Woman in Augustine and Thomas Aquinas*. Washington, DC: University Press of America, 1981.
Bowker, John W. *The Sense of God: Sociological, Anthropological and Psychological Approaches to the Origin of the Sense of God*. Oxford: Clarendon, 1973.
Butler, Judith. *Gender Trouble: Feminism and the Subversion of Identity*. Thinking Gender. New York: Routledge, 1990.
Butler, Sara, MSBT. "*Quaestio Disputata: 'In Persona Christi'*—A Response to Dennis M. Ferrara." *TS* 56 (1995) 61–80.
Coakley, Sarah. "The Eschatological Body: Gender, Transformation and God." In *Powers and Submissions: Spirituality, Philosophy and Gender*, 153–67. Challenges in Contemporary Theology. Oxford: Blackwell, 2002.
———. "The Woman at the Altar: Cosmological Disturbance or Gender Subversion?" *ATR* 86 (2004) 75–93.
———. "The Identity of the Risen Jesus: Finding Jesus Christ in the Poor." In *Seeking the Identity of Jesus: A Pilgrimage*, edited by Beverly Roberts Gaventa and Richard B. Hays, 301–19. Grand Rapids: Eerdmans, 2008.

---

47. I have attempted to capture something of the complexity of the issue of locating Jesus's presence and identity in Coakley, "Identity of the Risen Jesus."

48. This paper is a lightly revised version of the first of my Hensley Henson Lectures, originally delivered in Oxford in January 2005. An earlier adjunct paper is Coakley, "Woman at the Altar." I want to express my deep gratitude here to both John and Margaret Bowker for their consistent spiritual support of generations of Anglican ordinands, both women and men.

———. *God, Sexuality, and the Self: An Essay "On the Trinity."* Cambridge: Cambridge University Press, 2013.

Congregation for the Doctrine of the Faith. *From "Inter Insigniores" to "Ordinatio Sacerdotalis:" Documents and Commentaries*. Washington, DC: United States Catholic Conference, 1996.

Crammer, Corinne. "One Sex or Two? Balthasar's Theology of the Sexes." In *The Cambridge Companion to Hans Urs von Balthasar*, edited by Edward T. Oakes, SJ, and David Moss, 93–112. Cambridge Companions to Religion. Cambridge: Cambridge University Press, 2004.

Daly, Mary. "The Qualitative Leap beyond Patriarchal Religion." *Quest* 1 (1975) 20–40.

Ferrara, Dennis Michael. "*In Persona Christi*: Towards a Second Naiveté." *TS* 57 (1996) 65–88.

———. "The Ordination of Women: Tradition and Meaning." *TS* 55 (1994) 706–19.

———. "A Reply to Sara Butler." *TS* 56 (1995) 81–91.

———. "Representation or Self-Effacement? The Axiom *In Persona Christi* in St. Thomas and the Magisterium." *TS* 55 (1994) 195–224.

Gardner, Lucy, David Moss, Ben Quash, and Graham Ward. *Balthasar at the End of Modernity*. Edinburgh: T. & T. Clark, 1999.

Henry, Astrid. *Not My Mother's Sister: Generational Conflict and Third-Wave Feminism*. Bloomington, IN: Indiana University Press, 2004.

Lacqueur, Thomas. *Making Sex: Body and Gender from the Greeks to Freud*. Cambridge: Harvard University Press, 1990.

Lang, Uwe Michael. *Turning Towards The Lord: Orientation in Liturgical Prayer*. San Francisco: Ignatius, 2004.

Mansini, Guy, OSB. "Representation and Agency in the Eucharist." *The Thomist* 62 (1998) 499–517.

Oakes, Edward T., SJ, and David Moss, eds. *The Cambridge Companion to Hans Urs von Balthasar*. Cambridge Companions to Religion. Cambridge: Cambridge University Press, 2004.

Pesarchick, Robert A. *The Trinitarian Foundation of Human Sexuality as Revealed by Christ according to Hans Urs von Balthasar: The Revelatory Significance of the Male Christ and the Male Ministerial Priesthood*. Tesi Gregoriana. Serie teologia 63. Rome: Pontificia Universita Gregoriana, 2000.

Turner, Victor W. *The Ritual Process: Structure and Anti-Structure*. London: Routledge & Kegan Paul, 1969.

Ware, Kallistos. "Man, Woman and the Priesthood of Christ." In *Women and the Priesthood*, edited by Thomas Hopko, 5–53. Crestwood, NY: St. Vladimir's Seminary Press, 1999.

Williams, Rowan. "Balthasar and the Trinity." In *The Cambridge Companion to Hans Urs von Balthasar*, edited by Edward T. Oakes, SJ, and David Moss, 37–50. Cambridge Companions to Religion. Cambridge: Cambridge University Press, 2004.

8

The Moral Imagination and a Sense of God

—Jane Shaw

IN RECENT YEARS, AS the humanities have come increasingly under attack at all levels of education, there has been a growing appeal to the importance of *imagination* in many arguments in defense of the humanities. In her recent book *Not for Profit: Why Democracy Needs the Humanities*, the American philosopher Martha Nussbaum argues for the importance of literature and the arts in cultivating an imagination—which is to say, an understanding of what is outside ourselves and outside our immediate experience. Factual knowledge and logic are not enough. We need to develop what Nussbaum calls a narrative imagination: "This means the ability to think what it might be like to be in the shoes of a person different from oneself, to be an intelligent reader of that person's story, and to understand the emotions and wishes and desires that someone so placed might have."[1]

This cultivation of the imagination, says Nussbaum, enables a person to go beyond the interest of self alone, and foster understanding between strangers. There is, then, a moral component to this imagination, expressed in Nussbaum's work through her interest in the communal good. She writes that "the ability to imagine the experience of another—a capacity almost all human beings possess in some form—needs to be greatly enhanced and

---

1. Nussbaum, *Not for Profit*, 95–96.

refined if we are to have any hope of sustaining decent institutions across the many divisions that any modern society contains."[2] Or to put it another way, "cultivated capacities for critical thinking and reflection are crucial in keeping democracies alive and wide awake."[3] Nussbaum falls into a long tradition, extending back (at least in modern society) to John Locke, that suggests the moral life can be taught as part of a broader education pattern.

The American novelist Marilynne Robinson echoes these themes when she writes: "I am convinced that the broadest possible exercise of imagination is the thing most conducive to human health, individual and global."[4] Like Nussbaum, she writes of the importance of imagination in relationship to democracy. "Democracy, in its essence and genius, is imaginative love for and identification with a community with which, much of the time and in many ways, one may be in profound disagreement."[5] She articulates the strong relationship between community and imagination, arguing that community itself is largely a product of our imagination: "community, at least community larger than the immediate family, consists very largely of imaginative love for people we do not know or whom we know very slightly."[6] Thus, she suggests that "the more generous the scale at which our imagination is exerted, the healthier and more humane the community will be."[7]

Both Nussbaum and Robinson therefore suggest that the context of what makes us—what we read and see and hear, and therefore how we empathize with others whose experience we could never otherwise know—is essential not only in forging our imaginations but in the very creation of our communities.

THE RELIGIOUS IMAGINATION AND THE SENSE OF GOD

The title of this essay is obviously a play on, and homage to, the title of John Bowker's important 1978 volume, *The Religious Imagination and the Sense of God*, a book regarded of such significance that it was republished as an Oxford Scholarly Classic in 2000. (In turn, this book was an expansion of parts of Bowker's Wilde Lectures, delivered in Oxford, and published as

2. Ibid., 10.
3. Ibid.
4. Robinson, *When I Was a Child*, 26.
5. Ibid., 27–28.
6. Ibid., 21.
7. Ibid., 29–30.

The Sense of God in 1973.) Bowker's aim was to explore the ways in which religious belief is transmitted in religious communities. How does a sense of God, he asked, occur in human consciousness?

In answering that question, and in employing behavioral-science methodologies, Bowker concluded that "the reality external to ourselves" (with the caveat "if it [that reality] exists" and "if the accounts of experiencing it are not false"), resembles something like "an information net into which we can be specifically linked and from which we can receive signal inputs."[8] How we respond to the "cues" from that information net and, indeed, understand it, depends on our context. Bowker's interest is focused on the *theistic* contexts in which we receive those cues, and in his book he looks at Judaism, Christianity, Islam, and Buddhism (arguing that the latter is, on balance, a theistic religion); that is, his primary interest is in the tradition which shapes not only us but also that which we call God—that "reality external to ourselves." Finally, he emphasizes how our experience reshapes the context and tradition in which we are embedded. As he puts it, "The points of departure are necessarily the cues which arise in the universe and its theistic traditions. If they become informative in the construction of our lives, they work in and through the accumulation of what we have so far become, but they may well transform or transfigure that material into a new outcome."[9] Our religious imagination is therefore forged by, and in turn fosters and shapes, the religious tradition in which we are situated. Context is, for Bowker, essential, as he seeks to understand how a person becomes religious.

In this essay, I will briefly explore the context in which we may find ourselves—or not—cultivating a moral imagination, and what place religion has in that. Bowker was interested in what shapes the religious consciousness, particularly perhaps the individual religious consciousness, and he looked at that from *within* several theistic contexts. My concern here is with the formation of knowledge about one another and therefore the building of community, and what part religion might play in that process.

THE MORAL IMAGINATION

The phrase "moral imagination" can be traced back to Edmund Burke (1729–97) the dominant political thinker in late eighteenth-century England. Burke, a conservative critic of the French Revolution, was concerned at the ways in which the revolutionaries were destroying the existing sense

---

8. Bowker, *Religious Imagination*, 313.
9. Ibid., 312–13.

of civilizing manners and morals, and feared that the emotions which would enable common life together were being eroded by cold reason. He uses the phrase "moral imagination" just once in his book of 1790, *Reflections on the Revolution in France*.

> But now all is to be changed. All the pleasing illusions, which made power gentle, and obedience liberal, which harmonized the different shades of life, and which, by a bland assimilation, incorporated into politics the sentiments which beautify and often soften private society, are to be dissolved by this new conquering empire of light and reason. All the decent drapery of life is to be rudely torn off. All the superadded ideas, furnished from the wardrobe of a moral imagination, which the heart owns, and the understanding ratifies, as necessary to cover the defects of our naked shivering nature, and to raise it to dignity in our own estimation, are to be exploded as a ridiculous, absurd, and antiquated fashion.[10]

There was a sense in which Burke was appealing to the status quo—the spirit of religion and manners in particular—as something that furnished a moral imagination. As David Bromwich writes about this passage, "the wardrobe furnishes *habitual* ideas that, item by item as they are picked out and worn, protect our shivering nature and make us know our duties. I exhibit a moral imagination when I act rightly by my selection from a pre-existing array of approved habits." Bromwich therefore concludes that Burke's moral imagination, precisely because it does not stray from well-worn tracks, "simply offers wisdom without reflection."[11]

This is undoubtedly the thrust of Burke's argument here, but the consequence of Burke's appeal may be, paradoxically, to take us beyond what is our individual (and thereby implicitly impoverished) experience, and therefore unexpectedly beyond the familiar. In writing of "a moral imagination, which the heart owns, and the understanding ratifies, as necessary to cover the defect of our naked shivering nature," surely Burke is also gesturing towards the possibility that our understanding goes beyond our private experience or even our ready-furnished set of "answers"? The result of such a possibility is that our emotional understanding, and therefore our ethical capacity, might be unexpectedly stretched beyond our limitations, and thus beyond ourselves.[12]

10. Burke, *Reflections*, 75–76.
11. Bromwich, *Moral Imagination*, 7.
12. Ibid., 15. Bromwich looks at Burke's earlier writings on the future of India and the East India Company in the 1780s and sees there a subtly different perspective, such

A wide range of writers has used the phrase "moral imagination" ever since Burke for numerous causes, ranging from conservative arguments for keeping intact a certain "canon" in the liberal-arts curriculum, to the "art and soul of building peace."[13] By evoking this much-used and multivalent phrase, I am asking: How does an understanding of what it means to be in another's shoes not only foster sympathy but also a sense of community that engenders action? In what ways are we motivated to think about and act on the interests of another as well as, or even over and above, our own interests?

OUR CONTEXT

The context in which defenders of the humanities, such as Nussbaum and Robinson, write is one of a perceived crisis in education: the arts and humanities (including the study of religion) are losing their place in the curriculum to the teaching of highly applied and profit-making skills. Nussbaum claims that this is a decision about the nature of education that we have neither deliberated upon nor chosen, and yet it limits our future.[14] The English literary scholar Helen Small has been critical of Nussbaum and others for articulating the context of these debates in terms of *crisis*, but nevertheless agrees that the humanities need to be defended against those who see them of no or little public benefit in economic terms, and she elegantly outlines the five main arguments in defense of the humanities as they have developed, especially since the nineteenth century.[15]

There is some agreement that this shift in educational focus has occurred in a context in which market values have come to govern our lives. Michael Sandel, the Harvard philosopher, writes in his most recent book, *What Money Can't Buy*, that in fact money can buy just about anything—from a prison-cell upgrade to access to a car pool lane when you are a solo driver to the right to emit a metric ton of carbon into the atmosphere (a bargain, at 13 euros), which is the right to pollute. We can also make money by standing in line on behalf of a lobbyist on Capitol Hill in Washington DC, renting out space on our body to display commercial advertising (Air Zealand recently rented someone's forehead for this purpose for $777) or serving as a human guinea pig in a drugs trial. Sandel argues that we have

---

that "the test of a moral imagination turns out to be justice to a stranger."

13. See for example, Himmelfarb, *Moral Imagination*; and Lederach, *Moral Imagination*. For a fuller discussion of the range of writers using this expression, see Lederach, *Moral Imagination*, 25–29.

14. Nussbaum, *Not for Profit*, 2.

15. Small, *Value of the Humanities*.

drifted—without deliberation or choice—from having a market economy into *being* a market society. And what we buy and sell we necessarily regard as commodities: in a market society that includes social relations. This mentality pervades all of society, including education.

Markets have moral limits. So, if a market society is our primary context, as Sandel would argue, then that makes it increasingly difficult for us to think what it might be like to be in the shoes of a different person, to understand their story, their emotions, their wishes. It makes it difficult for us to go beyond our own interests and act on behalf of others, especially those who cannot afford to enter this market society at any significant level. It makes it hard for us to follow the Golden Rule of most of the major religions, which is to treat others as we would like to be treated ourselves. There is not much room for imagination or social relations in the kind of market society Sandel describes, unless they are oriented towards making money or using capital to gain an advantage or achieve a goal. Robinson writes wistfully of her American context:

> I note here that recent statistics indicate American workers are the most productive in the world by a significant margin, as they have been for as long as statistics have been ventured. If we were to retain humane learning and lose a little edge in relative productivity, I would say we had chosen the better part.[16]

If economics is often cited as the primary contextual element for the decline of the humanities, then we must too consider the religious context. Robinson points to the fact that the intellectual model for this sort of imaginative learning was—at least for most of the older universities and colleges in the USA—"a religious tradition that loved the soul and the mind and was meant to encourage the exploration and refinement of both of them."[17] We might agree that this is true for older universities and colleges in England and Europe, as well as the USA. I do not think it is controversial to say that this has largely been lost on most campuses, on both sides of the Atlantic (except for certain ceremonial occasions) as skepticism about institutional religion has increased, a certain form of religious belonging has declined, and universities have struggled with the question of how to embrace religious pluralism—especially if they were founded as Christian institutions. Consequently, younger generations do not have even a vicarious sense of the religious. Recent attendance figures for churches in the UK indicate that

---

16. Robinson, *When I Was a Child*, 24–25.
17. Ibid., 24.

"decline" has occurred not because people stopped going to church but because new generations never began the habit of church attendance.[18]

And yet, in the quest to articulate the importance of imaginative understanding in the task of community building, language that has had religious or, at the least metaphysical, connotations has often been evoked. Our philosophical and theistic context kicks in. For example, language of the soul occurs early in Nussbaum's argument. She writes:

> But we seem to be forgetting about the soul, about what it is for thought to open out of the soul and connect person to world in a rich, subtle and complicated manner; about what it is to approach another person as a soul, rather than as a mere useful instrument or an obstacle to one's own plans; about what it is to talk as someone who has a soul to someone else whom sees as similarly deep and complex.[19]

Nussbaum's choice of the word "soul" is interesting: she says, in something of an understatement, that the word "has religious connotations for many people."[20] She neither rejects nor insists on those religious connotations, but what she is pointing to, by the use of this word "soul" is "the faculties of thought and imagination that make us human and make our relationships rich human relationships, rather than relationships of mere use and manipulation."[21]

Rowan Williams, in his book *Lost Icons* (written a decade before Nussbaum's book on the humanities), suggests why a return to the language of the soul may be occurring in many contexts. "'Soul' is—at least—a religious style of talking about selfhood," he writes. It is useful, says Williams, for countering the wholly secular language for the self, which has become trivializing and reductionist.[22]

Nussbaum's use of the word "soul" is an attempt to evoke the deep way in which connections between people occur; she is gesturing towards the capacity for understanding the other, especially those whose experiences are outside our usual borders. By her speaking of "a rich and engaged life," I take Nussbaum to be promoting a way of being that is outward-looking; that places us in dialogue and community with others. It is, if you like, a task of deep translation from one to another. And by using the word "soul" she may be suggesting that it has a moral or transcendent component, or both.

18. See, for example, Church of England, *From Anecdote to Evidence*.
19. Nussbaum, *Not for Profit*, 6.
20. Ibid.
21. Ibid.
22. Williams, *Lost Icons*, 7.

An essential part of this "rich and engaged life" is to pay profound attention to one another's stories. The American playwright and actress Anna Deavere Smith does precisely this in her plays: *Fires in the Mirror*, about the race riots between Jews and African Americans in Crown Heights, Brooklyn, New York (1991); *Twilight, Los Angeles*, about the race riots in that city (1992); and *Let Me Down Easy*, about the crisis in the American health-care system (2012). In the preparation for her plays, she interviews hundreds of people in a community, or multiple communities, from widely divergent backgrounds and viewpoints, and brings their stories to the stage, performing each character herself. She has written of this process, "To me, the most important doorway into the soul of a person is his or her words. . . . I suppose that words could also be the doorway into the soul of a culture."[23] Words, of course, both engender and require translation in order for common understanding to be reached.

THE TASK OF TRANSLATION

In the last pages of *The Religious Imagination and the Sense of God*, Bowker quotes the sculptor Henry Moore describing the problem of carving a Madonna and Child for Saint Matthew's Church in Northampton. Moore's question was how to translate the Christian tradition's understanding of "Madonna and Child" in such a way that the sculpture remained within that tradition, and was not just an "everyday Mother and Child," as Moore put it, and yet was distinctively different from past representations of that theme.[24]

The artist is always engaged in this translational act. In part, this is about taking a theme or trope that has currency in one culture and making it intelligible to the audience (whether they come from that culture or not) in such a way that it has impact. The artist's work is often about relating different cultural worlds one to another. In short, it is about activating our imaginations such that we are taken beyond our own immediate experience.

The religious person frequently finds him- or herself engaged in this translational task in the context of the twenty-first-century West. As fewer people grow up with any knowledge of the theistic contexts that Bowker outlined in his 1978 book, so the cultural resonances of those traditions have less and less effect. To use Bowker's language, we are less attuned to the signal inputs from the religious information net, and so cues of a religious sort are fewer and fewer in our society.

---

23. Smith, *Talk to Me*, 12.
24. Bowker, *Religious Imagination*, 315.

RELIGION AND THE MORAL IMAGINATION

At the core of all the major religious traditions is an engagement with the other, a sense of opening ourselves to strangers as well as friends, often manifested in the practice of generosity, in every sense of that term. The Buddhist nun Tenzin Palmo writes in her book *Reflections on a Mountain Lake: Teachings on Practical Buddhism*, that in the popular mind, Buddhism is primarily associated with meditation; but there are in fact six perfections, or *paramitas*: transcendental qualities that are needed for making progress towards enlightenment. The very first of these is giving, or generosity; while meditation is only number 5 of these six qualities. She writes beautifully about this practice of generosity:

> Giving is placed first because it is something we can all do right now. We don't have to be ethically perfect, we don't have to be great meditators, we don't have to develop great patience and avoid anger in all circumstances. We can be extremely flawed, extremely problematic people, but still be generous. Giving opens up our heart, which is another reason why it is placed first.[25]

We find this emphasis on reaching out to others, not only in Buddhism, but also at the heart of all three of the main monotheistic religions: Judaism, Christianity and Islam. In the Jewish and Christian traditions, the language and practice of commandment has been at the heart of the ethical life and its necessary engagement with others. For Judaism, the keeping of the law was and is, as Bowker reminds us, "the means of faithfulness." Its observance helps shape community. The commandments "are the language of response. They offer the means of creating, in the midst of time, a representation of obedience and community—a demonstration of community in a world which is otherwise full of hatred and division."[26]

Medieval and early modern Christianity refashioned the commandments in its own particular image—as a series of commands to teach morality to the masses, rather than as a set of communitarian religious practices. Walk into any rural medieval or Reformation-era church in England that has not been greatly renovated, and you will most likely see a large board or painting on the wall listing the Ten Commandments. These were to be learned by all villagers; they were the main guide to living. Their prominent display in the parish church said something about the Christianity that was taught there: that it was practical and rule-bound. Their display

---

25. Tenzin Palmo, *Reflections*, 46.
26. Bowker, *Religious Imagination*, 41.

also indicated the nature of medieval and early modern society: that it was ordered and hierarchical, and that the keeping of that order at a micro level (by individuals, within households) was essential to the keeping of order at the societal level—within the village, the county, the country as a whole. In a great chain of being extending down from God through the monarch and the ruling elite and down to the lowest farm worker, society's hierarchy was to be maintained through the following of rules and thus the keeping of good order. Morality was not to be imagined but to be obediently accepted as given.

In the modern, democratic world, the posting of the Ten Commandments would not be regarded as an effective way for the churches to communicate with or to the wider world. The old order has been profoundly challenged; unquestioned obedience to one's elders and so-called betters is no longer a lynchpin of society. This is not to deny that many churches still rely on commandment and obedience as a way of teaching morality, not least the fundamentalist churches; but this method often results in the development of "us" and "them" camps: those who obey the commandments, and those who do not. Such a method of teaching morality usually results in a narrowing of a community rather than its expansion. This mentality is something that Robinson regrets for its "us" and "them" way of being (those who obey the tribe's rules and those who do not), and because it leads to a shrinking rather than an expansion of community. "As we withdraw from one another we withdraw from the world, except as we increasingly insist that foreign groups and populations are our irreconcilable enemies. The shrinking of imaginative identification which allows such things as shared humanity to be forgotten always begins at home."[27]

Jesus was, as Bowker reminds us, first and foremost a teacher, working within "the boundary conditions of Israel."[28] Jesus developed his ethical stance in relation to the community in two particularly distinctive ways. First of all, he worked within the law of his inherited religious tradition, while at the same time placing a special emphasis on two commandments: Love God and Love your neighbor as yourself. The commandments of the Hebrew Scriptures are pedagogical—teaching the people of God how to order the household, and thus shape community, as a part of the larger whole. Jesus was often speaking to small groups of people, sometimes just his disciples. He used the language of commandment because that was the language of his scriptures, but he was often pointing to a rather "flatter" reality. He was talking friend to friend. In the Gospel of John, in the long

27. Robinson, *When I Was a Child*, 31.
28. Bowker, *Religious Imagination*, 129.

discourse to his disciples on the night before he died, he said, "This is my commandment, that you love one another as I have loved you" (John 13:34). This suggests that a successful love relationship is when you put yourself in someone else's shoes: "Love one another as I have loved you."

Jesus uses the language of friendship, "I do not call you servants any longer ... , but I have called you friends" (John 15:15). The servant/friend distinction is surely significant here: servants do for others what they have to do by their terms of employment; friends do something for each other—often, at least; one might even say *usually*—because they would *like* to do it. A moral imagination is at the heart of this action of loving another as yourself. It requires an imaginative stepping into the other's world and asking what love might mean in the context of their lives.

Jesus did not rely solely on the language of commandment. He also taught ethics through the telling of parables, creating open and ambiguous imaginative stories into which his listeners could enter. John Dominic Crossan defines a parable as a metaphor expanded into a story, or, more simply, he suggests that a parable is a metaphorical story. He contrasts an ordinary story—which wants you to focus internally on itself (to follow the development of character and plot, to wonder what will happen next and how it will all end)—with a metaphorical story, which always points externally beyond itself, to some different and much wider referent.

This distinction between a metaphorical story and a so-called ordinary story may be drawn too sharply by Crossan, but the important point is the emphasis on the direction of the story towards an other. The word "metaphor" comes from the Greek *meta* meaning "over" or "across" and *pherein* "to bear" or "to carry." A metaphorical story therefore sees something as another, carries one thing from its territory into another territory. As Crossan says, "'away-from here' is the destination of any parable."[29]

Human beings have a tendency to fix meaning, to find a one-size-fits-all explanation; but a parable can open the way for us to identify with each element or character in its story, even when, and perhaps because, we find each of those "characters" troubling or strange. The result is that parables do not tell us what to think, but rather encourage us to fuse our horizons (to use Hans-Georg Gadamer's term) with that of another.[30] Parables open up a space for us to imagine something beyond ourselves. Parables are multi-layered and open to widely divergent interpretations. What you see isn't necessarily what you get, and suddenly you find yourself stirred up, thinking and feeling, in a new way.

29. Crossan, *Power of Parable*, 8–9.
30. Gadamer, *Truth and Method*.

This parabolic style is an effective way of opening up the possibility of a moral imagination, with or without "the sense of God," and it has been translated into, and by, the arts in modern culture. In the visual arts, one sees it for example in the work of William Hogarth, in his series of paintings and engravings, *The Harlot's Progress* (1730) and *A Rake's Progress* (1733). Told visually, as modern morality tales, they tracked the rise and fall of, respectively, Moll Hackabout and Tom Rakewell, and thus related the story of modern urban life and its moral dangers. The contemporary artist Grayson Perry reworked Hogarth's *Rake's Progress* in his recent set of six tapestries, *The Vanity of Small Differences* (2012), designed in conjunction with his Channel 4 television series on class and taste. Here, Tim Rakewell's progress through the British class system is depicted in order to give the viewer an insight into our internal longings and their relationship to class mobility in a consumerist society. Both Hogarth and Perry evoke a response to the moral questions of their day by inviting us into the worlds of others visually without telling us how to identify with the different characters. The effectiveness of Perry's work is due, in no small part, to the many conversations he had with groups of people from different segments of British society in preparation for creating his tapestries. In this way, his work, based on interviews, is akin to the drama of Anna Deavere Smith.

Smith, by her use of people's stories in this way, develops a modern form of parabolic art, which leads us to embrace the stranger—or at least think about what the stranger's experience might be. Take her play, *Let Me Down Easy*. One could say that it is about the health-care system; and it is—but to leave it at that would be like saying most of Jesus's parables are about farming. Through the stories of twenty characters, she tells us something about ourselves, and how we think and feel about health, life, and death. The genius of Anna Deavere Smith is not only that we are suddenly in the theater with the late Governor of Texas, Ann Richards, or the cyclist Lance Armstrong or the supermodel Lauren Hutton, and therefore in the presence of the familiar, but also that she knows exactly which stories of theirs to select and tell so that we encounter the strange through that familiarity.

Smith does not tell us what to think about the health-care system; she gives us stories to startle us into thinking in new ways about it—and thus about life and health and death. Through our experience of the play, she prompts us to think and feel differently, as all good art does, about something we thought we already knew. Thus, as audience members, we relate not simply to *one* of Anna Deavere Smith's twenty characters in the play *Let me Down Easy*, but find parts of each of them understandable, and parts of each of them strange, in ways that prompt us to rethink our assumptions and ideas about health, living, and dying. It is an art form that encourages us to cross over from our own safe islands and embrace the strangeness of another's story. In her performances, Smith does not so much walk in another's shoes, though she does that, as inhabit or walk in their *words* and therefore their souls. The *New York Times*, reviewing her play *Fires in the Mirror*, wrote that "she does people's souls."

THE MORAL IMAGINATION AND A SENSE OF GOD

In the conclusion to his book *The Religious Imagination and the Sense of God*, Bowker writes that "the continuity of a religious tradition depends on the appropriation of what has up to that point been fundamentally resourceful, and on the translation of those resources into the construction of utterance in life."[31] He concludes in something of a surprise turn (but less elusively than in his earlier work, *The Sense of God*) that this "essentially is the work of prayer." The point of prayer, he says, is to

> realize and lock into the information net, which already exists long before we do anything about it; and it is to allow those informational cues . . . so to rest and move and live within the disposition and intention of our brain behavior, that we—the very subject of that behavior—are moved beyond the inherited point of our departure into a new and volunteered dependence—until, indeed, we realize in ourselves the meaning of Augustine's otherwise unverifiable assertion, 'God is the only reality, and we are only real insofar as we are in his order, and he in us.'[32]

Just as Bowker turns to prayer rather surprisingly at the end of his exploration of how the religious imagination develops, so I want to make a (possibly) surprise turn to grace at the end of this article, as we think about the parallel case for developing the moral imagination. All the reading, all the art, all the liberal humanities curriculums of all the world's universities, make little difference in forging humanitarian communities unless they lead to change—which means that we have to change.

The development of a moral imagination requires the capacity to pay careful attention to the other, especially the stranger, and their stories—which may occur via the entry into a story, as encouraged by a parable or a parabolic art form. It also requires the expansion, rather than the narrowing, of our communities. And, finally, it needs something that emerges from these two aspects of story and community but which cannot be contained

---

31. Bowker, *Religious Imagination*, 315.
32. Ibid., 313.

in any formula—that is the impulse to act with the others' interests at heart rather than our own.

That requires the aha moment. The Christian tradition articulates this as grace, and the history of Christianity is filled with stories of those whose hearts were turned, with the result that their actions changed, no one more famous, perhaps, than John Newton, eighteenth-century slave owner turned abolitionist and author of the hymn "Amazing Grace." How does the moment of change, the change of heart, come about? How do the experiences stack up to help us create a moral imagination that enables us to act differently? Grace being a gift of God, we cannot force it. Ariana Huffington, founder and editor of the online newspaper the *Huffington Post*, when interviewed by Anna Deavere Smith, talked about how people develop what she calls their spiritual instinct: "How do you get people to make it part of their lives because you can't tell people 'It would be a good idea if you believed in God.' I mean, it's grace."[33]

Huffington suggests that this "getting to God" can happen through art: "when you do it through poetry and the theater you can get to a part of us that is not as barricaded as if you do it through [newspaper] columns or speeches. You know, people in a dark theater are more vulnerable in a positive way . . . . Through the play you get to the consciousness in a way that you can't do it through, ah, preaching or prose or this or that."[34] In other words, we do the footwork, but the moment of realization, of turning one's heart, comes perhaps when we least expect it. The development of a moral imagination can, of course, occur without any sense of God at all.[35] But what I hope what this article has illustrated is that both the moral imagination and the religious imagination need the right contextual conditions to flourish, and the sharing of those contextual conditions can only be mutually beneficial.

BIBLIOGRAPHY

Bowker, John W. *The Religious Imagination and the Sense of God*. Oxford: Clarendon, 1978.

———. *The Sense of God: Sociological, Anthropological and Psychological Approaches to the Origin of the Sense of God*. Oxford: Clarendon, 1973.

Bromwich, David. *Moral Imagination: Essays*. Princeton: Princeton University Press, 2014.

33. Smith, *Talk to Me*, 216.

34. Ibid., 217.

35. For an interesting exploration of the relationship between the two, see, for example, Temple, *Kingdom of God*.

Burke, Edmund. *Reflections on the Revolution in France* [1790]. Mineola, NY: Dover, 2012.

Church of England. *From Anecdote to Evidence—Findings from the Church Growth Research Programme 2011-2013*. London: Church of England Publishing, 2014. Online: http://www.churchgrowthresearch.org.uk/UserFiles/File/Reports/FromAnecdoteToEvidence1.0.pdf/.

Crossan, John Dominic. *The Power of Parable: How Fiction by Jesus Became Fiction about Jesus*. New York: HarperOne, 2012.

Gadamer, Hans-Georg. *Truth and Method*. New York: Crossroad, 1985.

Himmelfarb, Gertrude. *The Moral Imagination*. Chicago: Dee, 2006.

Lederach, John Paul. *The Moral Imagination: The Art and Soul of Building Peace*. Oxford: Oxford University Press, 2005.

Nussbaum, Martha C. *Not for Profit: Why Democracy Needs the Humanities*. The Public Square Book Series. Princeton: Princeton University Press, 2010.

Robinson, Marilynne. *When I Was a Child I Read Books*. London: Virago, 2012.

Sandel, Michael J. *What Money Can't Buy: The Moral Limits of Markets*. New York: Farrar, Straus & Giroux, 2012.

Small, Helen. *The Value of the Humanities*. Oxford: Oxford University Press, 2013.

Smith, Anna Deavere. *Talk to Me: Listening between the Lines*. New York: Random House, 2000.

Temple, William. *The Kingdom of God*. London: Macmillan, 1913.

Tenzin Palmo. *Reflections on a Mountain Lake: Teachings on Practical Buddhism*. Ithaca, NY: Snow Lion, 2002.

Williams, Rowan. *Lost Icons. Reflections on Cultural Bereavement*. Edinburgh: T. & T. Clark, 2000.

PART 4

Neuroscience and Theology

9

Brain Battles
Theology and Neuroscience

—William J. Abraham

The debate about the relation between science and theology has taken a whole new turn in the last ten years or so. We have entered a third phase in the discussion. The first phase was the discussion on the interaction between theology and cosmology. Traditional readings of Genesis, developed by the learned Archbishop Ussher of Dublin, posited that the world began in 4004 BC [sic]; this was clearly incompatible with the proposal that the earth is roughly 14 billion years old. The issue had to be thought through and it was. The second phase was the discussion posed by the challenge of evolution within biology generated in the late nineteenth century. The debate on this one lingers on, but as far as mainstream Christianity is concerned the issue is settled: some version of theistic evolution is the favored option. The main alternatives to this, that is, the young-earth option and the Intelligent Design option, are not really taken seriously in mainstream Christianity. Indeed they tend to be treated with disdain and contempt. Before I identify a third phase of the discussion it is good to pause and get a feel for what kind of issues sit below the surface of these old and hoary debates. What is it that generates and sustains the ongoing discussion between theology and science?

In the North American scene, one cannot discount the background music of how best to manage the relation between faith and politics. The science-religion debate intersects with the debate about the secularization of politics, with the ongoing, dynamic negotiation of the separation of church and state. Yet another factor in the neighborhood of secularization is more broadly cultural: that is, the debate on theology and science touches on the quest in the West for a viable *Weltanschauung* or comprehensive worldview beyond Christianity. The collapse of Christendom (in the case of the United States the second disestablishment of mainstream Protestantism) has left a void in which many look to science as the best bet on developing an intellectually satisfying vision of ourselves and the universe.[1] Intelligent lay folk in the churches I know best often take this option unwittingly. Science tells you the truth about the universe par excellence. This turn to science as the final revelation of the truth is most visible in the rise of the New Atheism, but this has traction precisely because it is now assumed that theology is epistemologically empty. Theology, it is generally believed even in the private university, deserves its lowly status at the margins of the academy or locked away in a private world that has no cognitive status in the real world of truth and knowledge. So we need to pay attention to the massive shift in intellectual sensibility in Western culture. Nor can one ignore the role of the media in seeking out the kind of emotive, if not sensational, issues that will whip up interest in the general public. There is a lively and polemical edge in the media that readily pounces on conflict and warfare. So there is an inescapable public dimension that is absent in Europe. In Europe the temperature of the debate and the noise level are much lower than they are in the United States.

However, these considerations scratch the surface. We need to get a sense as to why theology and science intrinsically interact, as to why this debate is not a mere epiphenomenon generated by other more primary realities. The debate arises because both theology and science make robust claims about the world. They are not isolated disciplines with a neat dividing wall of separation. Consider theology as that discipline committed to studious reflection on God and on all things insofar as they relate to God, and I mean "all things"; science in turn is one of our very best ways of gaining information about the natural order. Hence the potential for conflict is intrinsically in play. Serious theologians are bound to make claims about, say, the created order and within that about human beings. These are precisely

---

1. The popular alternative is to construct a comprehensive vision of existence around freedom and the tenets of liberal, capitalist democracy.

the objects of scientific investigation; so it is obvious that the potential for competing descriptions and explanations exists *ab initio*.

This is patently clear in the case of the first two phases of the discussion. Theologians claimed that God created the world in 4004 BCE; this turned out to be false, hence the lively debate. Theologians claimed that God created Adam and Eve, the first human agents, directly from the dust of the earth; evolutionary theory challenged this by positing that human agents arose indirectly through a combination of natural selection, random variation, and the survival of the fittest.[2] Beyond that, the theory of evolution challenged conventional ways of understanding the meaning and origins of the Bible. Thus it raised questions about how to distinguish the literal from the figurative; it also raised questions about how to understand the divine inspiration of Scripture; it cut into claims about the uniqueness of human beings in the wider scheme of creation; and it wreaked havoc on the kind of appeal to divine design that had become conventional in Victorian England.

The same logic of interaction is in play in the third phase of the debate on the interaction between science and theology, namely, the impact of developments in neuroscience. It would be fair to say that neuroscience is now sweeping through the academy like a hurricane. Its impact is felt very naturally in psychology, beginning with clinical psychology, but it has reached as far as the study of literature.

It is clear that John Bowker presciently recognized that studies of the brain were one of the new frontiers in the discussion of the relation between science and religion.[3] The caution he expresses is as important today as it

2. OED: evolution is "(in general) the proposition that all living organisms have undergone a process of alteration and diversification from simple primordial forms during the earth's history; (in particular) a scientific theory proposing a mechanism for this process, now *esp.* that based on Darwin's theory of the natural selection of genetically inherited and adaptive variation."

3. I was a doctoral student at Oxford in philosophy of religion when he gave some of his Wilde lectures. At the time I was both encouraged and astonished at the depth and range of his work. I do not recall which set of lectures I attended, but the impression that he left has remained with me across the years. As I talked with Maurice Wiles at the time, he noted that he had attended a session where there was a range of specialists gathered to discuss the public lectures. At that session, he reported that not a single expert faulted the materials that had been drawn from their respective disciplines. This clearly impressed Maurice Wiles, as it did me. At the time, the graduate students in philosophy of religion whom I knew were wrestling with the long-standing critique of theology that had developed from within the empiricist tradition. The sense was that while there was to be relief up ahead we were still operating with our backs against the wall. Bowker's lectures were a breath of fresh air. He struck me as one of the most learned scholars I had ever heard; yet his lectures were a model of modesty, clarity, intellectual humility, and fecundity. There was not a whit of defensiveness; yet there was a quiet boldness and confidence that was a source of intellectual hope for the future

was thirty years ago. This caution comes through very powerfully in his remarks on the physiology of the brain and the claims of religious experience. He notes that

> our present knowledge is minute. Perhaps for this reason many of the current debates about brain behaviour—particularly the debates about Skinnerian behaviourism—have not advanced much further than the level of cheese-mites and the cheese:
>
> > The cheese-mites asked how the cheese got there.
> > And warmly debated the matter:
> > The orthodox said it came from the air,
> > And the heretics said it came from the platter.[4]

The situation has changed dramatically from the early 1970s, but the need for caution remains as great as ever. The necessity of caution is reinforced by the inescapability of extensive collaborative work across several disciplines, a feature of the discussion which Bowker himself exemplified in the extraordinary range of data and warrants he brought to bear on his account of the sense of God.

My interest focuses more narrowly on the impact of neuroscience on theology; and my aims are modest, as they should be at this stage of the discussion. Even then the range of relevant disciplines in play is daunting, as I shall argue later. I want to do four things in what follows. First, in line with my opening comments, I want to identify where neuroscience and theology overlap. Prima facie they do not overlap at all, so we need to pause and get our bearings with some care. Second, I want to summarize the most radical version of the appeal to neuroscience, which is developed intentionally as a challenge to theology. Third, I want to draw attention to a very important theological response to that challenge that has surfaced in and around the work of Nancey Murphy, who has provided a substantive contribution to the discussion. Fourth, I want to sketch the contours of a research agenda that charts an alternative way to proceed. Finally, I shall stand back and make some summary comments on the nature and significance of this work.

Our first assignment is to get clear on how theology and neuroscience interact; that is, what claims do theologians make that overlap with the kind of claims that crop up in neuroscience? Initially this does not look very promising. Neuroscience focuses on the nature of the brain. Do theologians want to say anything about the brain? Surely we are no more interested in

---

of theology. I continue to cherish the memory of those days as a quiet landmark in my own intellectual journey even though my work has not drawn specifically on his research and writing as a primary resource.

4. Bowker, *Sense of God*, 136.

the brain that we are, say, in elephants' tentacles. What subsection of theological studies or systematic theology does that topic fall into? What does Scripture or the great theologians of the tradition have to say about the brain? The answer, of course, is nothing!

Well not so fast! Once we turn from the abstract idea of neuroscience to what neuroscientists and some of their philosophical friends say, then the picture changes dramatically. What is at issue is a theological vision of human nature. Neuroscience overlaps with theology because neuroscientists develop comprehensive visions of human nature. And human nature is most certainly on the theological radar screen. Yet we need to be even more precise. Theologians develop two quite different networks of claims about human nature. The first involves various doctrines of sin. Think of the proposals of Augustine or Pelagius or John Wesley or Reinhold Niebuhr or Judith Plaskow. In this instance, what is on offer is a vision of the human predicament nested in a wider analysis of creation, freedom, fall, and redemption. The focus of these claims is soteriological. The focus of the second kind of claim is broadly metaphysical; that is, it involves a vision of the human person, or of the human agent, as an ultimate factor or feature of the universe as a whole. Here think of the claim that human beings are made in the image of God and are best thought of as embodied souls, or a combination of minds and bodies, or as bodies with a special kind of Aristotelian form. One way to make the point would be to say that over and against natural agents, human beings are irreducibly personal agents endowed with various capacities and with the ability to make choices.

Once one puts the issue in this latter fashion, it becomes immediately clear that while we can *logically* distinguish between these two kinds of claims, they cannot *ontologically* be separated. The soteriological and the metaphysical begin to bleed into each other. Thus, doctrines of sin lead into doctrines of liberty and determinism that are highly ramified and contested. Christian theologians in the West have in fact been very leery of doctrines of freedom. Think of Luther's polemic against Erasmus. Or think of the soft determinism of Calvin and Edwards. Or think of the current work of Eleonore Stump in the deployment of the recent insights of Harry Frankfurt about first-order and second-order volitions. Frankfurt is a determinist. Stump rejects determinism; but you can see the issue of determinism is entangled in the neighborhood. The debate about the relation between sin and determinism from the theological side has been driven by an effort to safeguard the doctrine of grace. Theologians have been more than ready to surrender doctrines of human liberty and freedom to do so. It is a matter of intense debate as to how we are to reconcile freedom and grace. So while we can rightly distinguish the soteriological from the metaphysical, we cannot ultimately separate them.

To come back to the intersection between theology and neuroscience, the debate to date has centered on how to bring into harmony some elements of what I am calling the metaphysical dimensions or focus of Christian claims about human nature with the robust claims of many neuroscientists. The sticking point is obvious: many theologians have been committed to a dualist vision of human beings and neuroscience *prima facie* is a committed foe of any and all forms of dualism as applied to human agents.

We can see this most clearly if we look briefly at the most radical version of the appeal to neuroscience. One point of entry into our research is to ask this question: what would it be like to have a grand theory of everything? A grand theory of everything would be a theory that basically accounts for everything; it would have depth, and breadth; it would have explanatory power all the way to the bottom and all the way to the top; it would leave nothing out; it would be intellectually robust; and it would be emotionally powerful.

Over the last three hundred years one such grand theory of everything has emerged within Western culture. It has four crucial components. As I identify these, we can see that its proponents are in search of the crown jewels in the life of the mind. First, ultimate reality is essentially matter from top to bottom. Everything that exists is ultimately reducible to physics and chemistry. We are complex units of particles and impersonal forces. And that includes you and me and your neighbor next door. This is the ontological component. It can also be identified as the reductionist component, where human agents are reduced not just for methodological purposes of more elegant research but in the stronger and more interesting sense that they are best understood and explained as fundamentally made up of or constituted by matter. The ontological heavy lifting is done at the level of physical reality.

Second, there is a deterministic component. Reality is essentially governed by physical laws from one end to the other. There are no uncaused events in the world; inside the world-system, everything arises out of the preceding physical conditions. There is no free will in any robust, libertarian sense. This is the deterministic component. Of course, things are more complex at the subatomic level; but even there we can here the echo of Einstein: God does not throw dice; the determinism is statistical not absolute.

Third, there is a causal-closure component: there are no causes outside the physical system as a whole. There is no human agency. There may be consciousness (the grand theory wobbles here), but it is merely an epiphenomenon. It is like the steam coming off the sausages on the grill; it is caused by what is happening beneath it and below it. There are no genuine causes other than those countenanced by the physical senses. This is the causal-closure component.

Fourth, there is a rationality component. This grand theory has been established by science. It is not a matter of dogma or human tradition or authority or revelation. It is serious science, pure and simple. And the relevant science doing the heavy-lifting is neuroscience. If you are a rational person you will sign on with enthusiasm; and the pay-off is that you will be emotionally satisfied. This is the rationality component.

What this summary makes clear is that there is much more to the intersection of theology and neuroscience than the findings of neuroscience. We have, in fact, a combination of scientific and philosophical theory and insight (or misperception); and it is the combination of these claims that leads to the intersection with theological claims about human nature. It should not surprise us in the least, then, that theologians who reject this radical version of the appeal to neuroscience do so by carefully sorting through the entangled components and proposing a very different way to absorb the findings of neuroscience. One web of intersecting claims replaces another web of intersecting claims.

One theologian who deserves special attention in this regard is Nancey Murphy. Trained to the doctoral level in both philosophy of science and in theology, she is well placed to make her mark on the discussion. In addition, her formation in both Catholicism and more recently in the Anabaptist tradition ensures additional layers of richness in her formation as a theologian. Over the years she has teamed up with a network of theologians, philosophers, and biblical scholars to spearhead a comprehensive response to the challenge posed by developments in neuroscience. They deserve much more extended articulation and attention that I can give here, but I do want to lay out the core of her proposals. Let me summarize her moves in a series of propositions.

First, the findings of neuroscience make it clear that human agents are initially best seen as physical organisms. Dualism is therefore false; the view that human agents are combinations of minds and bodies is rejected; so too is any belief in human beings as involving a trichotomy of spirit, mind, and body.

Second, theologians can readily dispose of dualism in their vision of human nature because it is a late development in the tradition that is not in keeping with the biblical materials on human nature but was really imported into the tradition in the interaction of early postbiblical theology with Platonic philosophy. Moreover, talk about human nature being constituted by souls and bodies was originally an unstable doctrine that got flattened into the standard version of Cartesian dualism that flourished in the tradition in the modern period. Hence Christian theology can dispense with dualism (whether Platonic or Cartesian) without shedding any theological tears.

Third, what motivates the adoption of physicalism and the rejection of dualism is a sincere desire to rid the Christian tradition of alien materials that are a hindrance to contemporary educated folk from coming to faith. Here we can see the apologetic side of Murphy's work; she does not want inappropriate intellectual stumbling blocks to stand in the way of a robust faith commitment.

Fourth, this commitment to physicalism should not be confused with reductionism. What is proposed is a vision of nonreductive physicalism. The former (reductive physicalism) is disastrous both for Christian theology and for the rationality of human thinking; nonreductive physicalism is not. What is on display in nonreductive physicalism is a vision of reality in which matter is organized into more complex configurations so that there emerge new forms or structures with their own integrity and reality. As you move up the hierarchy of being (my language), you also encounter new causal factors that emerge at each new level. While there is a clear commitment to emergence, we emphatically do not have the emergence of some new "stuff" like a mind or soul; rather we have emergence of new levels of structure and organization. New configurations of structure constitute new causal factors so that you have both upward causation and downward causation. Life (itself a new configuration of emergent complexity) produces new sorts of causal interactions. When you have more complex structures, it is not that there are new causal forces (psychic forces or vital forces or minds or souls); rather, the causal forces of physics will enter into vastly more complex interactions. The laws of physics do not predict the new configurations and interactions; but whatever emerges does not violate the laws of physics.

Fifth, and finally, all this is entirely compatible with what theologians want to say about human agents and their place in creation. Thus theologians can still with integrity be committed to bodily resurrection in eschatology rather than the Greek notion of the immortality of the soul. They can be more biblical in their thinking about human agents; they can avoid interventionist conceptions of divine agency. And they can sustain all of the traditional features of human agents as being unique in creation as a whole. Thus human agents have the capacity to operate on the basis of moral reasoning. They can act on the basis of goals and principles. They are free (but not causally undetermined). They have consciousness. They can relate to God and engage in worship, and they can see the world as open to divine action at its most basic level (at the quantum level).

I have chosen to review the work of Nancey Murphy because it is by far the most sophisticated and interesting effort on the part of theologians to deal with developments in neuroscience. There is a pleasing boldness in her work that is has both a specificity in the claims advanced and a readiness to take the discussion all the way to the bottom. Thus, Murphy has developed a full-scale epistemology of theology that replicates her work in the epistemology of science; and this in turn is deployed to deal with recent journeys into postmodernity familiar to virtually all students of theology. She is also keen to pursue the ethical and spiritual dimensions of the turn to neuroscience.[5]

What we actually have on offer here is a comprehensive research program that involves interdisciplinary work in biblical studies, the history of doctrine, neuroscience, philosophy, and theology. This means that it would be utterly futile as well as unproductive to offer any kind of quick or decisive refutation of her claims. Research programs do not work that way. Indeed it is imperative that such research programs be envisaged and pursued with aggressive tenacity and persistence. This applies both to the materialist research program I outlined earlier and the Christian materialist research agenda of Murphy and her colleagues. Research programs like this are the lifeblood of the academy and of the journey to discovery. It may be unfortunate that the price we pay for these programs is that they appear dogmatic (actually, they really are dogmatic). They are initially unfalsifiable (follow Quine and make the necessary adjustments in the wider web of belief), emotionally charged, impervious to evidence, intellectually self-serving, and even bigoted. In this respect science turns out to be like theology across the centuries. Happily, given secularization, the state stops us from killing each other across the board in the academy, but there are other ways by means of which to ward off attacks from opponents in competing research programs: demonize, deny tenure, get control of editorial boards, exclude from doctoral programs, spread disinformation, cut off funding, and the like.

Which brings me to the constructive proposal: we need a radically different research agenda. The initial motivation for this revolves around three considerations. First, both these proposals are at the end of the day committed to a vision of full-scale determinism. Neither can support the kind of robust vision of human freedom and agency that is vital for morality,

---

5. Murphy's first book, *Theology in the Age of Scientific Reasoning*, received the American Academy of Religion's Award for Excellence. Most recently, she coedited *Downward Causation and the Neurobiology of Free Will*. Other recent books include *Did My Neurons Make Me Do It?* For coauthored and coedited works, see the bibliography at the end of this essay.

for theology, and for our medical and political practices. Second, the forms of reductionism involved are ultimately a form of elimination that fails to deal with irreducible features of our human and cultural landscape. The obvious anomaly at this point, which is virtually recognized by everyone, is the phenomenon of consciousness. Third, neither is ultimately compatible with the fullness and robustness of the canonical faith of the church which has its own reliable warrants, and which therefore, from the theological side of the aisle, deserves a full run for its money.[6] All that is needed to motivate an alternative research agenda is not some apodictic disproof of the current options. It is enough that within this highly contested arena we satisfy two conditions: first, there is enough skepticism and informed counter-intuition to be worried about the foundations of the research programs available; and second, we can begin to lay out the contours of an alternative research agenda. I have already indicated that the first condition is satisfied; it remains to provide a very brief sketch of an alternative research agenda. To that I now turn.

What would the research involve? It would begin with a new series of ingenious experiments in neuroscience that show that you can change your brain states by mental action. The crucial researchers here have been Jeffrey Schwartz and Mario Beauregard.[7] As a result of their research we can now actually measure the two crucial factors in play. On the one hand, we can measure the density of focused attention, and, on the other hand, we can measure the changes in the brain. The crucial finding from this research is this: the mind really can change the brain. This is a dramatic discovery. Notice that this move is not a matter of cooking the results in neuroscience; we can begin with state-of-the-art work in neuroscience with professional scientists whose competence is unquestioned.

The obvious objection at this point is, of course, that correlation does not mean causation. This is indeed correct. However, I am not speaking here of correlation and event causation; we are already in the world of agent causation. We are not talking of one event following by another; we are speaking of human action making a difference in brain states. This is a crucial causal statement. So at this point we need to draw on expertise in the arena of action theory that has been in play since at least the days of Thomas Reid.[8]

---

6. For an articulation and defense of canonical theism, see Abraham et al., *Canonical Theism*.

7. For a more popular and accessible version of their research see Schwartz and Begley, *Mind and the Brain*; and the work by Beauregard and O'Leary, *The Spiritual Brain*.

8. For a comprehensive review of this field see O'Connor and Sandis, *Companion*.

We can tackle the worry about causation from the side of science as well. Dig down deeper into the brain to the subatomic level and we enter the field of quantum physics. What do we find there? We find that the revolution from classical physics to quantum physics reveals a world that is open to human agency. Our observations actually change and stabilize the happenings at the subatomic level. Technically what is involved is the collapse of the wave function. The issue to be pursued at this point is a very simple one: could it be that the results of the work in neuroscience are best explained by saying that the changes in the brain involve the stabilization of the wave function at the subatomic level? To be sure, we face at this juncture a contested interpretation of quantum physics. However, it is a thoroughly plausible interpretation; it is a live option. To tackle the tangled issues in this arena we need to draw on specialized expertise in the philosophy of physics to critically examine what is at stake.

The claim that we can change brain states by human agency has got legs, that is, scientific legs. Does all this make a difference? Does belief in human agency matter? To answer this, we stay at the level of science—this time the science of psychology. Suppose you tell one group of students that they are determined, that they have no agency. Suppose you tell another group of students that they have agency, that they are genuinely free. What do you find? The first group is much more likely to cheat than the second. So these proposals really do matter. To put it mildly, it would appear that common sense and common law are dead right about their fundamental intuitions on the importance of free will and human agency.[9]

The envisaged research program has moved from human agency down to the subatomic level; we then moved back up to the psychological level. We now press our explorations up into the philosophical, religious, and theological arenas. We need a group of philosophers who can work on the mind-body problem, on the metaphysics of personhood, on the philosophy of action, and on epistemological matters. At the religious level we need the input of Buddhist scholars.

How do we get from all this science to theology? Christian theology has long grappled with the idea of human agency. There are libraries of critical reflection on it. At a minimum, theologians have insisted that human agents are made in the image of God. So, there is an immediate connection to divine agency. There is a wealth of material on divine agency and divine action that is relevant. God creates and sustains all that is; the world is mind-dependent at its deepest levels. I personally would be keen to work on

---

9. Important research related to this domain has been done by Jonathan Schooler. See http://www.psych.ucsb.edu/people/faculty/schooler/index.php.

sorting out how to develop a vision of divine agency that is compatible with the quiet revolutions happening within earshot of us all in neuroscience and quantum physics.[10] Moreover, it has been a long-standing intuition of a host of Christian theologians that the mystery in divine agency and reality is mirrored in an irreducible mystery about human agency and human reality. What should we make of this? Is this an escapist strategy, or does this metaepistemic observation find deep echoes in our efforts to develop a comprehensive metaphysics of human agency that should be taken seriously? Hence, I am interested in sorting out the epistemological considerations that enter into the debate at various levels.

We should be clear what this agenda would not involve, what it would aggressively forbid. The last thing we need is one more tired debate about the relation between religion and science; what I am proposing is not some kind of shot-gun wedding between science and religion. This research agenda is driven by a network of experiments in neuroscience. It insists on a relevant range of academic expertise within and without science. We need a wide range of difference of opinion: agnostic, Buddhist, Jewish, and Christian. This is one way to counter the bad side effects of most research agendas in this domain.[11] Second, this is not another tired effort to deal with the New Atheism. I find it interesting and salutary that John Wesley, in his treatment of science in his own day, revised the standard vision of natural philosophy by eliminating the drive to use science to combat atheism. He was content to explore the power, wisdom, goodness, and kindness of God in his *Survey of the Wisdom of God in Creation: Or, a Compendium of Natural Philosophy*.[12] We need to lower the temperature and get more expertise and intellectual virtue at the table. This is a positive research program that seeks to find a natural home for human agency in a scientific vision of the universe. It rigorously follows the evidence wherever it leads. It is clearheaded; it is robust; it is fallible; it is revisable; it is rational.

Now I hear the critic whisper: you say this is fallible and revisable; so, what if all this turns out to be wrong? Let me in conclusion give two quick

---

10. I am currently engaged on a long-haul, four-volume research agenda focused on divine agency and divine action.

11. John Bowker captured the important place of diverse conceptual commitments in our understanding when he noted with respect to our labeling experience in this way, "the warrant for a particular label does not lie in the experience itself, but in the conceptual background, the conceptual foundations, which create particular expectations and supply particular experiences to *any* experience." See *Sense of God*, 141. The emphasis is as in the original.

12. See the splendid review of the issues at stake in interpreting Wesley in Felleman, "John Wesley's Survey of the Wisdom of God in Creation," 68–73. Wesley edited out the references to atheism from his sources.

answers to that question. First, if all this turns out to be wrong, we can take a break and make a fresh start, or we can throw our intellectual weight behind other research agendas that are out there. This is what all good researchers and academics do. Second, if all this turns out to be wrong, we face a dilemma. On the one hand, if the only thing that exists is matter, then it does not matter if our proposals turn out to be wrong. We are just a bag of molecules or bundles of sensation or puppets of deterministic forces. We are complex configurations of physics and chemistry. There are no agents, decisions, actions, values. Many researchers think that they can still help themselves to these notions after embracing physicalism; I find this unpersuasive. So, the results do not matter one way or the other. If we fail for whatever reason, the whole agenda collapses; it will not matter, for all we are is matter. On the other hand, if I am on the right lines here, then it really does matter. We are genuine agents; we can ask genuine questions; we can make real decisions; we have value; we have real freedom and real responsibility. This vision is not make-believe; it fits with the best science we can muster. It should be an essential element in any grand theory of everything. And I would add, for any serious theologian it is going to be an essential element in any robust theological anthropology of the twenty-first century.

BIBLIOGRAPHY

Abraham, William J. et al., eds. *Canonical Theism: A Proposal for Theology and the Church*. Grand Rapids: Eerdmans, 2008.

Beauregard, Mario, and Denyse O'Leary. *The Spiritual Brain: A Neuroscientist's Case for the Existence of the Soul*. New York: HarperCollins, 2008.

Bowker, John. *The Sense of God: Sociological, Anthropological and Psychological Approaches to the Origin of the Sense of God*. Oxford: Clarendon, 1973.

Felleman, Laura Bartels. "John Wesley's Survey of the Wisdom of God in Creation: A Methodological Inquiry." *PSCF* 58 (2006) 68–73.

Murphy, Nancey. *Bodies and Souls, or Spirited Bodies? Current Issues in Theology*. Cambridge: Cambridge University Press, 2006.

———. *Theology in the Age of Scientific Reasoning*. Cornell Studies in the Philosophy of Religion. Ithaca, NY: Cornell University Press, 1990.

Murphy, Nancey, and Warren S. Brown. *Did My Neurons Make Me Do It? Philosophical and Neurobiological Perspectives on Moral Responsibility and Free Will*. New York: Oxford University Press, 2007.

Murphy, Nancey, and William Stoeger, SJ, eds. *Evolution and Emergence: Systems, Organisms, Persons*. Oxford: Oxford University Press, 2007.

Murphy, Nancey et al., eds. *Downward Causation and the Neurobiology of Free Will*. Berlin: Springer, 2009.

Murphy, Nancey et al., eds. *Physics and Cosmology: Scientific Perspectives on the Problem of Natural Evil*. Scientific Perspectives on the Problem of Natural Evil 1. Notre Dame: University of Notre Dame Press, 2007.

O'Connor, Timothy, and Constantine Sandis, eds. *A Companion to the Philosophy of Action*. Blackwell Companions to Philosophy 46. Oxford: Blackwell, 2010.

Schwartz, Jeffrey, and Sharon Begley. *The Mind and the Brain: Neuroplasticity and the Power of Mental Force*. New York: Regan, 2002.

10

The Origin of the Sense of God
Causation, Epistemology, and Ontology

—Quinton Deeley

INTRODUCTION

In his Wilde Lecture series of 1972 and 1978 John Bowker addressed "the origin of the sense of God in human consciousness"—in other words, the origin of the concept, imagination, or direct experience of God.[1] There are and have been many senses of God or gods, but a predominant theme in theistic traditions has been the sense of God as an object of awareness that is transcendent yet evokes the language of personal relationship and agency—what John has termed "responsive transcendence."[2] Collectively, the Wilde lectures articulate key themes and methods of John's work in theology and religious studies, and in particular how to account for the sense of God as responsive transcendence.

In this chapter, I will summarise these themes and their development in subsequent writings, before going on to consider recent research into how a sense of God arises in light of John's approach. The focus throughout will

---

1. Bowker, *Sense of God*; and Bowker, *Religious Imagination*.
2. Bowker, *Religious Imagination*, 27.

be on the fundamental question of the origin of the sense of God in human consciousness, holding in view John's own emphasis that the naturalistic question of the origin of the sense of God raises further questions not just of epistemology but also of ontology—in other words, of knowledge of the existence and nature of God. Part of my aim will be to show the implications that questions of ontology have for the origin of the sense of God in human consciousness, whether or not God exists as God independently of cognition. Yet, to investigate the origin of the sense of God is to investigate the cause or causes of the sense of God; so to begin we will consider the nature of causation.

CAUSATION AND CONSTRAINT

Causal theories of the sense of God matter to theology because of the ontologies they imply or presuppose—for example, whether God is invoked as a cause of the sense of God, or whether natural processes are considered sufficient. One of the key presuppositions of causal accounts of the sense of God is the very notion of causality itself. Causal explanations tend to emphasise immediate, active contingencies or processes that produce an outcome. This often leads to the isolation of single causes of complex phenomena with the attendant risk of falsely dichotomous explanations ("violence: is it born or bred?").[3] Multifactorial explanations are a partial antidote to this, and are more widely accepted in fields such as medicine and psychiatry than was the case even a generation ago.[4] More subtly, understanding the contribution of passive causes ("background" contextual conditions) is critical to the explanation of complex phenomena such as human biology or behavior. Overemphasis on apparent active, immediate causes can obscure the dependence of a phenomenon on a range of contextual conditions, without which an apparent active cause would have no effect or different effects entirely—for example, the effect of a gene is critically dependent on the system in which it is embedded.[5]

In *The Sense of God*, John proposed an alternative approach to the explanation of behavior to circumvent the biases introduced by the specification of "causes," and instead to accommodate a broad recognition of relevant conditions and influences. The term "constraint" was adopted from cybernetics, defined by one of its founders, Ashby, as "the science of

---

3. Bowker, *Is God a Virus?*
4. Harland et al., "Study of Psychiatrists' Concepts of Mental Illness."
5. Bowker, *Is God a Virus?*

communication and control in animals and man."[6] When analyzing the function of machines, "cybernetics envisages a set of possibilities much wider than the actual, and then asks why the particular case should conform to its usual particular restriction."[7] A set of possible outcomes is restricted into a specific outcome by constraints, whereby a constraint is any feature of a system that makes a difference to the occurrence of a given outcome. As such, the notion of constraint opens the explanation of any complex phenomenon to a wide recognition of potential influences; in a BBC radio debate with E. O. Wilson, the founder of sociobiology, John referred to this as "opening explanation at the seams."[8] However, to consider what constraints influence the sense or gods or God, it is first necessary to have a way of determining what the contents of such experiences are.

PHENOMENOLOGY AND THE APPEARANCE OF GOD

In *The Sense of God*, John discussed the method of phenomenology originating in the work of Edmund Husserl to understand how a sense of God appears in consciousness. Husserl sought a foundation for knowledge through the analysis of experience:

> there is only the stream of consciousness, "the flowing conscious life," which represents my "I-ness" at any particular moment. The only fundamental fact of which I can be sure is that I experience my own consciousness. What I experience is less immediately certain. Our access, therefore, to the only certain foundation of all knowledge must lie in a much closer attention to what consciousness is.[9]

The analysis of *cogitationes*, appearances in consciousness, is conducted with an *epoche*, a "bracketing out" of assumptions about their existence, truth, or value: "phenomenological experience as reflection must avoid any interpretative constructions. Its descriptions must reflect accurately the concrete contents of experience, precisely as they are experienced."[10] Nevertheless, attention to consciousness reveals its *intentionality*, that it is always consciousness of something: the object of an appearance in consciousness is its *cogitatum*. Yet the objects of awareness are experienced as changing

---

6. Bowker, *Sense of God*, 88, quoting Ashby, *Introduction to Cybernetics*.
7. Ibid.
8. Bowker, *Licensed Insanities*, 108.
9. Bowker, *Sense of God*, 170
10. Ibid., 172, quoting Husserl, *Paris Lectures*, 13.

awareness. As John put it, "I move out to designate the world, but the appearing world moves in to give my consciousness particularity and being."[11]

The "moving in" of God as an object of awareness is central to the argument of both *The Sense of God* and *The Religious Imagination and the Sense of God*. In the former, John reviewed explanations of the behavioral sciences of that time of how senses of God or gods arise. The approaches included Durkheimian sociology, Levi-Straussian structuralism, psychoanalysis, and psychopharmacology (in particular the effects of LSD and other hallucinogens). In each case, it was argued that each of these disciplines had—for different reasons—not only failed to explain the sense of God as a dependent variable, but had in fact arrived at "an entirely new concern with the differentiating consequences of the responsive objects of encounter."[12]

Part of the argument related to the insufficiency of monocausal explanations (and hence was an argument for opening explanation to multiple constraints); and part of the argument related to ways in which each theory accommodated the contribution of information derived from sources external to the subject to the formation of representations of any kind—including representations of God or gods. Much here depends on the meaning of "information" and "external to the subject"; but for the present purpose, let us consider the naturalistic component of the argument. In the case of sociology, Swanson's Durkheimian attempt to correlate specific senses of gods (e.g., belief in a high god) with particular social structures generated a moderate correlation coefficient—suggesting that constraints other than social structure must be operating (quite apart from the other methodological problems with the study).

This led to consideration of Berger's "sociology of knowledge" argument in *The Social Reality of Religion*[13]—that the sense of God is an entirely social construction—and his subsequent qualification of that account in *A Rumor of Angels*.[14] In this latter work, Berger came to recognise that the dialectical relationship between the production of social knowledge and individual cognition must allow individual construals of meaning that are not reducible to shared knowledge to nevertheless influence it—raising the question of what motivates attributions of meaning in addition to social learning. Levi-Straussian structuralism proposed that myths arose through the mediation of binary oppositions (e.g., birth/death, ingroup/outgroup), but failed to accommodate the incorporation of idiosyncratic but affecting

---

11. Bowker, *Sense of God*, 173.
12. Ibid., 181.
13. Berger and Luckmann, *Social Construction*.
14. Berger, *Rumor*.

details into the abstract systems of meaning it attempted to specify. Object-relations theory in psychoanalysis emphasized the contribution of the object (e.g., the behavior of the mother) to the representation of the mother, and by implication the representation of other internal objects (including gods or God). Accounts of the experiential effects of hallucinogens emphasised the contribution of culturally informed cognitive appraisal (or "labeling") of states of arousal engendered by hallucinogens), again pointing to the effects of learned information in forming the content of religious and any other kinds of experience. In summary, the appearance of God or gods did not conform to the predictions of theories (where predictions could be made), or the theories themselves had moved in the direction of taking into account the contribution of the external world, information, or the construal of meaning to differentiating objects of awareness (including God or gods) into their specific forms.

An effect of this converging emphasis on the relationship between information, the attribution of meaning, and the content of theistic experience was to underline the importance of analyzing religions as systems for the protection, organization, and transmission of information from one generation to the next. This perspective began to be developed in *The Sense of God* but took more explicit form in the subsequent Wilde lectures and book, *The Religious Imagination and the Sense of God*. The latter also built on an observation in *The Sense of God*, that "a critical focus of the sociological and anthropological study of religion must always be the inner logic through which a sense of God develops in relation to its previous context; it is never wholly 'unheard of'; there is always enough precedent for disagreement to take place."[15]

The Religious Imagination attends to the "inner logic" of four major religions—Judaism, Christianity, Islam, and Buddhism—where existing senses of God or gods came under severe crises of plausibility, and the changes within theistic understanding that occurred within each tradition in response to these crises. *The Religious Imagination* therefore complemented *The Sense of God's* focus on the behavioral sciences by providing more detailed accounts of the informational resources and related senses of God or gods within specific traditions. Analysis of different trajectories of the sense of God or gods in the *Religious Imagination* illustrates the reciprocal influences between the sense of God as a set of tradition-specific concepts, imagery, expectancies, and beliefs, and the sense of God as an object of direct experience, an agentive Other, who is experienced as taking initiative in acting in and through human lives and in the process transforms

---

15. Bowker, *Sense of God*, 41.

existing senses of what God is—the "responsive transcendence" that is a constitutive feature of theism.

INFORMATION, PHENOMENOLOGY, AND ONTOLOGY

The "moving in" of God—the sense of God as an agentive Other—raised the question of ontology: what must be the case for the appearances of God or gods in consciousness to behave as they do? John approached the relationship between experience, cognition, and ontology from a number of perspectives. One orientation was derived from Husserl's phenomenological method, which enabled Husserl to recognize consistencies in appearance which revealed essential structures: "the stream of consciousness is permeated by the fact that consciousness relates itself to objects.... It is the ability to pass over—through synthesis—from perennially new and greatly disparate forms of consciousness to an awareness of their unity."[16]

The recognition of essential structures was supported by intersubjective report, which belonged to the experience of the intending subject: "I experience the world not as my own private world but as an intersubjective world, one that is given to all human beings and which contains objects accessible to all."[17] A "first level" of phenomenology led to the determination of the essential structures of objects of consciousness, while a "second level" of phenomenology allowed inference to an ontological ground to account for the intersubjective reliability and persistence of some appearances. This established the possibility of what Husserl termed 'returning reality to the world' for some appearances on the basis of a careful determination of their essential structure, which—in principle—could be extended to the appearance of God of gods. Argument for the possibility of inferring an ontological ground correctly referred to as God to account for "the differentiating consequences of the responsive objects of encounter"[18] runs through *The Sense of God* and subsequent writings, and is illustrated for example by John's comment on a poem by Emily Dickinson in *Licensed Insanities*:

> what, then, is happening within the experience which produces this and her other poetry? It is possible to interpret her, isolated in Amherst, as a neurotic recluse who was driven to write poetry as a substitute for the unrequited love in her life. And that may indeed be so. But what does she encounter which, as a consequence of its own nature, evokes the poetry about itself,

16. Bowker, *Sense of God*, 174, quoting Husserl, *Paris Lectures*, 18.
17. Ibid., 175, quoting Husserl, *Paris Lectures*, 34.
18. Bowker, *Sense of God*, 181.

and creates such differentiation in her reflection? If the answer is "nothing," then it is indeed very difficult to account for the immensely well-winnowed traditions of prayer and spirituality, in which the nearest resemblance or analogy lies in the encounter between humans which has evoked the language of love.[19]

Yet there are challenges to the inference of an ontological ground for theistic experience. One problem is posed by inconsistencies in the appearance of God or gods, which raises questions about what features of theistic appearance should be identified as constituting its 'essential structure.' Even if an essential structure or perhaps a family of structures of theistic appearance can be determined (cf. *The Religious Imagination*), the possibility remains that they may be motivated not by the reality they purport to be about, but by other processes, constraints, or causes. Phenomenology's derivation of ontology from the determination of an essential structure of theistic appearance would bias ontological inference to a correspondent pre-intentional ground, but in fact the perceived unity of the intended object (e.g., God as imagined or perceived) may result from an act of cognitive synthesis rather than lie in or beyond the world. While phenomenology may support the possibility of inferring ontology from experience, it would seem that other approaches are needed to critically explore the question of how theistic appearances may be variously grounded or motivated.

An alternative framework to articulate the relationship between experience, reference and ontology was derived from the Anglo-American philosophical tradition.[20] "Critical realism" describes an approach in the philosophy of science which attempts to accommodate both the social construction of representations of the world in science and other domains of world-picturing, while allowing that the world sets limits on what can be reliably or usefully asserted about it. Hence, while the history of science amply demonstrates how representations of reality are approximate, provisional, corrigible, and wrong (at least from the perspective of later generations), it is nevertheless the case that they are wrong in relation to a reality or realities independent of those assertions; in other words, scientific theories are predicated to account for observable features or conditions of the world, which constrain what can be appropriately asserted about them. Indeed, regularities in the world are a condition both of reliable assertions to be possible, and for unreliable assertions to be demonstrated as such.

When this critically realist approach is extended to reports of religious belief and experience, it suggests that "although there cannot be any

19. Bowker, *Licensed Insanities*, 94.
20. Ibid., 63–65, paraphrased here.

apprehension of God which is not mediated by our concepts, it does not follow that there is no reality in the case of God apart from our concepts."[21] And, further, that "that which evokes the term 'God' or 'gods' may set limits on experience and reports, however provisional and corrigible those reports may turn out to be."[22] Like phenomenology, critical realism therefore provides a framework for articulating the notion that the sense of God as concept, imagery, intuition, or perception, may relate to a precognitive or prelinguistic "interactive reality correctly referred to as God."[23] Yet, like phenomenology, the general framework provided by critical realism does not in itself address the specific point about how, in a mechanistic sense, representations of a transcendent agent could relate to ontology, whereby an x independent of cognition constrains or motivates the content of cognition and experience.

The specific relationships between information, cognition, and ontology have perhaps been pressed most closely through a distinct line of argument that was present in *The Sense of God* and *The Religious Imagination*, then developed in *The Sacred Neuron*.[24] In *The Sense of God*, John asked

> whether the sense of God is simply built up from an extensive patterning of stable, consensual cues which then receive (but do not actually demand) theistic interpretation, or whether some of the cues, so to speak, arrive from that reality in existence to which a term such as "god" is appropriately applied, so that those cues arising from the external universe demand (but do not always receive) a response of faith.[25]

This seems to imply two types of ontological source for the sense of God: (1) inference from naturally occurring cues to the existence of God and related notions and (2) a class of cues which imply a more specific initiative or intervention by God in life or the world. We will consider each in turn. The "building up" of a sense of God from cues in the universe suggests both the evocation and construction of a sense of God from cues (whether sensory or conceptual) that occur in self, world, or other—even if the inference of God is not strictly entailed. There is no inherent tension with naturalism here, to the extent that "the cues" belong in principle to ontologies accepted by science or secular perspectives. Naturalism differs from theism to the extent that theism infers a transcendent ground from the

21. Ibid., 74.
22. Ibid.
23. Ibid., 108.
24. Bowker, *Sacred Neuron*.
25. Bowker, *Sense of God*, 157.

cues, which naturalism rejects. The "building up" of the sense of God (and related notions) can occur by analogy with processes observed in the world. For example, in the chapter "Death, Burial, and Cremation,"[26] John cites the example of how naturally occurring phenomena might support by analogy both the inference of personal continuity through death and related burial customs—such as "burying a body gains suggestive confirmation from the burying of a seed and the growth of a new plant, with comparable natural cues identified for cremation and water burial."[27]

There is also a more direct evocation of a sense of God from natural cues which recalls "the natural knowledge of God" of natural theology. The cues or attributes recognized in contemporary versions of natural theology include the existence of the universe; its conformity to order; the existence of humans and other living creatures, and other evidence of apparent design; and the sense of beauty and goodness.[28] However, the way in which philosophical theology treats God as a good explanatory hypothesis does not capture the phenomenology of the sense of God—for example, the sense of conviction or attendant emotion associated with the attribution of God, and the way that the sense of God goes beyond an explanatory function for specific aspects of the world but links together many concepts, images, value-judgments, sentiments and dispositions in tradition-specific ways.

The question of how beliefs and value judgments are linked to emotions and experience more generally is considered by John in *The Sacred Neuron*. This work is principally concerned with how human beings arrive at value judgments about what is true, beautiful, and good, and related notions; but the arguments can equally be extended to the origin of the sense of God. On the basis of recent research in cognitive neuroscience, *The Sacred Neuron* argues that the separation of reason and emotion that has been so widely proposed in Western and other accounts of the person is mistaken. Instead, rational evaluation ("cognitive appraisal") of features of the world typically occurs in conjunction with emotional responses in relations of mutual influence. Value judgments cannot therefore be parceled into rational (factual) and emotional (value) components; they are integrated both in experience and its underlying neurobiology.

In the case of the origin of the sense of God, this means that attributions of God will typically already be invested with emotion and associatively linked to many other concepts, presuppositions, and interpretive biases that reflect enculturation into a religious tradition, rather than applied as

26. Ibid., 66–85.
27. Ibid., 69.
28. Mackie, *Miracle of Theism*.

post-hoc interpretations to uninterpreted primary experiences. This does not mean that experience and judgments cannot be subject to post-hoc interpretation; rather, that conscious experience already incorporates interpretation, and that cognitive appraisal is closely integrated with emotional processing.[29] Consequently, the formal argumentation of natural theology is a high-level abstraction from how a sense of God typically arises as a cognitive-affective response to the world.

Another part of the argument of *The Sacred Neuron* follows on from John's earlier interest in the evocation of the sense of God by cues arising from the universe. John proposed that the psychosomatic responses contributing to value judgments are "tied to properties that do lie within the objects themselves, whether or not they are being perceived by some observer."[30] John describes these evocative features of the world as "conducive properties" because they conduce or lead to characteristic responses in observers. Conducive properties evoke responses (and therefore vocabularies) of approval and disapproval in ways that are frequently (if not universally) shared.

The grounding of value judgments in conducive properties is critically important for understanding the origin of the sense of God because the concept, imagination, and experience of God are extensively linked to value judgments in ways that vary across religious traditions and through time. Value judgments may be partly evoked by the orchestration of conducive properties in the form of reinforcing sensory-affective stimuli in ritual, symbolism, and other religious contexts. Reinforcing stimuli that are widely enlisted in religious practice include

> motion, color, luminosity, emotive facial expressions of masks, accentuated sexual characteristics (cosmetics, oils), sudden loud noises (fireworks, bells), prosodic accentuations of language (singing, chanting), pain (flagellation, circumcision), temperature (baptism by immersion), smells (incense, perfume), taste (ritual foods), and multi-sensory repetitious stimuli which activate arousal systems.[31]

Religions typically conjoin such sensory-affective stimuli with context, narrative, and symbolism to create a distinctive range of moods, emotions, motivations, and meanings. Liturgy, text, and story also adjust the sense of "is" and "ought" by evoking imaginative and empathic engagement with their content and imagery. For example (and it is just one example), Jesus

---

29. Bowker, *Sacred Neuron*.
30. Ibid., 41.
31. Deeley, "Religious Brain," 257.

reconstituted the sense of what God is of his time and place by linking it to a distinctive ethical orientation expressed through imagery and examples drawn from familiar features of human experience: "for I was hungry and you gave me food, I was thirsty and you gave me drink, I was a stranger and you welcomed me, I was naked and you clothed me, I was sick and you visited me, I was in prison and you came to me" (Matt 25:35–36).

The evocation and qualification of the sense of God by the tradition-specific orchestration of conducive properties in narrative and practice underpins the intentionality of the sense of God, what the sense of God is variously about, and how it relates to aspects of self, world, and others. In this sense, religions can be understood as a consequence of long-running processes of what John termed "somatic exploration and exegesis"—in other words, the exploration and interpretation of what can be experienced inwardly in meditation, prayer, or related practices, and outwardly in relationships and in interaction with the world.[32]

Over and above the binding together in religious story, context, and practice of cognitive-symbolic and sensory-affective stimuli to support a particular imagination and attribution of God, a fundamental source of the sense of God relates to apparent evidence of more specific initiatives by God in life or the world. These experiences, behaviors, and events are taken as direct cues or signs of the specific rather than more general agency of God; and they include the broad category of revelatory experiences, without which the sense of God would not exist in its familiar forms, and possibly not at all. John characterizes these cues as constituting "feedback" in *The Sense of God*:

> all theistic traditions have at some point suggested discernible (claimed) effects of God, ranging from trances, ecstasies, speaking in tongues, to individual conviction, answers to prayer, and the slow sea-change of human nature. This means that there must be sufficient feedback into experience, whether social or individual, for plausibility to be maintained.[33]

The conflict between naturalism and theism is perhaps sharpest in relation to experiences and events which are interpreted as specific initiatives of God in life or the world, because what is at stake is whether the law like regularities of nature (as conceived at a given time) have been disrupted through purposive and specific incursions of theistic agency—what the Elizabethan physician Edward Jorden termed "the immediate finger of the Almightie" when considering how cures of apparent cases of demonic

---

32. Bowker, *Is God a Virus?*, 151–53.
33. Bowker, *Sense of God*, 84.

possession are attributed to supernatural causation.[34] A fully successful naturalistic account of claimed specific effects of theistic agency—for example, the communication of revealed information via human intermediaries such as prophets—would be able to explain how such experiences arise without invoking supernatural agency. Recent research is relevant to understanding this aspect of the origin of the sense of God in human consciousness.

EXPERIMENTAL MODELING OF SUPERNATURAL AGENCY

Reports of supernatural agents (such as God or gods, demons, or spirits) speaking or acting through people to reveal important truths are present across cultures and periods of history in institutions and practices such as prophecy, mediumship, shamanism, or spirit possession.[35] Ethnographic and other accounts suggest that such messages may be communicated in speech, writing, or action; and occur primarily through the attribution and experience of direct supernatural control or influence over motor function (e.g., movements producing speech or writing) or thought, imagery, and perception. The experience of control by a supernatural agent may also be associated with loss of the sense of ownership of the contents of consciousness (e.g., this is not "my" thought, speech, or action but that of a supernatural agent)—and in some cases, loss of awareness and/or memory for the experience of altered agency.

The capacity to represent supernatural agents as exercising effects on experience and behavior presupposes the ability to represent agency in general, understood as purposive behavior determined by mental states such as beliefs, goals, desires, motivations, and so on. This ability has been termed "mentalizing," "perspective-taking," or "Theory of Mind," and is supported by a distinct neurocognitive network.[36]

Cognitive anthropologists and psychologists in the cognitive science of religion have analyzed the respects in which concepts of supernatural agents differ from more typical "intuitive" assumptions about persons as agents[37]—for example, by violating normal assumptions in certain respects (such as an agent that can be everywhere at once, violating normal assumptions about

34. Jorden, *Briefe Discourse*.
35. Rouget, *Music and Trance*; Vitebsky, *Shamanism*; Aune, *Prophecy in Early Christianity*.
36. Deeley, "Religious Brain."
37. Boyer, *Religion Explained*; Barrett, *Why Would Anyone Believe*; Deeley, "Cognitive Anthropology of Belief."

the physical embodiment of persons; or a statue that can think, transferring agentive attributes to physical objects). These analyses and experimental studies have provided insights into what renders notions of supernatural agents conceivable, salient, communicable, and memorable—as such, specifying additional constraints on how a sense of God or other supernatural agents arise in consciousness.

Given the ability to represent agents in general, and supernatural agents in particular, a further question concerns how such representations can influence the subjective sense of control and ownership of mental contents or behaviors such as thought, speech, or writing. Colleagues and I have investigated this question by creating experimental models of different kinds of possession and revelatory experience employing suggestions in highly hypnotisable subjects and functional magnetic resonance imaging (fMRI).[38] The premise is that suggested changes in experience in highly hypnotisable subjects can be used to model dissociative processes occurring in "altered states of consciousness" because both engage similar cognitive and neural mechanisms.

An initial study employed suggestions and fMRI to investigate brain activity when varying the experience of moving a joystick from normal voluntary movement to different experiences of loss of self-control.[39] We included a suggestion to model spirit possession based on a first-person report of the experience of possession by a *zar* spirit in Northern Sudan.[40] In our experiment, the *zar* spirit was represented by an engineer conducting experiments into limb movement. In the "possession" condition, the engineer had found a way to enter the participant's body and mind to control her hand movements from within. She is aware of the thoughts, motivations, and feelings of the engineer, but unable to control her movements, which are under the control of the engineer. The suggestions resulted in realistic, vivid subjective experiences of the intended effects, and significant reductions in feelings of control and ownership of hand movements.

Compared to a condition of impersonal control of hand movement (attributed to remote control by a malfunctioning machine), we found an increase in functional connectivity between M1 (a key movement implementation region) and BA 10 (a prefrontal region supporting the representation of agency). These results demonstrated that experiences reproducing key characteristics of spirit possession can be elicited by suggestion, and

38. Deeley et al., "Using Suggestion"; Deeley et al., "Modelling Psychiatric and Cultural Possession"; Walsh et al., "Using Suggestion."

39. Deeley, "Using Suggestion," is based on research supported by The Psychiatry Research Trust.

40. Boddy, *Wombs and Alien Spirits*.

that brain regions supporting representations of independent agents can be functionally coupled to motor systems (potentially explaining how it is possible for control of movement to be experienced as reassigned to another agent). Also, compared to the experience of normal voluntary control of joystick movement, involuntary movement was associated with reduced functional connectivity between motor planning brain regions (supplementary motor area, SMA) and regions involved in movement execution (e.g., premotor areas, M_1 and S_1). This indicates a mechanism by which involuntary movements (i.e., movements accompanied by a loss of the usual sense of control) can occur, which can be attributed to different causes (for example, impersonal control by a machine or personal control by an agent). Finally, reduced awareness of hand movement was associated with decreased activity in brain areas involved in bodily awareness (BA 7) and sensation (insula), suggesting a mechanism for the loss of awareness sometimes reported in association with episodes of possession or other types of involuntary behavior.[41]

However, these initial studies were of simple actions (joystick movement) rather than of the more complex cognitive and motor behavior of inspired or revealed writing. Writing involves the integration of thought content and movement. Reports of inspired or automatic writing indicate that it can involve experiences of external control of thought, and/or loss or control of hand movement (analogous to the symptoms of "thought insertion" and "alien control of movement," respectively, in schizophrenia). For example, supernatural control of both thought and hand movements was described by Mabel Barltrop (Octavia), the founder of the Panacea Society: a Southcottian prophetic movement in Bedford in the early twentieth century.[42] Her account is relevant because she described her experience of inspired writing in some detail, although other recent accounts—such as those of Vassula Ryden—exemplify similar forms of revelatory experience.[43] In 1916, Mabel Barltrop began to "receive messages from the Lord," which took the form of inspired writing. In *Brushes with the Bishops* (1919), she described how she became "a Scribe of the Lord" after a period of prayer: "Immediately I found myself writing . . . ; I had not the least idea whether I was going to write prose or verse . . . ; also I did not have to wait for a word or to alter a word, the rhyming word was mostly in my mind before I got to the end of the line."[44]

41. Rouget, *Music and Trance*.
42. Shaw, *Octavia*.
43. Hvidt, *Christian Prophecy*.
44. Besma [pseud. for Barltrop], *Brushes with the Bishops*.

Suggestions and fMRI were employed to create an experimental model of inspired or automatic writing attributed to an external agent (reproducing key components of the type of experience described by Mabel Barltrop and other practitioners).[45] The engineer returned, this time to insert thoughts and control hand movements as participants engaged in a writing task in the scanner. While loss of control of both the thought and motor components of writing were associated with distinct differences in brain activity, both involved reduced activity in supplementary motor area (SMA). This extended the findings of our initial study modeling spirit possession by indicating that SMA plays a key role in modulating the sense of control of ownership of both thought and movement. On this interpretation, the sense of loss of control of thought or movement is mediated by reduced SMA activity in conformity with the content of the suggestion, in which causation is attributed to an external agent. We also found that a "mediumistic" condition of reduced awareness of both the thought and motor components of writing was associated with reduced activation in BA 7—providing further evidence of the potential involvement of this region in the loss of awareness sometimes associated with possession, mediumship, or comparable experiences.[46]

The culturally influenced attributions and expectations of those reporting revelatory experiences may engage similar cognitive and neural processes as the targeted suggestions in our experimental models. At the very least, the experiments show how processes engaging beliefs, imagination, and expectations can lead to changes in experience that resemble possession and revelatory experience in important respects, and pick out brain processes by which such experiential changes may occur. Nevertheless, this proposal does not entail that possession or revelatory experiences (such as inspired writing or speech) involve hypnosis. One category (such as inspired writing, clinical dissociation, or hypnosis) cannot be reduced to another because all acquire context and tradition-specific meanings, values, and purposes.

For example, the presence of strongly held beliefs and authoritative social practices in religious contexts as opposed to temporarily imagined scenarios in hypnotic contexts may affect the threshold for experiencing the respective phenomena, quite apart from any differences in their attributed significance.[47] Also, hypnotic suggestions involve explicit verbal instruc-

45. Walsh et al., "Using Suggestion." Research for this study was supported by the Panacea Society, now the Panacea Charitable Trust.
46. Rouget, *Music and Trance*.
47. Deeley, "Hypnosis."

tions, whereas culturally influenced alterations in experience and behavior may more commonly involve expectancies based on imagery, symbolism, and implicit social modeling and learning.[48] In broad terms, these experiments provide examples of and brain mechanisms for how experience can conform to ideas and expectations, and as such are relevant to the explanation of a large class of culturally orchestrated or informed religious experiences, ranging from inspired writing, to glossolalia, spirit journeys, and possession cults.

An alternative (and commoner) approach to the "neurobiology of religious experience" rests on an implicit analogy between religious experience and epilepsy—that is to say, religious experience is a dependent variable that arises from the (mis)firing of neurons in discrete brain areas (such as the "God spot") with a cultural "overlay" of interpretation.[49] However, the contribution of meaning-based processes to the form, content, and attributed significance of experience is relevant even in cases where "bottom-up" changes in brain function (e.g., due to epilepsy or drug taking) produce characteristic alterations in consciousness (such as an altered sense of body boundaries or time). Whether the initial constraints on religious experience are "top-down" (meaning-based) or "bottom-up," brain processes contribute to the differentiation of experience and behavior within a wider network of constraint, which includes attributions of meaning from early stages of processing as well as extrapersonal influences (such as context or group processes).

The experiments show that subjectively realistic experiences of control of thought and movement by an external agent can be produced by suggestion without any such agent existing in reality. This implies that convincing experiences of responsive transcendence could be created by suggestive processes via the modulation of brain systems such as mentalizing or action-control networks without an independently existing transcendent agent contributing to the experiences. What if any implications do these findings therefore have for the real existence of God as an agent of revelatory experiences, such as inspired speech or writing?

Addressing this question partly relates to the respects in which agency is attributed to God in revelatory experiences. In "The Nature of Women and the Authority of Men,"[50] John considered the nature of revelation in relation to arguments against the ordination of women based on the au-

---

48. Deeley et al., "Modeling Psychiatric and Cultural Possession"; and Walsh et al., "Using Suggestion."

49. Ramachandaran and Blakesee, *Phantoms in the Brain*.

50. Bowker, *Is God a Virus?*, 195–264.

thority of Scripture. One question which arises in relation to the content of revealed texts is the sense in which the words of Scripture are the "Word of God." As John put it, "for almost two thousand years, many Christians thought that the books of Scripture had been directly dictated by the Holy Spirit, and that the biblical writers simply took down the words as inerrant recorders"—a view expressed as recently as 1920 in the encyclical *Spiritus Paraclitus*, which states that "the books of Holy Scripture were written under the inspiration of the Holy Spirit, by His instruction, stimulus, and even dictation, and were indeed written and produced by Him."[51] An alternative view, predominant in Protestant theology since the Reformation, and now widely accepted in all parts of the church, is that the Spirit operated in the writers' minds not through dictation but accommodation, so that God "completely adapted His inspiring activity to the cast of mind, outlook, temperament, interests, literary habits and stylistic idiosyncrasies of each writer"—a relationship termed "concursive activity."[52] As John once put it in discussion, "Scripture is a consequence of the intentionality of God to move its authors to produce works of significance and difference."[53] Consequently, both dictation and concursive accounts of revelatory experiences raise the question of how perceived effects of God as an agent independent of cognition should be interpreted in light of the experimental modeling of automatic writing outlined above.

From a naturalistic perspective, the experiments illustrate how imagined objects of belief can be experienced as external to the subject and influencing cognition. They are experienced "as if" they are external agents; but they are social, cognitive, and neural constructions or projections (to use Freud's earlier terminology). The "reality in effect" of the intended object is due to this remarkable human capacity for agentive representations to be experienced as external realities which can affect cognition as virtual, independent agents. The experiences are vivid, and the effects are real but their origin in socially embedded cognition is concealed. The construal of reality and the effects on behavior may even in some cases be profound or impressive, but the revelatory experiences are nevertheless a form of misattributed creativity rather than evoked by or derived from a supernatural reality outside cognition.

John's critically realist theological view, by contrast, is that God may be a constraint on the sense of God—for example, in the case of revelatory experience. In this latter case, God as an agent does not bypass cognition but

---

51. Ibid., 259.
52. Ibid., 260, quoting Packer, *"Fundamentalism" and the Word of God*.
53. Bowker, supervision, Trinity College, Cambridge c. 1987.

acts through it, in which case theological criteria of coherence and evaluation of effects become the basis for judging the truth and value of specific claims to revelation: "by their fruits ye shall know them" (Matt 7:20). In this view, "the reality in effect of the object of belief" can at least partially originate in God, rather than in all cases be entirely attributed to a cognitive representation of God among other naturalistic constraints.

Against this, it might be argued that naturalistic accounts are sufficiently powerful to render theistic effects on the experience of God implausible, even if they cannot be disproved. Yet, plausibility is a complex property of propositions. In *The Web of Belief*, Quine and Ullian observed that the belief status accorded to a given proposition is validated in relation to other beliefs, and, conversely, that any given belief "can be held unrefuted, no matter what, by making enough adjustments in other beliefs."[54] The plausibility of a proposition is influenced by wider commitments and foundational assumptions. The weight attached to specific assumptions, the sense of their authority or reality, is a critical constraint on the interpretation placed upon a wide set of features of self, world, or others—extending to how the world is interpreted as variously disclosing the presence and action of God or its converse. Religions (and other organized ideologies and cultural systems) are in the business of creating, influencing, and managing assumptive worlds through social, cognitive, and neural processes and their respective interactions.[55] Yet, plausibility can still collapse for those inside a strongly-bounded system despite these procedures—either because engagement within the tradition creates dissonance (cf. *Religious Imagination*), or in the face of dissonance with the broader ecology of authoritative knowledge. An alternative orientation within theology is to open a religion's closed circle of coherence to reappraisal and correction through engagement with the system on its own terms but also in relation to construals of the world originating outside the system. John's justification of Christian belief is an exemplary illustration of this approach to interpreting religious belief and practice in relation to a changing worldview.[56]

THE ORIGIN OF THE SENSE OF GOD

What, then, is the origin of the sense of God in human consciousness? While the differentiation of particular senses of God or gods occurs within

54. Quine and Ullian, *Web of Belief*.
55. Deeley, "Religious Brain."
56. E.g., Bowker, *Is God a Virus?*; Bowker, *Licensed Insanities*; Bowker, *Sacred Neuron*.

specific contexts (including what John termed the "inner logic" of traditions), general constraints can be identified. The concept, imagery, and experience of God or gods as responsively interactive transcendent agents enlist a particular cognitive scaffolding: the capacity for symbolic cognition and communication as the basis for the creation and transmission of symbolic culture; the capacity for representing agency; and the ability to modify general schemata of persons as agents to create distinctively supernatural properties (such as disembodiment, or the transfer of agentive properties to inanimate objects).[57] The capacity for representational redescription (including analogy and metaphor) and associative learning vastly expands the potential meanings, referents, emotions, motivations, and behavioral dispositions or effects that can be borne by God or gods.[58]

In this way, representations of God or gods act as dynamic placeholders within mind and culture for widely ramified semantic fields, from highly concrete representations of otherworldly agency to metaphors for an intuited totality of being lying beyond epistemic limitations. Bringing such diverse referents into conjunction in concept, shared narrative and practice, and individual negotiations of meaning allows their attributed senses to be cross-influenced (for example, the sense that the fundamental nature of reality is love, or some other property that is normally ascribed to persons as agents). The tenacity of God or gods is at least partially attributable to this dynamic, contextually responsive polysemy, which cannot be borne by humans as agents or by the ontological referents of secular naturalism in the same way. The grounding of senses of God in conducive properties—including properties orchestrated in narrative, ritual, and other practices—further qualifies and reinforces them. The cognitive capacity for agentive representations to be experienced as independently acting or communicating through human intermediaries critically reinforces the centrality of God or gods as bearers and creators of individual and collective meaning.

A further reflection following from John's charting of the birth and death of gods, and of collapses of plausibility in religions and sciences, is that the world in itself does not unequivocally dictate a single system of interpretation, despite the ways in which given features of the world motivate responses. Rather, the world admits a range of systematic interpretations that are distinct even if there are points of resemblance, compatibility, or intersection with other systems. This does not mean that experience and interpretation are unconstrained, or that people cannot change perspectives or be persuaded from one view to another. Nor does it mean that all

57. Deeley, "Cognitive Anthropology of Belief."
58. Deeley, "Religious Brain."

accounts of the world are equally coherent, justified, or persuasive (at least in light of what has been shown to be reliably the case about different aspects of the world through the broad project of science).

The diversity of worldviews does draw attention, though, to Quine and Ullian's "web of belief" and how cultural systems make available sets of interlocking concepts and practices which provide a context for the formation and/or interpretation of specific facts or experiences. In this context, theology defends the possibility of religious belief to allow an interpretation based on faith to be applied to the world (where "faith" refers to accepting or granting authority to a given body of religious ideas and practices as a basis for life). A Wittgensteinian recognition of how a body of concepts and practices constitutes a "form of life" is relevant, because it draws attention to the internal logics and distinctive trajectories of lives lived within a given tradition—that the differences do make a difference.[59]

Against this background John's theology has implications for a life of faith. It is a theology that recognizes that we see through a glass darkly. It is moved by the spirit rather than the letter of the law, the challenge being to live out the implications that "God is love" in a complex world of profound suffering where understanding is not fixed. A critically realist theology sits uneasily with the sense of absolute conviction and ultimacy that is evident in much (but not all) religious belief and experience. It is more consistent with apophaticism and a sense of the mystery and unknowability of God, of human epistemic limitations in the face of whatever is ultimately the case—*Deus semper maior*, as John says.[60] Conversely, the unknowability of God is qualified by the example of Christ, who—from a Christian perspective—showed what a life lived in relation to God looks like, providing examples and principles as a model for engagement with the world, and also—from a Christian perspective—indications of the nature of God. Yet John has been equally able to authoritatively and empathetically articulate the views of non-Christian religious traditions. The value of his work does not therefore only consist in its immense intellectual range and creativity, involving a cross-civilizational knowledge of religion, philosophy, languages, arts, and science, but also in the humanity as well as critical perspective that he has brought to the broader understanding of religions.

BIBLIOGRAPHY

Ashby, W. Ross. *Introduction to Cybernetics*. London: Chapman & Hall, 1964.

59. Bowker, "Can Differences Make a Difference?"
60. Bowker, "Introduction: The Unknowable."

Aune, David E. *Prophecy in Early Christianity and the Ancient Mediterranean World.* 1991. Reprinted, Eugene, OR: Wipf & Stock, 2003.

Barrett, Justin L. *Why Would Anyone Believe in God?* Walnut Creek, CA: AltaMira, 2004.

Berger, Peter L. *A Rumour of Angels: Modern Society and the Rediscovery of the Supernatural.* London: Penguin, 1970.

Berger, Peter L., and Thomas Luckmann. *The Social Construction of Reality.* London: Penguin, 1967.

Besma [pseud. for Barltrop, Mabel]. *Brushes with the Bishops.* London: Cecil Palmer and Hayward, 1919.

Boddy, Janice. *Wombs and Alien Spirits: Women, Men, and the Zar Cult in Northern Sudan.* New Directions in Anthropological Writing. Madison: University of Wisconsin Press, 1989.

Bowker, John. "Can Differences Make a Difference? A Comment on Tillich's Proposals for Dialogue between Religions." *JTS* 24 (1973) 158–88.

———. "Introduction: The Unknowable as Invitation in Science and Religion." In *Knowing the Unknowable: Science and Religion on God and the Universe*, 1–34. London: Tauris, 2008.

———. *Is God a Virus? Genes, Culture, and Religion.* Gresham Lectures 1992–93. London: SPCK, 1995.

———. *Licensed Insanities: Religions and Belief in God in the Contemporary World.* London: Darton, Longman & Todd, 1987.

———. *The Religious Imagination and the Sense of God.* Oxford: Clarendon, 1978.

———. *The Sacred Neuron: Extraordinary New Discoveries Linking Science and Religion.* London: Tauris, 2005.

———. *The Sense of God: Sociological, Anthropological and Psychological Approaches to the Origin of the Sense of God.* Oxford: Clarnedon, 1973.

———. *The Sense of God: Sociological, Anthropological and Psychological Approaches to the Origin of the Sense of God.* 2nd ed. Oxford: Oneworld, 1995.

Boyer, Pascal. *Religion Explained.* London: Vintage, 2002.

Deeley, Quinton. "The Cognitive Anthropology of Belief." In *The Power of Belief: Psychosocial Influences on Illness, Disability, and Medicine*, edited by Peter Halligan and Mansel Aylward, 33–54. Oxford: Oxford University Press, 2006.

———. "Hypnosis." In *Encyclopedia of Sciences and Religions*, edited by Anne L. C. Runehov and Luis Oviedo, 1031–36. Dordrecht: Springer, 2013.

———. "The Religious Brain: Turning Ideas into Convictions." *Anth and Med* 11/3 (2004) 245–67.

Deeley, Quinton et al. "Using Suggestion to Model Loss of Control and Awareness of Movements: An Exploratory fMRI Study." *PLoS ONE* 8(10). http://www.plosone.org/article/info%3Adoi%2F10.1371%2Fjournal.pone.0078324/.

Deeley, Quinton et al. "Modelling Psychiatric and Cultural Possession Phenomena With Suggestion and fMRI." *Cortex* 53 (2014) 107–19. http://www.ncbi.nlm.nih.gov/pubmed/24632378/.

Harland, Robert et al. "A Study of Psychiatrists' Concepts of Mental Illness." *Psych Med* 39/6 (2008) 967–76.

Husserl, Edmund. *The Paris Lectures.* 2nd ed. Edited and translated by Peter Koestenbaum. The Hague: Nijhoff, 1967.

Hvidt, Niels Christian. *Christian Prophecy: The Post-biblical Tradition*. Oxford: Oxford University Press, 2007.

Jorden, Edward. *A Briefe Discourse on a Disease Called the Suffocation of the Mother*. London: Printed by John Windet Dwelling at the Signe of the Crosse Keys, Powles Wharfe, 1603.

Mackie, John L. *The Miracle of Theism: Arguments for and against the Existence of God*. Oxford: Clarendon, 1982.

Packer, J. I. *"Fundamentalism" and the Word of God*. London: Inter-Varsity Fellowship, 1958.

Quine, W. V., and J. S. Ullian. *The Web of Belief*. 2nd ed. New York: McGraw-Hill, 1978.

Ramachandran, V. S., and Sandra Blakeslee. *Phantoms in the Brain: Human Nature and the Architecture of the Mind*. London: Fourth Estate, 1999.

Rouget, Gilbert. *Music and Trance: A Theory of the Relations between Music and Possession*. Chicago: University of Chicago Press, 1985.

Shaw, Jane. *Octavia, Daughter of God: The Story of a Female Messiah and Her Followers*. New Haven: Yale University Press, 2011.

Vitebsky, Piers. *Shamanism*. Norman: University of Oklahoma Press, 2001.

Walsh, Eamonn et al. "Using Suggestion to Model Different Types of Automatic Writing." *Con Cog* 26 (2014) 24–36.

Part 5

Comparative Religion

11

The Idea of Constraint
A Hindu Example

—Gavin Flood

As an undergraduate at Lancaster University, I was riveted by John Bowker's lectures. One question he raised has stayed with me: "What are the constraints that control an eventuality into its outcome?" John Bowker always emphasizes the necessity to specify constraints operative within any system, including religions. To specify constraints is to understand the world in a more nuanced way that reflects its complexity. Thus, rather than speaking of a cause, to specify a constraint is broader, more inclusive, and in the end closer to the truth of the world. As John Bowker says, "If I push a book, the fact that the book moves is indeed because I pushed it, but also because both I and the book are constrained by (amongst much else) the laws of motion."[1] Even in such a simple example as pushing a book, the search for a single cause is insufficient; and, already in this mundane case, the specification of constraints would be enormous. How much more so in the case of religions, where a simple causal explanation is always insufficient; and the specification of constraints, or rather networks of constraint, becomes an enormously complex task that is never completed. In any explanation we must, as Bowker says, choose from a range of constraints that we judge to

---

1. Bowker, *Is God a Virus?*, 5.

be relevant; and we should be "sufficiently but not recklessly generous" in our specification.[2]

Although the idea of constraint highlighted by Bowker is new in the sense that it is linked in to natural science and the philosophy of science, it is nevertheless something that has been recognized in different cultures throughout history. Theologies of religions have themselves developed ideas that are somewhat analogous to Bowker's constraint. In their analysis of human experience, various thinkers in the Hindu and Buddhist world came up with accounts of the human that can be understood more in terms of constraint than of cause. In this paper, I wish to describe one such account that claims that the nature or networks of constraint upon the person that limit the person into a fundamentally deluded condition can in fact be used to free the person from this state of ignorance. Although this Hindu view entails a distinct metaphysics and cosmology that are a long way from contemporary Western understandings, there is a parallelism in recognizing the complexity of forces operative in the human case. Such a study can provide support for a claim about a fundamental constraint upon us, namely social cognition.

A HINDU ACCOUNT OF CONSTRAINT

Writing in Kashmir in the early eleventh century, the polymath Hindu philosopher Abhinavagupta had spent his life analyzing human experience and reading this experience in the light of what he believed to be divine revelation from a transcendent reality he called Shiva. He had written on aesthetics and the classification of aesthetic emotion in his younger years—how laughter is transformed into comedy, how desire is transformed into the erotic, and how grief is transformed into tragedy—and then wrote systematic expositions of revealed texts, promoting his own nondualistic interpretation. Now in his later years, he turned his thinking to the textual source of his philosophical tradition and composed his most mature and thoughtful work, the commentary on the verses of his great grand teacher Utpaladeva (925–75 CE). Utpaladeva had composed a text called *Verses on the Recognition of the Lord* (*Īśvarapratyabhijñā-kārikās*); and Abhinavagupta's commentary was both a reflection on the text and an argument against its detractors, most notably the nontheistic Buddhist philosophers. The verses themselves are about the need to recognize God in and as world. The human subject is in fact ultimately identical with God who is glossed as pure consciousness (*caitanya, saṃvid*) and the limited sense of "I" is but a constriction of God's

2. Bowker, *Sacred Neuron*, 84.

cosmic and absolute subjectivity or "I-ness" (*ahantā*). The purpose of life is the recognition (*pratyabhijñā*) of the Lord or that the Lord is in fact both self and world, which recognition is freedom from suffering in the cycle of reincarnation. Abhinavagupta expounds these ideas in developing a theory of the human person through specifying a network of constraints that result in the eventuality of the human subject. We might class these constraints as cosmological and psychological.

For Abhinavagupta, the cosmos is ordered in a hierarchical sequence with "pure" levels (i.e., less solidified) developing into the more solidified, "impure" world that we inhabit. Other classes of beings inhabit "higher" invisible worlds; and they too are constrained by cosmological forces. These invisible beings also inhabit this world; but we cannot see them, although they can affect human life. In one rendering of the cosmological hierarchy that specifies categories that govern each level of the cosmos, certain powers come into play that limit a soul and control the way it inhabits a body. These cosmological powers of limited agency (*kalā*), time (*kāla*), limited knowledge (*vidyā*), causal restriction (*niyati*), and attachment to sense objects (*rāga*) "cover" the soul and limit its true powers of spontaneous freedom as God. All this is particularly accounted for in his earlier work; but in his later text, Abhinavagupta is more concerned with a different network of constraints that we might call "psychological." That is, he begins with a phenomenology of human experience and attempts to specify the constraints within the person that result in who they are in their particularity. All experience depends upon God, but this theistic view is modified in the sense that this God is pure awareness identical with the self; theistic language in the end has to give way to nontheistic language for Abhinavagupta.

Human experience is ultimately the experience of transcendent consciousness becoming reflexively aware of itself. Our limited experience of the world is the contraction of pure consciousness—first through the cosmological network of constraints and second through an inner or psychological network of constraints. Regarding the latter Abhinavagupta specified three: the power of knowledge or cognition (*jñāna*), memory (*smṛti*), and exclusion (*apohana*). These powers are necessary conditions for us to experience a world. The Sanskrit term *jñāna* has a double meaning of both knowledge and cognition as it denotes both the quality of apprehending the world and knowledge of the apparently objective world itself, a world apparently beyond the self. Memory gives us a sense of who we are in providing continuity with the past: it gives us identity and continuity of thought process. These three powers, although limiting constraints, are actually powers derived from God. In Utpaladeva's text, where these three constraints first appear, we read a claim that they are powers of God:

> Thus the functioning of the human world—which stems precisely from the unification of cognitions, in themselves separate from one another and incapable of knowing one another—would be destroyed if there were no Great Lord (Maheśvara) who contains within himself all the infinite forms, who is one, whose essence is consciousness, possessing the powers of knowledge, memory and exclusion.[3]

Utpaladeva claims that our experience of the world is unified and that our cognitions of the world form a coherent pattern—not because the cognitions are mutually aware of each other, but because they are given coherence by, to use a Bowker phrase, a putative theistic reality. Abhinavagupta's commentary on this passage brings out the idea that human experience assumes a certain unity or consistency. Our cognitions of the world are related to each other; and this continuity is because they are related to each other through the Lord, who is in fact our true self. The self, which is God, is a substratum that unifies otherwise disparate cognitions. Our ability to experience a world is guaranteed by the Lord, which is the highest level of constraint, who functions within the person through the powers of knowledge, memory, and differentiation. Abhinavagupta offers an exposition of these powers.

How do objects of consciousness appear? Or, in other words, how does the world arise as a focus of experience? In order to account for our experience, Abhinavagupta claims that objects of consciousness are constituted within consciousness itself, and cannot be external to it. The Buddhists had thought this too—the Yogācāra tradition had denied the external reality of the world—but Abhinavagupta is critical of them. According to the Buddhists, consciousness is constantly changing from one moment to the next (the doctrine of momentariness); but given this, there could be no continuity in the flow of the objects of consciousness according to Abhinavagupta unless there were a substratum or self.

If the Buddhist view were correct, that there is simply a flow of momentary thoughts not linked to a self, then memory would be unstable. To circumvent the problem of how we account for the continuity of experience, Abhinavagupta posited that the flow of the objects of consciousness must themselves be constituted within consciousness, a position the Buddhists would accept, but that this flow must be happening to someone. And against realist philosophies that maintained the external reality of the world, he argued that consciousness must include objective reality within it as it differentiates objects through the power of knowledge. The truth of the objects

---

3. Utpaladeva, *Īśvarapratyabijñākārikā*, 1.3.6–7.

of consciousness is only constituted within the interiority (*antahkṛta*) of consciousness.

But how does consciousness, which is resting within itself, manifest its objects? It does this through the powers of knowledge or cognition, memory, and exclusion. The internal self-luminosity of consciousness remains constant even though the flow of its objects changes. This flow appears to be distinct, but in truth is part of consciousness itself—the "this" only appears to be distinct from the subject, the "I." This orientation of the object towards externality (*bahirmukha*) is the way in which consciousness appears to itself: in reality, the objects are constituted only in interiority (*antaḥmukha*). When I imagine an apple, it appears to be external but in fact is only within consciousness.[4]

Although the Buddhists accept that the object is internal to consciousness, they do not accept that there is a constant, unchanging subject, because the subject is constituted only by its objects. But if this were the case, argues Abhinavagupta, there could be no continuity of experience. One contender to account for continuity is memory, but memory alone is not enough because it has to be rooted in a subject: there need to be memories of someone. So, to account for continuity, we need the notion of a self. If memory is the residual trace (*saṃskāra*) due to previous experience (*pūrvānubhavasaṃskārāt*), then the direct object (*viṣaya*) of that experience becomes the object of memory.[5] But to become the object of memory, there must be a subject for whom and of whom there are memories. To the Buddhist claim that all experience can be accounted for in terms of the chain of residual traces with no need to posit a subject, Abhinavagupta retorts that memory is a quality (*guṇa*); and a quality cannot stand independently but needs a substratum (*āśraya*) to be embedded in and that substratum is the self (*ātman*).[6]

Other schools of Hindu philosophy would accept this, but some such as the Vaiśeṣika and Sāṃkhya would maintain that each of the selves is separate and distinct. My experience is unique to me as a distinct self. Having established the need for a subject of experience, Abhinavagupta does not want to stop there. This is no individual self but is part of a broader, cosmic picture: a self-luminous consciousness outpouring itself into the flow of its intentional objects and, indeed, consuming them, and absorbing them back into itself through and because of its power of spontaneous freedom (*svatantra*). As there are infinite possibilities of which particular

4. Ratié, *Le Soi*, 176.
5. Abhinavagupta, *Īśvarapratyabijñāvimarśinī*, 1938: 1.2.5.
6. Ibid., 99.

objects appear to consciousness, the powers of knowledge and memory are necessary: knowledge to illuminate particular objects, and memory to link the objects of experience with a subject.[7]

But the powers of knowledge and memory are not sufficient constraints in themselves to ensure appearances to consciousness and to account for human perception. We need something more that controls events into their particularity; and that is the power of exclusion. This power of exclusion we might also translate as the power of differentiation, especially as Abhinavagupta glosses *apohana*, "exclusion," with *pariccheda*, "cutting."[8] *Apohana* is the power that differentiates and particularizes forms into their unique appearance. But differentiation in the flow of appearances—one object of consciousness from another and one subject from another—does not entail ultimate separation, says Abhinavagupta. In reality there is no differentiation; and appearance is just that, mere appearance (*avabhāsamātra*). The appearances to consciousness are in fact identical to that ultimate reality just as subjects; they are not deprived of reality. Indeed, this is in marked contrast to another idealist, non-dual system in Indian philosophy: the famous Advaita Vedānta in which appearance is illusion (*māyā*). For Abhinavagupta, the world or flow of objects of perception is not unreal, not an illusion; but it is identical with absolute consciousness. The world is not deprived of reality, but the world is that very reality. The being of consciousness is precisely its appearance, as Ratié observes.[9]

Consciousness contains within itself the whole universe or mass of objects but only causes some to appear as distinct for a subject through the powers of knowledge, memory, and exclusion. Consciousness can become aware of its projecting itself apparently externally in what appear to be new cognitions (*navajñāna*); and while these new cognitions arise and pass away, the perceiving subject in its self-luminosity does not. Memory allows us to recognize that these new cognitions are identical with universal self-luminosity in the sense that appearances to consciousness are always in the present; but once new cognitions have gone into the past, they are only accessible through memory—which recognizes that they are past experiences of a subject, a subject that is cosmic and self-luminous. What makes one object appear in contrast to another is the power of differentiation, which again is within consciousness itself or, in theistic language, it is the Lord who knows, remembers, and differentiates and thereby exercises his power

7. Ibid., 1938: 1.3.7, p. 141.
8. Ibid., 142–43.
9. Ratié, *Le Soi*, 183–84.

of freedom.[10] How do we know all this? In the end, Abhinavagupta has to resort to the revelation expressed in the texts of his tradition and the experience of enlightened persons.

So far, we have discussed the three constraints of knowledge, memory, and differentiation; but these are set within a temporal context, within the flow of time. Indeed the very notion of an appearance to consciousness entails the idea of temporality, the broadest constraint within which appearances arise. Time is the succession of appearances that result in, for example, the statement "I am standing here" (*iha tiṣṭhāmi*) along with other experiences of near and far, and all types of relation (*sambandha*).[11] Our experience of the world constrained by knowledge, memory and exclusion is set within the horizon of time, which is characterized by relationality between appearances and between apparently distinct subjects of experience.

According to the Buddhists, there can be no relation between a self that does not exist and objects of consciousness including other selves. For Abhinavagupta by contrast, the idea of relation is central in establishing the truth of the self. Relation is central to our experience of the world; it is "the practicable life of this entire world" (*sakalalokayātrānuprāṇitakalpa-*):[12] one of the most important relations being between cause and effect. But the relation between subject and object is not simple; and in Abhinavagupta's analysis is constrained by interest and motivation. Thus, for example, terms such as "pot" can give rise to different human responses depending upon situation and motivation. A man who is brokenhearted, Abhinavagupta touchingly says, for whom "there is nothing," simply sees the pot as bare existence. The thirsty man sees a container for water, while a trader sees gold in the pot, and so on.[13] Our perception of the world is colored by our motivation and who we are as persons. The particularity of each situation constrains the experience of the appearances to consciousness.

The particularity of each human experience is constrained by these individual and cosmological factors. We are affected by residual traces of experience from past lives and a sense of the continuity of the self such that we can be aware "I who was fat am now thin," or "I who was a child am now young or old."[14] In the end, such particular perception is a constraint upon the absolute freedom of the Lord. The use of the first-person pronoun "I" is a limitation on the absolute subject that is God. Through particular-

10. Abhinavagupta, *Īśvarapratyabhijñāvimarśinī*, 1938: 1.3.37, pp. 141–43.
11. Ibid., 2.1.7, p. 22.
12. Ibid., 2.2.6, p. 54.
13. Ibid., 2.3.4, p. 99.
14. Ibid., 1.6.5, pp. 314–15. *yo 'haṃsthūlaḥ... ahaṃ sthūlaḥ....*

izing myself in a certain situation and time, I am limiting the experience of absolute subjectivity; but this limitation, through complex sets of constraints, is beyond my power to change except through the slow process of spiritual redemption involving ritual and meditation practices. Those who practice a discipline—one of the ritual and meditational practices described by Abhinavagupta—can learn to perceive the constraints affecting their life and through that recognize the transcendent power that animates all particularity. Abhinavagupta speaks of yogis who reverse the cosmic unfolding into limitation through a process of meditative ascent back to the source of all life (the source that is absolute subjectivity or "I-ness"). The path to enlightenment is an "ascent higher and higher."[15]

Abhinavagupta has a vision of the human person as the result of networks of constraint that form the person into his or her particularity. These constraints that produce the form of life that a person is, are, for him, the outpouring of the spontaneous and unlimited freedom of God. Manifestation is the self-limiting of God as limited subject and world. God chooses self-limitation as person because God's nature is spontaneous freedom. The limited human faculties of willing, knowing, and doing (constricted by the network of constraints) reflect God's same unlimited powers. But the constraints that enable the world to be experienced—the powers of knowledge, memory, and exclusion as we have seen—also allow us to transcend limitation and experience our true nature as one with God, and to perceive our limited powers of willing, knowing, and acting as ultimately God's powers. Through putting these faculties into the service of a spiritual discipline, through what Bowker has called "somatic exploration,"[16] we can come to realize our true nature.

FREEDOM THROUGH CONSTRAINT

From this account of Abhinavagupta, we can see that one of the main tasks the Hindu philosopher set himself was the specification of constraints in the human case. What is it that constitutes experience? How can life be transformed and limitation overcome? What forces keep us bound in the cycle of suffering? Furthermore, the identification and specification of constraints operative at a cosmological and individual or psychological level have a soteriological function in that to know how experience arises is to begin to know how to deconstruct it, to know how to return to a deeper sense of subjectivity that, for Abhinavagupta, is the source of life. Constraint

15. Ibid., 1.6.5, p. 322.
16. Bowker, *Sacred Neuron*, 151–67.

that is a limiting factor can, in fact, become a force for liberation. Here the very structure of the world is a manifestation or emanation of a pure power that the tradition identifies as a conscious power, as a combination of light (*prakāśa*) and awareness (*vimarśa*). In the human case, the level and degree of constraint that produces human experience is very high, as we have seen; and conversely the deconstruction of constraint in order to realize our innate freedom is paradoxically through a process of strict constraint in the form of ascetic and ritual practice. The higher the restriction, the greater the freedom in the sense that restriction at one level leads to freedom at another.

For Abhinavagupta the very structure of the universe, the constraints that operate within it to create the myriad forms of the world, including human and animal life, is used as a way of salvation. The structures of the universe—that we might even call laws of nature, although for Abhinavagupta these laws of nature entailed a hierarchical cosmology—are recapitulated in human life and consciously recapitulated in the ritual context. To follow a path to the realization of God, which is the recognition of oneself as God, is to use those very powers of the cosmos that constrain us into who and what we are. The human experience of willing, knowing, and doing reflects divine qualities; and through these faculties, through the limitations of the human condition, the person can be freed from those very constraints.

Abhinavagupta divides the paths to the realization of God into three groups that use the faculties of willing, knowing or cognizing, and acting. The path of will (*icchā*), the "will-means" (*icchopāya*), uses innate human emotional force, an upsurge of emotional power, to shatter ordinary discursive thought to realize the truth of God behind thought. Thus, Abhinavagupta says that a man on seeing a loved one unexpectedly experiences the arousal of emotion that momentarily shatters discursive thought. The path of knowledge or cognition (*jñānopāya*) uses a pure thought, such as "I am God" or "I am omniscient," to existentially realize its truth on the model that a pure thought gradually purifies all others in a temporal sequence.

The path of action (*kriyopāya*) uses the usual structures of meditation, asceticism, and ritual—such as mantra repetition and other kinds of yoga—to gradually realize the truth of God within. Indeed the daily ritual procedure to be performed by the devout follower of Śiva would have been to visualize the structure of the universe pervading the body and then symbolically destroying it in the imagination: the purification of the elements in the body involved imagining the body being burned to a pile of ash before a new, pure body could be constructed. Here the constraints of the hierarchical universe that are, as it were, behind every human appearance, are symbolically presented in the ritual and transcended. These time-consuming procedures were intended to free the practitioner. The highly disciplined life of the Śaiva ascetic is geared towards the maximum constriction at a worldly level to achieve a higher freedom. Through these practices the practitioner is using the very structure of the universe, and the constraints that bind a person into the cycle of suffering, as a way of freeing a person from that cycle.

CODA: CONSTRAINT AND SOCIAL COGNITION

So far, I have presented a Hindu philosopher's account of the human in terms of constraint: how Abhinavagupta's views accept the idea of a network of constraints that control the particularity of the human into what it is. Paradoxically, this structure of the universe can itself be harnessed to free the person from the limitation that those constraints impose. Through conforming to the structures of the cosmos, the practitioner believes that he (and it is usually a male Brahman) can access the powers of the universe within himself to become freed from suffering and ignorance, to realize his true identity which is, indeed, to recognize himself as God.

But what are we to make of this in the twenty-first century? How do we understand Abhinavagupta today; and can we who live so far away from him in terms of the worldview we live within have any sympathy for his project? Does the translation of his concerns inform us about our own? These are not easy questions—although I do think we can have sympathy with his view and, if not conceding to it (how could we concede to a premodern cosmology of the kind he or any premodern theologian presents?), we can understand the broader purpose of his analysis.

Drawing on knowledge that Abhinavagupta could not have had, we might say he recognizes certain structures in human life that we now know are neurologically grounded. In highlighting knowledge, memory, and exclusion or differentiation, he is acknowledging our powers of functioning successfully in the world: we need cognition; we need to remember who we are and what we are about; and we need to differentiate between situations. In a word, he is recognizing the importance of human judgment.

In recent years there has been a rapid expansion in what we know about neurobiology and the new field of social cognition. We now know much about the brain and its interaction with the environment, even though the relation of consciousness or experience itself to brain states remains a mystery.[17] We know that the brain is of fundamental importance in how religions work;[18] and we know how important the brain is in the face-to-

---

17. Zeman, *Portrait*.
18. Bowker, *Sacred Neuron*; and Deeley, "Cognitive Style."

face human encounter from infancy. Human beings need to interact at the face-to-face level, particularly babies with the mother, in order for the brain to develop properly. Second-person neuroscience is at the forefront of this burgeoning field of inquiry[19] that has wide ramifications for other fields of study, particularly the study of religions.

Furthermore, we know that there are systems in the brain: the mirror neuron and mentalizing systems that enable us to creatively interact and come to judgment about each other in the context of complexity. We are hardwired to interact and to cooperate in the complex ways that we do. All human beings have known this; but now there is evidence to demonstrate that this is the case. Thus, we know that coming to judgment in complexity involves the frontal medial cortex that has the function of "valuation" and establishing "meaning for me" in complex human exchanges.[20] Taking Abhinavagupta's account of the human, we might say that although we no longer believe in the hierarchical cosmology he presented, what he is describing is the way human beings come to judgment about particular situations through using knowledge, memory, and discrimination. Furthermore, in his account of religious or soteriological practices prescribed by his tradition, he is implicitly recognizing the importance of the way religions abstract from the immediate human encounter to create a broader community. In Abhinavagupta's worldview, that community is not only those within the tradition but the wider cosmos peopled by innumerable invisible beings. That is, if the face-to-face is the realm of the ethical, the immediacy of human encounter and the place where we make judgments, we might say that Abhinavagupta presents an account of how his tradition attempts to both control the face-to-face and extend or abstract the face-to-face to a wider community.

Abhinavagupta did not know about social cognition as we do, but he did know about human interaction; and he knew deeply what his tradition meant and how its practices were intended to transform persons. Might we claim therefore that Abhinavagupta's account of human particularity in terms of knowledge, memory, and exclusion is drawing on our hardwired capacity for social cognition? That is, the capacity to know another person, to remember who we and they are in the context of our broader life, and to experience the particularity of our situation as it is in itself (the power of exclusion) are recognized by him. Through their analysis, he thought we could achieve freedom and deeper integration with the cosmos that he regarded as God. His tradition becomes an extension of community beyond

19. Chantel-Goldman et al., "Non-Local Mind."
20. Seitz et al., "Value Judgments"; and Kuzmanovic et al., "Matter of Words."

the face-to-face to a kind of collective body in which person and world are integrated; such an integration he regards as recognizing our true identity as God and thereby putting an end to suffering.

Although this is a somewhat cursory analysis, my Bowkeresque reading wishes to claim that, in recognizing the importance of constraint in his account of the human, Abhinavagupta is recognizing a fundamental feature of religions that informs judgment and develops and controls the face-to-face encounter. The paths that he describes are ritual structures that take communities beyond the immediacy of the here and now and impose order upon the hardwired spontaneity of human life. As John Bowker has shown, we now have a better vocabulary for describing human interaction and ways we encounter the world; yet this does not detract from Abhinavagupta's account, but rather increases our admiration for his fundamental insight into the nature of the human and the forces that make us who we are.

BIBLIOGRAPHY

Abhinavagupta. *Īśvarapratyabijñāvimarśinī*. Edited and translated by R. C. Dwiwedi et al. *Bhāskarī*, 3 vols (1938, 1950, 1954). Delhi: Motilal Banarsidas, 1986.

Bowker, John. *Is God a Virus?: Genes, Culture and Religion*. Gresham Lectures 1992–93. London: SPCK, 1995.

———. *The Sacred Neuron: Extraordinary New Discoveries Linking Science and Religion*. London: Tauris, 2005.

Chatel-Goldman, Jonas et al. "Non-Local Mind from the Perspective of Social Cognition." *FHNS* 7/107 (April 2013) 1–7.

Deeley, Quinton. "Cognitive Style, Spirituality, and Religious Understanding: The Case of Autism." *JRDH* 13/1 (2009) 77–82.

Kuzmanovic, Bojana et al. "A Matter of Words: Impact of Verbal and Non-verbal Information on Impression Formation in High-Functioning Autism." *RASD* 5/1 (2011) 604–13.

Ratié, Isabelle. *Le Soi et l'Autre: Identité, différence et altérité dans la philosophie de la Pratyabhijñā*. Jerusalem Studies in Religion and Culture 13. Leiden: Brill, 2011.

Seitz, Rüdiger et al. "Value Judgments and Self-Control of Action: The Role of the Medial Frontal Cortex." *BRR* 60/2 (2009) 368–78.

Utpaladeva. *Īśvarapratyabijñākārikā:The Īśvarapratyabhijñākārikā of Utpaladeva with the Author's vṛtti; Critical Edition and Annotated Translation*. Serie orientale Roma 71. Rome: Instituo Italiano per il Medio ed Estremo Oriente, 1994.

Zeman, Adam. *Portrait of the Brain*. New Haven: Yale University Press, 2008.

12

Al-Ghazālī and the Progress of Islamic Thought

—David Thomas

Al-Ghazālī was probably the single greatest theological mind in Islam. His works are known and studied by Muslim thinkers of all traditions, and his name is familiar to nearly all Muslims, whether they know his teachings or not. While this is generally not the case outside Islam, his writings were known to Thomas Aquinas, with whom he is often compared because of the breadth of his contribution to his religion, and he is the one Muslim mentioned in Bertrand Russell's *History of Western Philosophy*,[1] while translations of his works not infrequently appear on booksellers' shelves.

Until 1973 I was among those who had never heard about al-Ghazālī. I had lived for two years among Muslims in Sudan, and been mildly intrigued by their faith. So, when I went up to Cambridge to study theology and saw options on Islam, I decided to take them. The lecture course on theological thinking in the early Islamic centuries attracted me most. It covered the first attempts to understand the Qur'ān in light of the rational thinking that was flowing into the Islamic world through translations from Greek in the late eighth and ninth centuries, and after them al-Ghazālī. John Bowker spoke about this figure with a hint of lyricism, and particularly about his

---

1. Russell, *History*, 444 (cited in Bowker, *Religious Imagination*, 196).

Iḥyā' 'ulūm al-dīn ("The revival of the sciences of religion"), his masterly *summa* on the branches of religious belief and observance in Islam, and on the inextricable relationship between outer acceptance and inner conviction that there must be between them for faith to be lively. In one lecture, he remarked without looking up from his notes, that this treasure of theology and spirituality was only accessible in Arabic (parts are now available in translation, and they are the ones that appear on booksellers' shelves); and then he spoke words to the effect that, for anyone who was serious, this should not cause a problem. That remark fired me to find out more. There followed doctoral research at Lancaster, where John Bowker had moved as professor; and then a decade later I began at Birmingham, where I now teach the thought of the early theologians of Islam. I owe John Bowker an immense debt, and I gratefully acknowledge his continuing influences on my approaches to Islam.

Any study of the crucial early centuries of Islam must give prominence to Abū Ḥāmid Muḥammad ibn Muḥammad al-Ghazālī. Born in 1058, he lived more than four hundred years after the Prophet Muḥammad, a period of time in which the community first founded in Mecca and Medina had expanded Islamic rule over a vast empire that stretched from Spain to Afghanistan. Over this period as well, the implications of the Qur'ān, the revelation he claimed was sent to him directly from God, had been unfolded into elaborate systems of legal and theological thought. It had not been a simple history, by any means. The Islamic Empire, which in its first two centuries had remained more or less unified, had increasingly divided into semiautonomous regional powers, and the position of the caliph in Baghdad had declined from executive ruler to powerless figurehead under the control of warlords and palace officials. While the caliph was widely acknowledged as a symbol of unity by al-Ghazālī's time, he was liable to lose his throne and his life if he did not follow the ruling of those around him.

In a similar way, the teachings of the Qur'ān had taken minds in many different directions, raising disagreement and dissension. Some Muslims maintained that the immediate meaning of the text must be adhered to above all else: speculation on difficult passages was to be resisted, and problems caused by such incidental difficulties as the anthropomorphic depictions of God that were found in it should be accepted as indications of a mode of existence into which human minds were not to inquire.

Such groups of conservative thinkers often looked back to the ninth century scholar Aḥmad ibn Ḥanbal (d. 855), whose resistance to more radical developments had earned him a whipping and imprisonment. The main group opposing him, who did more than any other to cause dissension, though not always intentionally, were known as the Mu'tazila, "seceders" because their supposed founder had withdrawn from a circle of scholars when he found he disagreed with them. They regarded themselves as defenders of the supreme transcendence of God and of the justice of his actions, and they championed the use of reason in interpreting the Qurʾān and drawing out the possibilities implicit in its teachings. Thus, with regard to the anthropomorphisms, such as God's hand being outstretched or his being seated on his throne, they insisted that these could not be taken literally because they risked similarity between God and human beings and must therefore be interpreted metaphorically: God's "hand" was his grace, and his "being seated" on his throne denoted his supreme power. More than this, they inferred from their definition of the absolute oneness of God that the Qurʾān could not be eternal because it would then be a second eternal entity alongside God. This made the Scripture less of an absolute authority for theological minds to contend with or for rulers to have to obey. In fact, the caliph of the day made it official policy that anyone seeking public office must affirm the createdness of the Qurʾān. It was Ibn Ḥanbal's disagreement with this principle that earned him his punishments.

The Muʿtazila's systematic application of rational categories of thinking to the Qurʾān incurred the accusation that such interpreters were effectively subordinating God's revelation to human reason. Indeed, their approach did lead in the direction of independent speculation into the nature of the world, free from the constraints of revealed truth. In this they resembled the philosophers, who form what may be regarded as a third stream in early Islamic religious thought. These scholars took the thinking of the ancient world, in the developed and often harmonized forms in which they found it, as their starting point; and from the ninth century onwards leading exponents established elaborate systems involving cosmological schemes and hierarchies of transcendent beings in which pure reason was dominant and the true vocation of the human was to align the innate rational faculty with the Intellects that governed the movements of the heavenly spheres, and so to aspire to connect with the ultimate Source from which all being emanated. True followers of truth would succeed in this endeavour by honing their rational faculties so that these could be activated all the more readily by the heavenly Intellects.

In this system there was no need for knowledge of a revealed kind, and so for Ibn Sīnā (d. 1037), the greatest of the Islamic philosophers in the era before al-Ghazālī, the figure of the prophet, while he was a unique individual in that "he hears the speech of God, exalted be he, and sees his angels that have been transferred for him into a form he sees,"[2] was directed

---

2. Avicenna, *The Metaphysics*, 359.

towards providing teachings of an essentially legislative kind: "He must lay down laws about men's affairs by the permission of God, exalted be he, by his command, inspiration, and 'the descent of the Holy Spirit' on him."[3] It was not the function of a prophet to divulge anything about God apart from the fact of his existence, because this is something beyond the ability of ordinary people, and it could lead them into confusion and disputes: "[The people's] complaints and doubts will multiply, making it difficult for a human to control them. For it is not for everyone that [the acquisition] of divine wisdom is facilitated."[4]

This kind of speculative activity established a divide between revelation and rational reflection, relegating the Qur'ān and other revealed books to the sphere of morals and ethics, and to the use of the common people, for whom the stories and examples in them would provide the most accessible form of truth, while the pursuit of pure rational discernment would remain the province of the few who possessed the necessary intellectual gifts.

By the eleventh century, these streams of thought in Islam were at such odds that they appeared virtually to offer distinct ways of comprehending the nature of the world and the activity of God within it. More than anything, the position of the Qur'ān and its teachings were threatened by the apparent supremacy of independent human reason, which the philosophers claimed could be informed and directed by the transcendent Intellects, and ultimately God himself, without need for revealed teachings. The situation was complicated further by yet another strand within Islam, the mystics, who sought personal experience of transcendent reality through elaborate forms of mental and physical preparation, and the ultimate goal of passing into annihilation in complete communion with the One. This was essentially a world-denying pursuit that attached little importance to the external religious observances that were laid down in the religious law that was derived from the Qur'ān.

This was in effect the religious world of Islam into which al-Ghazālī was born in 1058. He remained in his native Ṭūs (in present-day northern Iran) as a student until his early twenties, when he went to Nīshāpūr to learn from one of the leading scholars of the time. He excelled, and when his teacher died in 1085, al-Ghazālī took his place. But his brilliance was mentioned more widely, and in 1091 he was called to Baghdad and installed as professor in the university that the ruling vizier had newly established. Here he wrote some of his greatest works, though he also experienced a growing spiritual crisis. He had set himself to discover what could be known with

---

3. Ibid., 365.
4. Ibid., 366.

absolute certainty, and his inability to reach an end in his search prompted him suddenly to abandon his position when one day he found he could not deliver his lecture: "God put a lock on my tongue so that I was impeded from public teaching. I struggled with myself to teach for a single day . . . but my tongue would not utter a single word."[5]

He gave up his post and took to a life of wandering: to Damascus, Mecca, and maybe further afield. After ten years he returned to Nīshāpūr and then back to Ṭūs, where he died in 1111. In these latter years, he wrote the *Iḥyā' 'ulūm al-dīn*, in which he combined the insights he had attained in his years of wandering together with the solid teachings of the Qur'ān to produce the classic that is still read widely by Muslims. These and other details are known thanks to a schematised autobiography that he wrote towards the end of his life, *Al-munqidh min al-ḍalāl* (*Deliverance from Error*), in which he explains that the solution to his existential and intellectual quandaries was to cease searching for solutions that could be reached intellectually, but to seek solutions by actually "tasting" what God is like through mystical experience. In this abandonment of the purely mental struggle of what can be grasped by the mind for the fuller experience of truth that can be absorbed by the whole person lies the crux of al-Ghazālī's life, and in many important respects the crux of Islam. Too far in one direction and the faith tips over into an entirely intellectual quest for propositional truth; too far in another and it becomes an obscurantist defense of scripture as a symbol rather than a comprehensible and dynamic source of guidance for real life; and too far in another and it descends into a sequence of experiences of the Other that have little relation to any doctrinal framework that can be built on the Qur'ān. Al-Ghazālī chose to follow the way of the mystics, subject to the constraints of the framework of communal observances and duties set by the Qur'ān. It is this that he presents in the *Iḥyā'*, and in doing this he lays aside, or appears to, the possibility of intellectual speculative endeavour. However, while he seeks to give the faith a new "life" that is informed and fed by scriptural teaching, he risks diverting it from intellectual discovery and the exploration of new possibilities of reality and the belief that is fashioned in light of them. He himself could never be accused of turning away from the excitement of new discoveries, though the alternative he favours could be interpreted as deterring Muslims from thinking outside the boundaries established by the traditional interpretations of the Qur'ān, and warning them to keep on the more obvious pathways of knowledge. The risk inherent in what he did and the possibilities that were raised in it are illustrated

---

5. Al-Ghazālī, *Deliverance*, 79. See Bowker, *Religious Imagination*, 193.

vividly in his intellectual encounter with philosophy, and the philosophers' spirited response.

In the period when al-Ghazālī was still professor in Baghdad, he was engaged in what he called the search for "the certain," making a deep study of the works of Islamic philosophers—especially the leading exponents, Abū Naṣr al-Fārābī (d. 950) and Ibn Sīnā (d. 1037). The outcome was a work on the discipline of philosophy in Islam: *Maqāsid al-falāsifa* (*The Intentions of the Philosophers*), followed by a searching critique of their discipline, *Tahāfut al-falāsifa*, which, alongside the *Iḥyā' 'ulūm al-dīn*, is his most influential work. Its title is often translated as *The Incoherence of the Philosophers*, though it can equally mean their collapse or breakdown. With it, al-Ghazālī was indicating from the outset the seriousness of his purpose, which was to demonstrate the groundlessness and error of key elements in the philosophers' enterprise.

The *Tahāfut* is frequently praised for the clarity of its approach. Al-Ghazālī divides it into twenty chapters, presenting in each what he regards as a key philosophical teaching and then refuting it. Of these twenty, three have usually been regarded as fundamental, because they contradict (or appear to contradict) traditional Islamic teachings based on the Qur'ān, and threaten to lead anyone who accepts them into error.[6] They thus expose the philosophers who promote them to the accusation of misguiding fellow Muslims. But al-Ghazālī is careful in his procedure, for rather than attempting to overcome his opponents with the bare authority of scripture or arguments based in tradition, which they could easily deny or reply to with verses favorable to their position, he counters their teachings by analysing them according to the philosophers' own methods and demonstrating their unsoundness and shakiness in their own terms. He upholds traditional Islam by showing that alternatives are unviable.

The three major teachings of the philosophers attacked by al-Ghazālī are the eternity of the world, God's knowledge of particulars, and survival after death. Concerning the first, for the philosophers the world must be eternal because God would otherwise have had to create it at a particular moment, requiring him to undergo a change from not creating to creating. This would subject him to a cause that was external to his being, which is impossible for God. The problem for traditional Islamic thinking is that this teaching appears to contradict the Qur'ān and it also posits the existence of eternal entities in addition to God. Al-Ghazālī replies that the philosophers cannot provide any cogent proof for their proposition, and there is therefore no reason to accept what they say rather than an alternative, such as that

---

6. Al-Ghazālī himself later summarised these very briefly in *Deliverance*, 66.

God may have eternally willed the existence of the world but only brought it into actual existence at a particular stage.

Concerning the second teaching, the philosophers argue that knowledge changes the knower, which for God is impossible. Since he is pure intellect, his knowledge is of universal principles not of individual phenomena, and his awareness of particular events (Ibn Sīnā gives the example of a solar eclipse) is through the concatenation of causes that bring them about rather than through the actual changing events themselves. Al-Ghazālī rejects this as pure guesswork, arguing that the philosophers have merely set up theoretical principles and forced God to conform. There is no reason to follow what they say.

Concerning the third teaching, for the philosophers the human body, as the material shell of the soul, disintegrates at death, and what survives is the soul with the intellect of the person. This has been influenced and activated by the heavenly Intellects, and it therefore continues eternally in conjunction with them. Al-Ghazālī rejects this as even more of a supposition than the previous one. He argues that there is no reason to postulate the existence of heavenly Intellects, and no evidence to support these teachings about this form of survival after death. Therefore, there is no more cogent reason to accept what the philosophers say than to believe what the Qur'ān teaches.

On the surface, al-Ghazālī's contention against the philosophers is that they have no sound basis for the suppositions they present as logically necessary facts. Their only authorities are their Greek predecessors, who have no greater stature than any other thinker; and their theories may only be accepted after thorough testing. But beneath this framework of argument, al-Ghazālī is seeking to discover what cannot be denied by reason, and his conclusion is that while the enterprise of philosophy may possibly be of use, or at least cause no harm, the conclusions to which the philosophers have come are both unfounded and potentially injurious. Thus, while philosophy as such may add to the sum of human knowledge in some respects, it is nevertheless dangerous because it takes the unsuspecting into realms where they could find themselves denying religious teachings.

This narrow distinction between what philosophy is and what the philosophers have done was not always appreciated. In fact, al-Ghazālī's attack on philosophy was popularly regarded as putting an end to it as a respectable Islamic activity. But his *Tahāfut* was potentially much more threatening to intellectual inquiry, because it could be taken to assert that, not only was the Qur'ān the main authority in matters of knowledge and understanding, but that any teaching that appeared to contradict its evident message or to venture outside it was wicked. To less subtle minds than al-Ghazālī's, his arguments strengthened the notion that the Qur'ān is not only the source of knowledge but is also its sum and safeguard, beyond which there was no need to look. This both threatened independent inquiry and made the Qur'ān the necessary centre of what legitimate inquiry could be.

The dangers arising from al-Ghazālī's cautionary demolition of philosophy in Islam did not escape a mind that was at least the equal of his own, and in some respects superior. This belonged to Abū l-Walīd Muḥammad ibn Rushd, a polymath whose single greatest achievement was to distinguish the true thought of Aristotle from the accretions of Neoplatonism with which it had become encrusted over the centuries. He was born in Spain in 1126, not long after al-Ghazālī died at the other end of the Islamic world, and he was soon recognized for his exceptional abilities in law and medicine as well as in philosophy. He came to know al-Ghazālī's criticisms, and he rebutted them with superlative skill in a work whose title indicates his attitude towards them, *Tahāfut al- tahāfut*, *The Incoherence of the Incoherence*, revealing the inconclusiveness of the theologian's refutation of philosophy that many thought had finished it off.

Ibn Rushd's work is as clear in its layout as al-Ghazālī's: he systematically presents the twenty objections of his opponent and carefully shows the misunderstandings in them, as well as some of the shortcomings of the earlier philosophers whom al-Ghazālī has refuted, and he explains how al-Ghazālī has not done justice to the true nature of the philosophical enterprise.

Ibn Rushd's spirited defense of philosophy in his great rejoinder is expressed just as vividly in a rather shorter work, *Kitāb faṣl al-maqāl wa-taqrīr mā bayn al-sharī'a wa-l-ḥikma min al-ittiṣāl* (*The Book of Distinction of Discourse, and the Determination of the Connection between Religious Law and Philosophy*), known as *Faṣl al-maqāl: The Decisive Treatise*.[7] This dates from the same time as *Tahāfut al-tahāfut*; and it complements it, in that while the much longer work is a detailed reply to al-Ghazālī's objections to the logical coherence of philosophy in Islam, this is a reply to the assumptions in al-Ghazālī's arguments that philosophy is un-Islamic in nature. Ibn Rushd contends that this judgement is based on a misperception of what philosophy is, and equally upon a narrow understanding of Islam. His defense is worth examining in detail because it seeks to preserve within the Qur'ānic framework a dimension of exploration that al-Ghazālī's arguments tend to exclude. Ibn Rushd has al-Ghazālī very much in mind as he writes, though his reply takes the debate onto a different level from mere reply to

---

7. Averroes, *On the Harmony*. See Leaman, *Averroes and His Philosophy*, 144–60.

the various points made by his opponent by drawing attention to the wider implications of the differences between the two positions.

Ibn Rushd begins by establishing that the pursuit of philosophy is not only permitted by the Qur'ān, but is actually required by it. At the outset he argues that if philosophy "is nothing more than study of existing beings and reflection on them as indications of the Artisan . . . and if the [religious] Law has encouraged and urged reflection on beings, then it is clear that what this name [viz. philosophy] signifies is either obligatory or recommended by the Law."[8] He supports this by quoting a number of verses that explicitly enjoin this "reflection on beings." Among them is this: "Have they not studied the kingdom of the heavens and earth, and whatever things God has created?" (Q 7:185). Here he concisely demonstrates that the purpose of philosophy, just like theology, is to show that the world is evidence for the existence and character of its Maker. None of the Mu'tazila or any other theologian could disagree.

He goes on to argue that, in order for philosophers to perform this task, they must be trained in the proper methods, and also that they would be remiss to neglect what predecessors had discovered. In this way, he justifies the use of specialized methods and techniques—and also study of Aristotle and other masters from before the era of Islam:

> It is evident that the study of the books of the ancients is obligatory by Law, since their aim and purpose in their books is just the purpose to which the Law has urged us, and that whoever forbids the study of them to anyone who is fit to study them . . . is blocking people from the door by which the Law summons them to the knowledge of God.[9]

Here he is suggesting that suitably qualified individuals should legitimately be allowed to pursue unfettered exploration into natural phenomena, because this will bring them to a knowledge of God that is analogous to what can be found through the study of the Qur'ān. Furthermore, it would be wrong to prevent this, both because the Qur'ān itself recommends it and because God is behind phenomena in the world as their "Artisan" and is discernible through them, just as he is discernible through the study of the Qur'ān. The importance of this point becomes evident as the argument progresses.

In the second major stage of his argument in *Faṣl al-maqāl*, Ibn Rushd develops the implications of his initial point more fully. He begins with the principle, "Truth does not oppose truth but accords with it and bears

8. Averroes, *On the Harmony*, 44.
9. Ibid., 48.

witness to it."[10] Thus, he continues, if there appears to be a conflict between knowledge that is reached by philosophical investigation and the Qur'ān, the solution will be to interpret the Qur'ān allegorically:

> Whenever a statement in Scripture conflicts in its apparent meaning with a conclusion of demonstration, if Scripture is considered carefully, and the rest of its contents searched page by page, there will invariably be found among the expressions of Scripture something which in its apparent meaning bears witness to that allegorical interpretation or comes close to bearing witness.[11]

This procedure may seem strange or arbitrary because it appears to subordinate the meaning of the Qur'ān to a hermeneutic that is external to it and also determined by human reason. One might expect that it should be the other way round, as al-Ghazālī suggests throughout the *Tahāfut*, because human reason is fallible while the Qur'ān is not. But Ibn Rushd has a good explanation for laying down this procedure, arising from what he sees as the purpose and aim of the Qur'ān. He argues that it was revealed for all people—hence, for those with diverse natural capacities and differing innate dispositions, and also in order to attract those with the ability to interpret its different teachings in ways that reconcile its apparent differences. His point is that the Qur'ān, with some verses that are clear in meaning and others that are less obvious, as it itself declares (Q 3:7), purposely draws people into exploring the different levels of its meanings according to the degree that their different abilities allow them. He backs up what he says by referring to the wide variety of disagreements over doctrine that have been witnessed in Islam since its inception and the practical impossibility of reaching complete unanimity, implying that differences have been willed by God, and that these are to be encouraged because different minds at different times and places must inevitably discern the truth of Islam in different ways.

Ibn Rushd illustrates what he means by briefly discussing the three accusations that al-Ghazālī had levelled against philosophers in *Tahāfut al-falāsifa*, thereby taking the argument right back to its origin. Al-Ghazālī appeared to show once and for all that philosophers tended towards presenting guesses as certainties and contradicting religious truths. But Ibn Rushd challenges the apparent finality of what his opponent had claimed by making the point that, because there have always been among Muslims diverse interpretations of the Qur'ān, and that the Qur'ān itself calls for

---

10. Ibid., 50.
11. Ibid., 51.

different ways of interpreting it, no one can condemn another who bases his views on a legitimate interpretation of the text.

Of course, this begs the question of what a legitimate interpretation is, and Ibn Rushd discusses this crucial matter. But before he does, he rather pointedly takes issue with al-Ghazālī's three main accusations.[12] On the first, the question of God's knowledge of particulars, he argues that the philosophers contend that God's knowledge is not like that of humans: "Our knowledge of [particulars] is an effect of the object known, originated when it comes into existence and changing when it changes; whereas glorious God's knowledge of existence is the opposite of this; it is the cause of the object known, which is existent being."[13] He not only corrects al-Ghazālī's misunderstanding, but also implies that the theologian has reduced God's knowledge to the same restricted mode as human knowledge.

On the second accusation, the eternity of the world, Ibn Rushd postulates a third logical form of being between what is created from something else in time by another being, and what is uncreated and "not preceded by time." This third form is "that which is not made from anything and not preceded by time, but which is brought into existence by something. This is the world as a whole."[14] This being so, the world resembles both what is generated (the theologians' position), and what is not (the philosophers' position), with the consequence that the opposing positions are not as different as they may appear, so that al-Ghazālī's accusation is not appropriate.

Ibn Rushd underlines his point that al-Ghazālī is rash in condemning the philosophers' argument about the preeternity of the world by quoting verses of the Qur'ān that suggest there were entities existent before God created. The verse "It is he who created the heaven and the earth in six days, and his throne was on the water" (Q 11:7), points to the throne and the water as being in existence before the world was created, and also to time (the six days) preceding the created heavens and earth. This bold move shows how confident Ibn Rushd is about the correctness of his position.

He pursues this further by arguing that some verses in the Qur'ān must be taken literally, while others must be taken figuratively by those who are qualified to do so, though not by those who do not have the right qualifications. The implication of what he contends is that the derivation of meaning from scripture is a much more complicated matter than simply reading the text as it stands, and further that different people with their various talents and acquired skills can legitimately find different meanings in the text. The

12. He replies to these at much greater length in *Tahāfut al-tahāfut*.
13. Averroes, *On the Harmony*, 54.
14. Ibid., 55–56.

Qur'ān cannot be regarded as a map with its teachings fully configured to anticipate all requirements and eventualities, but it is more an array of basic possibilities that provides guidelines for aspirant explorers who must use it inductively (though appropriately) to find the meaning that is best suited to their purposes. It provides a series of congruent explanations and not a readily accessible single interpretation of reality that precludes exploration outside the boundaries it has apparently set.

On the third of al-Ghazālī's condemnations of the philosophers, that their teachings about the afterlife run counter to the Qur'ān, Ibn Rushd takes the same position as on the other two accusations: that there is nothing so unequivocal about this in the Qur'ān that an accusation of unbelief about any particular position would be justified. But this only holds for interpretations of verses that are agreed among qualified philosophers. The general population will not have the knowledge to understand the allegorical interpretations of scripture that lead to agreement with the insights of philosophy on this matter; so, these should be kept away from the uninitiated, whom it would be wrong to expose to matters too recondite for them to appreciate, and that might lead them into unbelief.[15]

It has become clear by this point at the end of the second stage of *Faṣl al-maqāl* that Ibn Rushd is far from being cowed by al-Ghazālī's accusations against philosophy, but that he places the whole issue in a different context from his opponent. For the earlier theologian, the Qur'ān sets the framework within which intellectual discourse is to be set, but for the Andalusī philosopher it is the starting point and informing inspiration for exploration, though with the condition that this should be an activity open only to the appropriately qualified. For ordinary people who could easily get lost in error, it should not be permitted.

Clearly, the nature of the Qur'ān and the correct way of interpreting it are central to Ibn Rushd's disagreement with al-Ghazālī. He focuses on these in the third and last stage of this short essay, and he begins by explaining that the primary purpose of the Qur'ān "is simply to teach true knowledge and right practice." These are the essentials of belief: as he says, knowledge is knowledge of God, and of happiness and misery in the life to come, while right practice "consists in performing the acts which bring happiness and avoiding the acts which bring misery."[16] (In a short digression that may be intended as a piece of mild sarcasm, Ibn Rushd explains al-Ghazālī's *Iḥyā' 'ulūm al-dīn* as a book that is centred on the two forms of right practice, which are acts of the body and acts of the soul, because people had aban-

---

15. Ibid., 60–61.
16. Ibid., 63.

doned the latter. In this way, he implies that the theologian was mainly concerned with the practical implementation of the literal injunctions of the sacred law rather than probing into the deeper consequences of its inner ramifications. This may be important for the masses, but hardly comparable with probing into the profound questions raised by the nature of reality, which was the province of philosophy.) However, the Qur'ān admits different kinds of interpretation, and when it comes to allegory, only certain people should be allowed to practise this: "the duty of the masses is to take [the sacred texts] in their apparent meaning . . . since their natural capacity does not allow for more than that."[17]

Ibn Rushd has already made the point that the allegorical meaning of scripture should be shielded from the general population of Muslims. Here he explains that the reason is that this form of allegorical interpretation comprises "rejection of the apparent meaning and affirmation of the allegorical one,"[18] which, in the mind of someone who cannot go beyond the immediate meaning, can lead to unbelief as they relinquish the one meaning without being able to apprehend the other. The Qur'ān actually supports this: "And they will ask you about the Spirit. Say: 'The Spirit is by the command of my Lord; you have been given only a little knowledge'" (Q 17:85). He develops his point further in the remainder of the work by showing how different sects within Islam have caused divisions through their efforts to ally ordinary people to their allegorical interpretations, and by insisting that while the meaning of the text that is available to ordinary people is sufficient for their needs, the deeper meaning is equally authentic and must also be investigated.

A remark Ibn Rushd makes in this third stage of his argument is revealing with regard to the personal approach to the Qur'ān that he himself favours. He says, "Since the primary purpose of scripture is to take care of the majority (without neglecting the elite), the prevailing methods of expression in religion are the common methods by which the majority comes to form concepts and judgements."[19] It is the aside that in the translation appears within brackets that is significant here because it suggests that, while the mass of ordinary people (including the theologians, who content themselves with drawing inferences from the immediate meaning of the text) should remain loyal to exegesis of the most obvious teachings in the Qur'ān, there are others who can be challenged and inspired by its sometimes indirect references. Ibn Rushd has alluded to this hidden layer of significance

17. Ibid., 65.
18. Ibid., 66.
19. Ibid., 64.

within the text throughout *Faṣl al-maqāl*; and here he implies that it stands as the key to a form of inquiry that goes beyond the obvious interpretation to a form of interrogation that many of the uninitiated would find uncomfortable and un-Islamic.

This is the point over which Ibn Rushd fundamentally disagrees with al-Ghazālī. The theologian had effectively sought to put an end to philosophical inquiry because it was demonstrably un-Qur'ānic and potentially un-Islamic. In his *Tahāfut al-falāsifa* he had strongly suggested that those with a philosophical bent were led away from Islam by the teachings of the ancient Greek masters, and they risked leading fellow Muslims astray with them. The consequence, whether he intended it or not, was that learning that could not be shown directly to reflect the Qur'ān was dangerous, and the implication that some might draw from his objections was that the Qur'ān alone was sufficient for knowledge of God and the forms of belief and conduct that could lead to felicity.

When inadequately understood, this attitude that clearly elevates revelation above human reason can threaten to rule out the exercise of reason completely. Curiously, it may seem, al-Ghazālī did not negate human spontaneity entirely but condoned it if it was channelled not through rational inquiry but through personal immersion in experiential faith. In *Al-munqidh min al-ḍalāl* he praises the way of the mystics in lavish terms: "I know with certainty that the Sufis are those who uniquely follow the way of God Most High; their mode of life is the best of all."[20] For him this is orthodox because it remains within the obvious confines set by the Qur'ān and the model of prophethood, though not every Muslim would agree.

As he shows in this short sequence of arguments, Ibn Rushd advocates a way that is different from the way of the Ṣūfī though analogous to it. Just as the mystical adept must learn from the master, so the philosophical initiate must learn from his predecessors; the mystic acquires techniques that equip him to proceed along the way of experience; and the philosopher learns new methods that allow him to discern new meanings in the world. The Qur'ān is the mystic's warrant for his ecstatic progression towards God; and, as Ibn Rushd shows clearly, here it is also the basis and guide for the philosopher's abstract reflections about the One. Moreover, just as philosophers can commit religious excesses in their speculations, so mystics can exceed the bounds of religious propriety. Ibn Rushd's contention is that in the right hands philosophy and rational exploration is as Islamic and as true to the Qur'ān as any other intellectual discipline in Islam; and it can actually glorify God more than others.

20. Al-Ghazālī, *Deliverance from Error*, 81.

However, whereas al-Ghazālī found an audience that greeted his prescriptions with enthusiasm, Ibn Rushd was hardly heeded. *Faṣl al-maqāl* may, in fact, have contributed to his downfall; and after his death it was hardly read.[21] But while, in its immediate terms, his response to al-Ghazālī and other detractors of philosophy was part of a distinctively medieval debate, its arguments contain a more wide-ranging significance. He provides justification in terms of the Qur'ān itself for a procedure of rational exploration that goes beyond the bounds set by orthodox Islam and that counters the narrowminded prohibition on exploration that appears to exceed these bounds. He affirms that the exercise of human reason is a gift from God, and he celebrates the ability of human ingenuity to discern unforeseen possibilities within the text of scripture. In essence, he shows how the Qur'ān anticipates and authenticates the whole range of knowledge that the human mind can attain, and thereby provides a way of relating the teachings that lie within its text to the ideas and intellectual needs of his own times, with neither the one being despised as irrelevant nor the other dismissed as ungodly. In many Muslim communities this need is as pressing today as it was when Ibn Rushd wrote. His wisdom is worth a fresh hearing.

BIBLIOGRAPHY

Al-Ghazālī. *Deliverance from Error: An Annotated Translation of "Al-munqidh min al-ḍalāl," and Other Relevant Works.* Translated by Richard Joseph McCarthy. Louisville: Fons Vitae, 2001.

Averroes. *On the Harmony of Religion and Philosophy: A Translation of Ibn Rushd's "Faṣl al-maqāl."* Translated by George Fadlo Hourani. London: Luzac, 1976.

Avicenna. *The Metaphysics of "The Healing": A Parallel English-Arabic Text.* Translated, introduced, and annotated by Michael E. Marmura. Islamic Translation Series. Provo, UT: Brigham Young University Press, 2005.

Bowker, John. *The Religious Imagination and the Sense of God.* Oxford: Clarendon, 1978.

Leaman, Oliver. *Averroes and His Philosophy.* Richmond, UK: Curzon, 1998.

Russell, Bertrand. *A History of Western Philosophy.* London: Allen & Unwin, 1954.

---

21. See Averroes, *On the Harmony*, 40–41 (editor's introduction).

13

God, Life, Love, and Religions among Indigenous Peoples of the World

—Darryl Macer

OUR PRECOLONIAL GOD

WHEN DID GOD REVEAL himself to the created? Most would agree it was before the nineteenth-century in America, when followers of the Mormon faith would claim that God presented Joseph Smith with a set of tablets. Many would claim it was before Moses received the tablets of the ten commandments from God at Mount Sinai. There have been many earlier and later saints; but just how do the major religions regard the saints and faiths of many Peoples around the world? Perhaps "ignorance" is the most common word we can use to describe the understanding of many Peoples by most others. Yet, religious faith is common among all Peoples of the world, although the details differ.

This paper is dedicated to a dear friend, mentor, and someone who inspired me to consider life and broaden my faith as our life paths encountered each other when I came as a doctoral student in molecular biology to Cambridge University: Canon John Bowker. This book to honor his eightieth birthday is a good opportunity for me, thirty years younger, to reflect on how this friendship has been linked to my scholarship and life ever since.

What I am doing now is establishing a global university on Sovereign land of Native American tribes in the United States, which may explain the link in the title to Indigenous Peoples. As Provost of the University, and Director of the Institute of Indigenous Peoples and Global Studies, I learn something new everyday still about the faiths, beliefs, and wisdom of different people. I will happily join in a premeal grace of the Apache chief facing East, where the sun rises, just as joyfully as welcoming the rising sun for a prayer with my dear friend in Japan, a samurai of Shinto faith with whom I had the privilege of sharing a common office wall for over a decade as professors at the University of Tsukuba. The fact that both faiths face East is not hidden on me, as one who grew up in Aoteoroa, New Zealand and climbed the roof of my house there to welcome the first sun in the world of any city for the new millennium in the year 2000 . . . also facing East. Actually, as I welcome many Muslims to American University of Sovereign Nations, I am also happy that it happens that Mecca also is in the East. It is nice[1] that Peoples of different faiths could prayer together on sacred mountains and lands together, despite the fact that their revealed faiths came through the wisdom of different saints.

Back in my Cambridge days, I was the Chair of the Cambridge Christian Society for two years, and also one of the cofounders of the Cambridge Christians in Science group, and still have a strong faith. Although there were those at that time, and still today, who preached an exclusive form of religious faith, one of the lessons I learned from John Bowker is a respect and love of learning about other faith systems. I remember his writing that 90 percent of the world's people follow a religion; and the same is true today. I have conducted research in around 50 countries of the world to date, and right now am learning more about many indigenous Peoples. My original passion for bioethics as an all-embracing discipline remains from my Cambridge days, and most of what I do I would call bioethics—encompassing the love of life, and the ways people relate to each other, and to other lives and nature.

Before this, I have spent a decade as UNESCO's Regional Adviser for Social and Human Sciences in Asia and the Pacific, conducting programs in over forty countries of the world—some small and others huge consortiums such as India and China. So many systems are trying to find their way in a postcolonial world to prosper, and some even attempting to rediscover themselves and find their identity and past heritage. One of the programs I developed was a dialogue between Asian and Arab philosophers to help

---

1. The word *nice* could be substituted by many more complex expressions; but, for the point of people around the world, why not use a word like *nice* or *beautiful*?

produce alternative materials for students to learn about philosophy from different traditions than the standard Anglo-American-European ones that dominate. The obvious interfaith nature of these philosophical reflections has links to the Cambridge days also. I remember the attitude of the fundamentalists on both sides of a joint meeting I organized as a student between the Christian and Muslim societies in Cambridge—an evangelistic exercise from both sides; but most people just had a great time together. The Asian-Arab philosophical dialogues were more a scholarly exercise by equally passionate people—not evangelizing the other but trying together to understand the revealed wisdom of different traditions and how it could help us all in our contemporary, postcolonial world.

BIOETHICS AS LOVE OF LIFE

The gift that we receive when we are born into this world is love. While it is a gift that few are deprived of—a deprivation that is in itself an insult to the humanity that our flesh embodies—it is a norm for all forms of life for the new life to be given a good start.[2] The ultimate gift that we can share with others is also love. If we ask people what images they have of love, answers might include: lovers, family, warmth, God, happiness, difficulty, and many others. Many of these answers come from the local encounters around us; and, in fact, the challenges for those who have tried to work on universal love is that it is difficult to empathize with others in a distant land unless we are in contact with them. Only when "they" become "us" can we empathize with others.

We can find various definitions of "bioethics." The simplest would be love of life.[3] Or less passionately, a consideration of the ethical issues raised by questions involving life ("bio"). It includes questions we face each day, like, What food should I eat? How is the food grown? Where should I live; and how much disturbance of nature should I make? What relationships should I have with fellow organisms, including human beings? How do I balance the quality of my life with development of love of my life, others' lives, and the community? These are just a few; you can think of many more. The history of bioethical reasoning is influenced by our genes, and the forces that shaped and continue to shape these genes into the people, society, and cultures that we have.[4] We now have the power to change not only our own genes but the genes of every organism, and the power to

---

2. Macer, *Bioethics Is Love of Life*.
3. Ibid., 1.
4. Macer, *Shaping Genes*, 340.

remodel whole ecosystems of the planet, which has made many focus on biotechnology applications. However, the key questions are more basic. We have the technology to conceive an embryo in vitro, to mix genes from different persons and beings and to offer life support to those whose body has temporarily failed. We have the power to remodel whole ecosystems of the planet. New technology has nevertheless been a catalyst for our thinking about bioethics, which have been stimuli for research into bioethics in the last few decades.

A fundamental way of reasoning that people have when making decisions is to balance doing good against doing harm. We could group these ideals under the idea of love, though the question of benefits for whom and harm to whom is central to deciding whether an action is one of love or not. One of the underlying philosophical ideas of society is to pursue progress. The most common justification for this is the pursuit of improved medicines and health, which is doing good. A failure to attempt to do good is a form of doing harm: the sin of omission. This is the principle of beneficence. This is a powerful impetus for further research into ways of improving health and agriculture and living standards.

Fritz Jahr[5] has urged people to turn to "bioethics" and conduct a review of the ethical relations of humans towards animals and plants, following the traditions followed for millennia in Africa, the Americas, Asia, and the Pacific—in fact, by indigenous persons across every continent. If one has ever walked in a jungle, or swum in a coral reef, the words—"The strict distinction between animal and human being [Mensch], dominant in our European culture up to the end of the 18th century, cannot be supported anymore"—would have not only resonated, but also made us wonder what sort of world tried to distinguish human beings from other animals in the first place.

Such thinkers had a biocentric or ecocentric worldview, influenced not only by a revealed God through nature but also by the increased understanding of biological evolution. The love of life has always been expressed by some in society, in each religion. There are several basic theories of bioethics, and the simplest distinction that can be made is whether they focus on action, consequences, or motives. Another separation that is used is deontological theories, which examine the concepts of rights and duties, and teleological ones, which are based on effects and consequences. If we use the image of walking along the path of life, a teleologist tries to look where decisions lead, whereas a deontologist follows a planned direction. All around

---

5. Jahr, "Bio-Ethik," 2–4.

the world people make moral decisions using a range of ideas, which are not as diverse from each other as their different etiquettes may demand.[6]

What future do we want? The pursuit of a good life is a goal that all persons can hope for. A good life should be understood in a holistic sense, and is clearly more than just a contented life, free of want and fear. At the international level, this is what the United Nations was established to help provide. This is also the duty of all governments to provide to their citizens, and those with the abilities to provide to those in need. Local wisdom provides a number of answers to the question of what a good life is. The extension of local wisdom to global love can be seen throughout history. In the words of Erich Fromm, "If I truly love one person I love all persons, I love the world, I love life. If I can say to somebody else, 'I love you,' I must be able to say 'I love in you everybody, I love through you the world, I love in you also myself.'"[7]

This reminds us of the words of Mo Tzu in the sixth century BCE from China referring to Confucian family-centered love:

> It should be replaced by the way of universal love and mutual benefit . . . . It is to regard other people's countries as one's own. Regard other people's families as one's own. Regard other people's person as one's own. Consequently, when feudal lords love one another, they will not fight in the fields. When heads of families love one another, they will not usurp one another. When individuals love one another, they will not injure one another. When ruler and minister love each other, they will be kind and loyal. When father and son love each other, they will be affectionate and filial. When brothers love each other, they will be peaceful and harmonious. When all people in the world love one another, the strong will not overcome the weak, the many will not oppress the few, the rich will not insult the poor, the honoured will not despise the humble, and the cunning will not deceive the ignorant. Because of universal love, all the calamities, usurpations, hatred, and animosity in the world will be prevented from arising.[8]

---

6. Macer, *Bioethics for the People*, 188.
7. Fromm, *The Art of Loving*, 63.
8. Macer, *Bioethics Is Love of Life*, 27.

OUR COMMON MIND AND HUMAN DIGNITY

There have been debates in almost every corner of the globe over the definitions of "culture" and "identity," and over the question, what is ethics? These social constructs all originate in our mind, a product of an individual's ontology, genes, environment, and relationships. The underlying heritage of ethics can be seen in all cultures, religions, and in ancient writings from around the world.[9] We in fact cannot trace the origin of bioethics back to their beginning, as the relationships between human beings within their society, with nature and God, are formed at an earlier stage then our history would tell us.

As countries have developed spaces to discuss their values, we have also seen the role of social science as a driver towards understanding of different social relations and patterns between and within cultures, and increased understanding of our views of nature. Creating a space is not so much a challenge from the use of technology, but rather a challenge from the growing knowledge of human nature and life itself. Bioethics is the concept of love, balancing benefits and risks of choices and decisions, in our ethical mind. This heritage can be seen in all cultures and religions, and in ancient writings from around the world.

One of the most interesting questions before a thinking being is whether we can comprehend the ideas and thoughts of other beings, and conversely whether they can also read our mind. In terms of evolution, there could be survival benefit by the capacity to be able to fully understand the thinking of others, both for direct competitive benefit and also for the spirit of altruistic cooperation. Although the human mind appears to be infinitely complex, and the diversity of human kind and culture has been considered vast, in 1994 I made a hypothesis that the number of ideas that human beings have is finite,[10] and in 2002 I called for a project to map the ideas of the human mind[11]—the behaviorome project (or human mental mapping project).[12] There are many opportunities offered by greater understanding of the human mind, but also many challenges to greater individual and cross-cultural understanding of human beings.

The term "love" is usually omitted from international law, whereas the concept of human dignity is often cited. Human dignity is arguably even more difficult to define than love. For example, article 11 of the *Universal*

---

9. Macer, *Bioethics for the People*.
10. Ibid., 168.
11. Macer, "Next Challenge," 12.
12. Macer, "Finite or Infinite Mind?," 203.

Declaration on the Human Genome and Human Rights states, "Practices which are contrary to human dignity, such as reproductive cloning of human beings, shall not be permitted."[13] Why cloning is always against human dignity is not clear. For example, if it was the only way a family could have a genetically related child, why is that against human dignity? Especially when using donated sperm and eggs or a surrogate mother is permitted in many countries, even for commercial contracts. Yet, at the time following the cloning of Dolly the sheep by nuclear transfer in February 1997, it became a popular call for many government leaders to say it was against human dignity. Still, across the world we can find many common expressions of dignity from many sources.[14]

Another expression of love of our own life that is dominant in medical ethics is the sanctity of life. This sanctity of life is also often imposed upon others on the behalf of the person who has their life threatened. The argument is also used by opponents of abortion, claiming the fetus also has a sanctity of life. Indian philosophy also includes the idea of to do no harm, *ahimsa*, as one guiding principle. Indian medical ethics today includes Hindu and Western influences, plus many folk traditions and other religious groups. India includes followers of many religions, and the long tradition of living together, and has a holistic environmental ethic.[15] In Jainism, patience is regarded as a good; and pleasure is a source of sin, so that true freedom is independence to outside things. Depending how removed we attempt to be from the material world, we might accept our fate without taking medicine. This reminds us of the Taoist idea to flow with nature.[16] However, there is a long tradition of use of curative and cosmetic remedies in Indian medicine, suggesting that, in India as elsewhere, people seek to cure sickness and enhance their body and emotions.

Part of the concept of dignity is linked to self-determination. Autonomy is applied to many life choices that are bioethical dilemmas. For example, personal transport in an automobile is associated with high environmental load. People are free to pursue sports that consume large amounts of energy, or to buy large cars or large homes that are beyond what is necessary for a comfortable life. Personal or cultural freedom in continuing to eat whale meat in Norway, Iceland, or Japan is considered more important than concerns that whales might have sanctity of life because of intrinsic moral status. Whale baleen used to be widely used in woman's corsets in

---

13. UNESCO, *Universal Declaration on the Human Genome*, 3.
14. Macer, *Asian-Arab Philosophical Dialogues*, 1–177.
15. Azariah, "Global Bioethics and Common Hope," 66.
16. Hsin and Macer, "Contrasting Expectations," 195–216.

the West, and today many endangered animals are used to make cosmetic products. We can see the evolution of law, however, in the 2014 decision of the International Court of Justice to stop the hunting of whales in the international waters of the South Pacific in order to end an intensifying battle between environmentalists of that region and whalers. Although the direct legal arguments can be interpreted in different ways, the ethical-political rationale is extending the concept of moral agency beyond human species. Similar arguments have been used for the Great Ape project, to call for laws against experimentation on great apes—including chimpanzees, gorillas and orangutans.[17]

There are precedents for limiting autonomy in behavior towards the environment. Personal taste in tropical timber products is one choice that has begun to be limited by restrictions on tropical-forest logging. Another limit is personal choice in use of ivory in statues and personal name stamps in many countries due to the endangered status of elephants. Limiting personal choice of human beings when those choices harm other beings is being accepted. This will be seen more in environmental ethics.

PRECOLONIAL AND POSTCOLONIAL VALUE SYSTEMS

Colonization has been a major force to articulate bioethical value systems that were previously implicit in the relationships of people and nature. Along with colonization came waves of Christian missionaries; and the Christian faith was readily adopted in a "local" form. Anthropologists also described a number of traditions, although some "sacred" knowledge is preserved among chiefs and only informed to those they decide to entrust such wisdom to. In my home, Oceania, as more persons left the shores of the islands to study, they started to document more of these diverse traditions, and in turn these values were discussed among many of the communities in a more articulated form.

"Bioethics" is both a word and a concept. Likewise, bioethics in the Pacific is identified closely with a broad concept of love binding all of life together, and the terms and values used to translate English words of bioethical principles in Pacific languages have deep historical roots. Although there were a wide variety of concepts prior to European colonization of the Pacific, the modern Pacific is predominantly Christian in faith, with a blend of indigenous culture and a theocentric approach to life ethics. Thus, although the actual word "bioethics" comes to us only from a German paper

---

17. Cavalieri and Singer, *Great Ape Project*, 11.

of 1927,[18] amplified by Potter in English,[19] the concept comes from human heritage thousands of years old; and there has been rejection of attempts to introduce the term "bioethics" when it is associated with universal ethical principles.

The concept of love as a binding force resonates well with many approaches of indigenous cultures. This includes more than humans, however, with strong love of animals who live on the land and in water, and a love of nature. In Maori, the word *aroha* is used to denote something broader than love, but including a oneness with nature and animals. Bioethics has origins in exploring human relationships with animals and with nature (ocean and land), and spirituality.[20] Love continues to be taught to children from a young age as a noble ethical character. In Tonga, *ofa*, which means all forms of love, and *fe'ofo'ofani*, caring love as a family, are some of the basic values taught to children from a young age, which influence their behavior. These concepts are expressed in the way that Pacific islanders care for the sick, often with practical expressions that family members will accompany the sick person to the hospital and a relative will always stay with the person day and night in the hospital.[21]

Stories explaining the deeds of past generations and the symbolic nature of the landscape can be found in songs, laws, history instruction, and social systems. It is not possible to trace the origin of bioethics back to their beginning, as the relationships between human beings within their society, within the biological community, and with nature and God are formed at an earlier stage then history provides.[22] Love is recognized as both the biological heritage given to humankind by genes, as well as a social heritage, as society tries to pursue harmony between individuals and communities.

In some countries, deliberate mistranslations were made if a written concept existed. For example, the Spanish missionaries in Mexico tried to eliminate the concept of reincarnation from Aztec and Mayan writings so that people could believe in the Christian concept of one life, one death and one judgment. Because Pacific values and beliefs are transmitted orally, many have incorrectly assumed that bioethics were effectively nonexistent

18. Jahr, "Bio-Ethik," 2–4.
19. Potter, *Bioethics*, 1–16.
20. Macer, *Bioethics Is Love of Life*, 3.
21. Mafi, "Polynesians often put family and community before their own health," 13–16.
22. Macer, *Bioethics Is Love of Life*, 124.

before the expansion of modern bioethics in the 1970s.[23] Ethics has a central place in all indigenous knowledge systems and processes.

> Each daily life event is seen through a lens of ethical values, mores, and codes of conduct developed over years. Indigenous ethical systems incorporate technical insights and wisdom-based observations of natural, social, and spiritual phenomena which, in turn, validate place and identity, as well as the survival of Pacific nations in our increasingly globalized societies.[24]

Ethical values and principles have developed in the context of epistemological systems and are central to how knowledge is gained and organized, how knowledge is used, and who has access to it. In the development of ethical principles for medical research, the Pacific Health Research Council in New Zealand wrote:

> Every Pacific society has a framework of knowledge that is systematically gathered and formulated within a paradigm of general truths and principles. Knowledge gathering and systems of validating knowledge and legitimizing information are processes that are often determined and regulated (but not exclusively) by a select group within the traditional hierarchy of knowledge with the aim of protecting the quality and wellbeing of people.[25]

The prime minister of Samoa, Tui Atua Tupua Tamasese Ta'isi Efi described the importance of the Samoan concepts of *tapu* (the sacred) and *tofa sa'ili* (the search for wisdom) in identifying ethical practices for application in research.[26] He argued that it is possible to find a middle ground between ideas and practices grounded in religion, the spiritual, the sacred, and science. Against the background of an exploration of different facets of the Samoan concept of *tapu*, which encompasses the sacredness of the origins of all things as well as the affinity between people, the cosmos, and animate and inanimate earthly phenomena, he envisages a Pacific bioethics that reaches out for wisdom. Such activity and the search for knowledge would be grounded in a sense of connectedness to all things, the awareness of people's responsibilities as protectors of the earth, attention to the sacred essence of all things, and a desire for increased understanding without ever presuming to know God.

23. Ibid., 15.
24. Fairbairn-Dunlop, "Pacific Ethics and Universal Norms," 9–13.
25. Health Research Council, *Guidelines*, 10.
26. Tui Atua Tupua Tamasese Efi, "Bioethics and the Samoan Indigenous Reference," 115–24.

There are a variety of approaches to deciding whether a practice is ethical or not. Are there indeed universal values which can be agreed upon across the many cultures of the world, and is there a universal language of making these values acceptable as well as applicable across the many communities? In the Western Abrahamic and post-Enlightenment worldviews, there is a strong belief that universal values can be realized through objective criteria. Contrastingly, the Indic systems believe that while universal values exist, they are not achievable because human beings apply their own subjective experiences and emotions to their knowledge of values. Therefore, whereas the former ascribes a degree of objectivity as a prerequisite for legitimacy, the latter considers subjectivity as a major influencing factor specific to individuals, groups, cultures, and so on.[27]

This worldview will tolerate many individual choices as long as they do not do harm, and will also tolerate belief in attempting to improve ourselves. Indic cultural systems would be uncomfortable with a "universal" set of values arrived at through a consensus of human reason or legitimized through divine revelation. A pluralistic approach exists in most Eastern civilizations, including in the Far East and China. It is understood that human society lives by a diverse set of values and philosophies, and universalism deprives some communities and people of their own value systems. Thus, Eastern traditions believe that universalism is an infringement on a human being's basic right to enjoy one's own value and belief system. People should be able to exercise their choices if they do not harm others.

Confucianism has two interesting characteristics that set it apart from Abrahamic and Indic traditions. First, it does not dwell on God or other metaphysical theories. This leaves the individual free to believe in any "spiritual" truth he or she may wish to follow, and enhancement is a common belief. Confucianism is a set of ethics on relationships between the individual and government, the individual and society, individual and family and the individual and friends. It describes how concepts such as compassion, honesty, justice, and work fit within these relationships. These sets of values and directions form the essential nature of Chinese society regardless of the "religion" of the person. In fact, if religion is usually both about a metaphysical theory and human relations, then Confucianism can be said to be a religion which does not concern itself with metaphysical aspects.

Second, Confucianism emphasizes harmony among humans and between humans and nature. Confucianism does not proffer divine origins of harmony, but rather a set of values derived from reason and a spiritual awareness. Harmony influences the ethics of Confucians towards nature and

---

27. Rai et al. *Universalism and Ethical Values for the Environment*, 16.

society. In the future, when differences between those who are enhanced and those who are not become significant, there will be some challenges to harmony for these reasons. Growing socioeconomic gaps however have been tolerated over time; so. we can question whether people will really apply concepts of justice to the way people think.

Aristotle in *Nicomachean Ethics* wrote that morality is the pursuit of a "final good" or "supreme good." This may be accepted widely, but the question is what this "good" is.[28] The final good was often interpreted as happiness, which leads us to one of the main teleological theories: utilitarianism. Utilitarianism looks at the consequences of an action, and is based on the work of Jeremy Bentham (1748–1832) and John Stuart Mill (1806–1873). They could have been rediscovering what Mo Tzu had taught in China in the sixth century BCE. The benefit of the community over individual is a widespread ethic across Asian countries, as is the sacrifice of individuals for the greater good. If a substantial majority of a community consider a practice to be ethical does it make it ethical? The principle of utility asserts that we ought always to produce the maximal balance of happiness/pleasure over pain, or good over harm, or positive value over disvalue. Harmony is an important principle in Asian bioethics.

DESCRIBING OUR VIEWS

A repository of worldviews[29] is being set up that will evolve as different sets of ethical values from the first principles widely held within the religion or culture of that region, people, or civilization are included. Once a repository is more fully developed, we may find that there may be similarities in all, there may only be similarities in some, or there may not be any similarities in the different perspectives, or that the small number of similarities does not warrant a unitary ethical system for the whole world.

There are implications for mind mapping our future relationships with nature and cultural identity as we explore. How should a culture that tries to maintain its cultural uniqueness by claiming everyone thinks the same, face up to the reality that in every culture the full range of idea diversity is found. This diversity is found in almost all groups, excluding those particularly finite groups that are formed to promote particular political aims, such as those who fight for or against abortion or euthanasia. Religions which have observed already that humankind is universal will have fewer challenges than religions which claim a special religious status for their

---

28. Macer, *Bioethics Is Love of Life*, 52.
29. http://www.eubios.info/repository_of_ethical_world_views_of_nature/.

"chosen" people. The question of how universal the human-idea map is, is of importance for the development of global society, when we're faced with dilemmas like should we have common guidelines to regulate the use of new biotechnology or assisted reproductive technology using cloning, for example. It is time to start thinking scientifically about it, whether or not science is finite or infinite. That is another question.

To compare mental maps allows comparisons of idea diversity between persons and species. This will allow the development of descriptive bioethics into a common framework for comparative ethics. This will aid in policy making to make policy that respects the diversity of people in a culture, and globally. This would help develop bioethics for the people by the people. The development of biotechnology and use of humans in clinical trials in many countries raises fundamental questions about whether the standards used should be universal or local. The development of guidelines should be culturally sensitive in the way ethical, social, and legal aspects are considered. Having a map of human ideas will enable us to reflect more diversity of ideas into policy frameworks. We will have to pay attention to ensure it is used well, and not used to dictate majority views to minorities.

We can see that the mental-mapping project will develop international bioethics, social and human sciences of the twenty-first century onto a more concrete and transdisciplinary basis. We need to develop a common language for studies of life and ideas, and it is hoped that these projects will allow this. There will be challenges for many aspects of our understanding of human beings—though we should be clear: there will always be more questions than answers for humans to attempt to understand ourselves and nature. This is clearly an issue of information ethics in collection, storage, and use. Already military uses have been debated at conferences on this project, as have many psychological consequences of the mental maps when they are available for human individuals, cultures, and in general. How should we proceed in these studies, also given that the mind of youth and aged persons also vary in the era of mundialization and globalization? There are many questions for us to discuss, and more contributions for the repository will be useful as we develop these processes.

ETHICS EDUCATION THROUGH GLOBAL AND LOCAL DIALOGUE AND DEBATE

What future do we want? The pursuit of a good life is a goal that all persons can hope for. We can consider the four imperatives of love for ethics, as self-love, loving others, loving life, and loving good. Love is not only a universally recognized goal of ethical action, but is also the foundation of normative principles of ethics. Global responsibilities for promotion of a good life for all (not only humankind) are necessary for our sustainable future.

A person's identity and ethic develops based on their own and other people's opinions, and grows as we face various dilemmas through our life. To have a balanced opinion from the community, it is important to hear from persons in a range of positions with different occupations. Interactive ethics education allows the classroom to be a place for moral exploration and clarification of values.

The common social goal to respect the moral choices of others has developed hand in hand with the emergence of increased media attention in pluralistic democracies to display the divergent views on many topics. These dialogues can show us that local wisdom from our corner of the world is similar to local wisdom from others on the other side of the globe, so that they now also join to "us" to construct a larger "us." These lessons also assist us in the development of a globally accessible multicultural and multidisciplinary curriculum that offers cases from many local wisdoms that can be shared.

We need to promote greater dialogue between different regions of the world, separate to the export of ideas from Europe that occurred during the colonial days, and more recently from North America as English has become the common language for globalization. What can we teach in a curriculum that covers many localities and local wisdoms? Consensus is possible after recognition of the individual yet connected history of relationships between different persons and communities, to try to preserve social harmony. This consensus building is seen even in countries that have structured paternalism affecting the relationships between persons. Public discussion of the ethics of science and technology in many societies is aided by the media.

CONCLUSIONS

Scholarship is so engrained in the fabric of the human mind that some have considered it the image of God; as Descartes said, "I think therefore I am." A mature society can discuss the benefits and risks of all choices and have public debate on these. The same is true in our individual moral education. Participation of the public in the societal decision-making process regarding new technology is essential. Community engagement is not only a question of knowing what is going on: but for a new technology to be accepted by the public, it is crucial to perceive the choice and influence.

Beyond that, scholarship is the capacity to show love, and in that there is some common understanding of love that should be central in a dialogue between cultures—of East and West, North and South, powerful and weak, and technophiles and technophobes. Human beings are one part of nature, closely interwoven with all species. Can we enhance all species to love more to enhance life? It is a challenge that many cosmetic choices are not beyond the economic choices that societies let individuals pursue; and if they do not directly harm others, perhaps we will see even greater evolution of our mind than we would like to! However, a lesson of indigenous culture is that most are evolutionary and prepared to survive through times when norms are thrown upside down and trampled on. That capacity for survival is something that gives us hope. That hope is also embedded with the humility that all of us and all societies have made moral mistakes; that should make us pursue greater wisdom for a better future.

BIBLIOGRAPHY

Azariah, Jayapaul. "Global Bioethics and Common Hope." In *Bioethics for the People by the People*, edited by Darryl R. J. Macer, 98–124. Christchurch, NZ: Eubios Ethics Institute, 1994.

Cavalieri, Paola, and Peter Singer, eds. *The Great Ape Project: Equality beyond Humanity*. London: Fourth Estate, 1993.

Fairbairn-Dunlop, Peggy. "Pacific Ethics and Universal Norms." In *Asia-Pacific Perspectives on Ethics of Science and Technology*, edited by Darryl R. J. Macer, 9–13. Bangkok: UNESCO, 2010.

Fromm, Erich. *The Art of Loving*. New York: Bantam, 1963.

Health Research Council of New Zealand. *Guidelines on Pacific Health Research*. Auckland, NZ: Health Research Council of New Zealand, 2005.

Hsin, H-S.D., and Darryl R. J. Macer. "Contrasting Expectations of Biotechnology for Medical Care in Taiwan between Seniors and Medical Students." *LHGR* 20 (2004) 195–216.

Jahr, Fritz. "Bio-Ethik. Eine Umschau über die ethischen Beziehungen des Menschen zu Tier und Pflanze." *KHN* 24/1 (1927) 2–4.

Macer, Darryl R. J., ed. *Bioethics for the People by the People*. Christchurch, NZ: Eubios Ethics Institute, 1994.

———. *Bioethics Is Love of Life*. Christchurch, NZ: Eubios Ethics Institute, 1998.

———. "Finite or Infinite Mind?: A Proposal for an Integrative Mental Mapping Project." *EJAIB* 12 (2002b) 203–6, http://www.eubios.info/mentmap.htm/.

———. "The Next Challenge Is to Map the Human Mind." *Nature* 420 (2002a) 12.

———. *Shaping Genes: Ethics, Law and Science of Using New Genetic Technology in Medicine and Agriculture*. Christchurch, NZ: Eubios Ethics Institute, 1990.

———, ed. *Asian-Arab Philosophical Dialogues on Culture of Peace and Human Dignity*. Bangkok: UNESCO, 2011.
Mafi, G. "Polynesians Often Put Family and Community before Their Own Health." *NZFP* 25/1 (1998) 13–16.
Potter, Van Rensselaer. *Bioethics: Bridge to the Future*. Englewood Cliffs, NJ: Prentice-Hall, 1971.
Rai, Jasdev Singh et al. *Universalism and Ethical Values for the Environment*. Working Group Report 1. Bangkok, UNESCO, 2010.
Tui Atua Tupua Tamasese Efi. "Bioethics and the Samoan Indigenous Reference." *ISSJ* 60.195 (2009) 115–24.
UNESCO. *Universal Declaration on the Human Genome and Human Rights*. Paris: UNESCO, 1997. http://portal.unesco.org/en/ev.php-URL_ID=13177&URL_DO=DO_TOPIC&URL_SECTION=201.html/.
UNESCO. *Universal Declaration on Bioethics and Human Rights*. Paris: UNESCO, 2005. http://unesdoc.unesco.org/images/0014/001461/146180E.pdf/.

Part 6

Culture

14

The Word Was Made Flesh
Life without Footnotes. John Bowker as Religious Broadcaster for the BBC

—DAVID CRAIG

THERE ARE FEW ACADEMICS of John's outstanding intellectual rigor who can make their arguments as accessible to a nonspecialist reader as to an audience at High Table or postgraduate seminar. Even fewer can communicate with an unseen broadcast audience. This was something John could do and regularly achieved with consummate skill. His first major Radio 3 talk was recorded in an airless cupboard, tucked away in a corner that served as the radio studio at Lancaster University. It was a program in the weekly series *Third Opinion* when contributors were asked to comment on the week's spoken output on Radio 3.

The script had arrived in good time and as a young, not-that-experienced producer, I had gone through it with a toothcomb, making many slight editorial alterations so that it would sound like an informal off-the-cuff reflection rather than a studied academic presentation: easy on the ear, memorable, and entertaining.

At our preliminary meeting, we worked through the first paragraph, explaining why such small alterations were necessary; and John grasped what was wanted. I left him with his original elegant paper. By return came back an almost perfect and broadcastable script. It had lost none of its rigor;

but it was couched in a way listeners could appreciate. Each of my preferences had been incorporated.

Academic presentations are the result of a life of research, pitting intellectual wits against others, questioning, cross-questioning, discovering new facts, propounding new arguments, and persuading the academic world that they advance one or other branch of learning. Academic writing is dependant upon corroborative footnotes, cross-referencing, extensive bibliographies, and pages of acknowledgments. Academic argument deploys lengthy sentences, subclauses, numbered points, lettered sub-divisions, and so forth, while any serious reading of such works involves page turning to check a note, a reference seeking for authorisation, or a bibliographic citation. None of these tools is available to a broadcaster.

Broadcasting depends on other conventions: broadcasters have to be their own experts, relying on no footnotes, bibliographies, or cross-referencing to support or substantiate a point. Any footnote must be included in the script, and any bibliographical reference translated into "as Shakespeare says in *The Winter's Tale* . . . ." Elisions, pauses, and unfinished sentences are all part of broadcasting. Instead, the name and provenance of the broadcaster is the guarantee of authority.

John's bibliography is in itself testimony to an almost unique breadth of theological learning. It encompasses in depth more areas than most academics could skim over. No treatment is shallow, unargued, or left to chance. Textual exegesis, philosophical argument, scientific investigation are all laid out, logically argued, and elegantly phrased. Quotations are from a wide range of original languages, revealing an unparalleled depth of study, knowledge, and memory.

But it was the experience of writing first for radio and then television that enabled John to translate so many theological arguments, religious practices, and philosophical precepts into personal experience and people. Interpreting the theoretical through the practical, John brought the everyday experiences of ordinary people into the public view. He did not patronize by interpretation; he put them in a context where their significance could shine.

The background against which the series was made was a divided nation. The 1980s had seen some of the most serious civil unrest in Britain's postwar history. Brixton in South London was an area with serious social and economic problems. The whole United Kingdom had been affected by recession, and the local migrant community was suffering particularly high unemployment, poor housing, and a higher-than-average crime rate.

The preceding months had seen growing unease between the police and the inhabitants of Lambeth. In January 1981, a suspected racially motivated arson had killed a number of black youths in New Cross. The police investigation was criticized as inadequate. Black activists, organized a march for the Black People's Day of Action on March 2. The marchers passed the Houses of Parliament and Fleet Street. Les Back wrote the local press for reporting the march respectfully, but he felt that the national papers had unloaded the full weight of racial stereotyping. A few weeks later, some of the organizers of the march were arrested and charged with inciting to riot. They were later acquitted. During the disturbances, police and members of the public were injured, and at least sixty private vehicles and fifty police vehicles were damaged or destroyed. Twenty-eight premises were burned and another 117 damaged and looted. Eighty-two arrests were made.

Between July 3 and 11 of that year, there was more unrest fueled by racial and social discord at Handsworth in Birmingham, Southall in London, Toxteth in Liverpool, Hyson Green in Nottingham, and Moss Side in Manchester. There were also smaller pockets of unrest in Leeds, Leicester, Southampton, Halifax, Bedford, Gloucester, Wolverhampton, Edinburgh, Coventry, and Bristol. Racial tension played a major part in most of these disturbances, although all of the riots took place in areas hit particularly hard by unemployment and recession.

On April 13, the then–Prime Minister, Margaret Thatcher, dismissed the notion that unemployment and racism lay beneath the Brixton disturbances, claiming that nothing whatsover had justified what had happened—although figures showed high unemployment amongst Brixton's black population. Overall unemployment in Brixton stood at 13 percent, with 25.4 percent for ethnic minorities. Unemployment among black youths was estimated at 55 percent. Rejecting increased investment in Britain's inner cities, Thatcher opined that money could buy neither trust nor racial harmony. The leader of Lambeth Borough Council, Ted Knight, suggested that the riots had been provoked by a police presence resembling an army of occupation. Thatcher thought the remark to be nonsensical and appalling. Such violent acts, that amounted to criminality, should never be condoned.

Small-scale disturbances continued to simmer throughout the summer. After four nights of disturbances in Liverpool during the Toxteth riots, beginning July 4, there were 150 buildings burnt and 781 police officers injured. CS gas was deployed for the first time on the British mainland to quell the rioting. On July 10, there was fresh rioting in Brixton. It was not until the end of July that the disturbances began to subside and the country began to evaluate the causes and extents of the riots. The riots were indeed seen by many as a racial and civil war. They raised many questions about civil society, ethnic diversity, educational opportunities, social achievements, and—somewhere amongst all these—the dangers inherent in serious religious commitment.

It had become apparent that the religious allegiances of the immigrant communities were far stronger than the laissez-faire Anglicanism of so many British citizens whose religion along with nationality came with their birth certificates and National Health Service number! In the 1980s, fundamentalism and extremist religion was limited to America's televangelists, the Taleban (a small, relatively unknown group in Afghanistan), stirrings of political Hinduism with the BJP [Bharatiya Janata Party], and nascent expressions of engaged Buddhism. Words like "Islamism" were not in common use; and phrases like "comparative religion" largely existed both in universities and among those engaged in interfaith discussion. The series *Worlds of Faith* came about first from an awareness that the religious element of society was being underplayed, and that, while News and Current Affairs Departments had acquired resources to approach the issue from a political, sociological, or economic angle, they were not competent to deal with the religious dimension. For a long time current affairs "did not do religion."

As the result of working with John, the producer was convinced that he—more than any other presenter—would grasp the sensitivities involved in making such a series, work with so wide a range of believers, and at the same time have the academic credibility to front such a treatment. There were many weekend-long conversations between presenter and producer as we tried to make some sense of the events unfolding within the country, and the commentaries, which lacked almost any reference to the power of religious engagement that undergirded the whole lifestyle of believers.

So, originally intended as a six-part Radio 4 series, *Worlds of Faith* was a serious attempt to provide a picture of the religious beliefs and practices of middle England, to widen the explanations for the unrest which news departments had covered in detail with appropriate political and social comment, and perhaps to provide some apologia for religion as a driving force.

Worlds of Faith was a breakthrough at different levels. One of the most significant was its use, not of academics, theologians, or scholars but of those who were practitioners of the faith: people whose worldview was focused through the prism of faith, for whom the daily, weekly, or annual practice of faith shaped their lives. The BBC has a history of using experts, initially as authorities in their own fields, voicing a received and approved intellectual position—then, as corroborative evidence for a less well-known speaker, or experience, usually prefacing such contributions with the patronizing "what he really means is . . ." followed by an authorizing, academic gloss which effectively diluted any real experience.

The contributions to *Worlds of Faith* came not on the whole from religious spokesmen, the priestly class: bishops, imams, rabbis, priests, or bhikkus. Rather, they came from the experiences of the Muslim doctor, the Hindu shopkeeper, the Sikh trader, the Catholic engineer, and from the experiences of a further hundred and fifty believers. Over three hundred hours of conversations were recorded with people from a broad social and geographical spectrum. Whole families were interviewed, contributing the understanding of what being religious actually meant in terms of time, financial commitment, engagement, and sacrifice.

The argument behind the series was that while it was relatively simple to know what a religion was through its religious texts, its creedal formulae, its main tenets and practices, it was far harder to understand what a belief in that religion implied—how religious faith was lived out in action, how transformative spiritual experiences effected life changes, or how inherited cultural practices dictated the minutiae of daily life.

Initially, we thought we knew what the areas of concern would be; but the further the interviewing process developed, the less sure we became! Committed to letting people speak for themselves and expressing their own concerns, feelings, and religious certainties, the contents of the interviewed dictated the priorities of religious practice and belief.

In broadcasting terms, it was absurd! In those days, documentaries were structured in advance; interviewees were selected to support the main argument. But it was only when at last all the material was gathered, some three hundred hours of recorded material, that we began to identify what the real concerns were, what the shape of the programs should be, what really mattered to people of faith, the tenets that dictated their lives for which they would ultimately be prepared to die—in effect, what their worlds of faith really were. It was impossible to condense the arguments into three hours of broadcasting; so, John went to the gatekeeper (the then-Controller of Radio 4 Monica Sims), explained the situation, and argued passionately that, because religion was the most important thing in the lives of so many people—indeed the very thing they would die for—it deserved adequate air time to put its arguments across. His commitment to the integrity of the programs prevailed; and we were sent away to make a thirteen-part series!

Recognizing that, for the most part, religions in the United Kingdom had been transplanted as the result of migration, it was important to identify how (while changing, Westernizing, and exchanging rural for urban) they had maintained their integrity in interpreting the changes of location, history, and event through the spectrum of an inherited religion. At the heart of survival was the maintenance of the religious practices brought from Jerusalem; from Uganda; from Tibet—from the experiences of partition, dislocation, exile, even persecution. Regardless of class, reason, or social status, religion was the focus of their lives.

At the center of each religion, some practice of prayer, meditation, or spiritual engagement was central; and, as people expressed the ways in which they reflected, it was hard at times to identify from which tradition specific witness came. Listening, thanking and interceding are common forms of prayer, and enlightenment. Unanswered prayer and periods of sterility are common in all traditions. *Worlds of Faith* dug deeper into spiritual experience. It sought understanding of these experiences and asked the one question a journalist should never ask: What did it feel like . . . ? Every response was different, personal.

However, one common and concrete spiritual experience was found in the significance of pilgrimage—whether to Jerusalem, Lourdes, Walsingham, Mecca, Amritsar, Radipura, or Auschwitz, Armenia, or Tabriz: locations of peace and presence where believers receive inspiration and make sense of otherwise inexplicable experiences. They are places where intensity of experience justifies the decision to die rather than to abandon faith.

More accessible, even rational, is the tangible: teachings manifest in writing; scriptures providing an authority outside the believer; a guide to everyday living. But therein lies inner conflict: in so many religions, divisiveness is caused by interpretations: differing textual exegesis citing conflicting authorities. While authority demands obedience, personal faith demands conscience—a tension which has to be lived out in daily life and practice with, in most cases, a physical focus.

Temples, synagogues, churches, chapels, gurdwaras, and prayer halls are locations for witness, communal worship, and social engagement as well as personal rites of passage. They provide the religious timetables that mark public and private expressions of faith and which, to believers, mean more than bricks and mortar or an address on the map. Death as a constant, and the questions of evil and suffering confront any believer. Central to every human life is the dichotomy of good and evil, clear in the opposing elements of the Hindu pantheon, apparent in human selfishness, unbearable in the Holocaust. The experience of religion suggests that there is no solution but an acceptance of the reality of both.

Transition to Western society creates intense pressures on traditional family life. In moving from a South Asian extended family to the limitations of a small west London apartment, Hindus and Muslims and the traditional observances of each group are challenged. When the inherently religious nature of motherhood has to be evaluated, some customs become illegal, others socially or legally unacceptable. Financial pressures dictate a lifestyle threatening religious observances and demanding new ways of parenting. Maintaining religious integrity has to be re-created.

Death comes as the end: regardless of religion or location, of tradition or observance. Therefore, the final rite of passage has a major religious significance. While Hindus, Sikhs, and Buddhists in general accept a rebirth, the monotheistic traditions to some extent believe in a form of life after death. For Jews, it is being remembered; for Christians, it is a concept of heaven; and for Muslims, the idea of returning someone to God: the graphic description of a Qur'anic paradise. In the individual observance of death, the familial responsibilities and the external rituals differ; but the imperative remains: custom, tradition, and religious duty must be fulfilled. For people of faith, the dead may be raised incorruptible; hell may be harrowed; mortals may be judged; and sins may—or may not—be forgiven. Which of these a believer accepts is not as significant as the fact they believe it.

This is the world of faith; this is the landscape which explains practise and custom, prejudice and pride, loyalty and passion, fundamentalisms and ideologies. This is a world inhabited by people who believe—often irrationally. Their personal lives are dictated by external rules, uncomfortable requirements, and demands on and limitations of their time and freedom. Often, the lives are translations or transplants from another continent where community, culture, and even weather permits and dictates religious observance. There is a divine irrationality behind the practice of religion, a "licensed insanity"—but to those who understand, there is a total logic which can be uncompromising and, perhaps, when interpreted, circumscribes explanations of urban rioting. This indeed does define the world of faiths.

15

"Such Was the World"[1]
A Verse Offering

—Eleanor Nesbitt

In recognition of the wide range of genre, as well as the diversity of focus, of John's publications, and the various projects in which he has involved me,[2] this contribution is a selection of poetic responses, in different moods and modes, to a few of the themes that John has addressed. These include the problem of suffering, the afterlife, the physiology of religion, winter, prayer, and animals. For nearly forty-five years, John and his multifarious writings have provided me, and no doubt many others, with encouragement as well as intellectual challenge, and offered inspiration and humor—a rare combination.

THE PROBLEM OF SUFFERING

"It is because suffering, in one form or another, is a common experience that religions give to suffering a place of central importance or consideration—indeed it is often said that suffering is an important *cause* of religion, since

---

1. Title of one of John Bowker's poems in *Before the Ending*, 28.
2. These include interviewing for Bowker, *Worlds of Faith*, and writing and serving as a consultant editor for Bowker, *Oxford Dictionary*, as well as contributing to Bowker, *World Religions*; and Bowker, *Cambridge Illustrated History*.

the promises held out by religion represent a way in which men [sic] can feel reassured in the face of catastrophe or death."[3]

Theodicy[4]

Cancer and evil . . .
Cancer and evolution . . .
Even cancer and even odds . . .
But cancer and God—or gods . . . ?

God contemplating and creating cancer?
God remonstrating, God berating cancer?
Is God inclement, impotent
Or just inconsequential?
Or is my cancer somehow Providential?

Thinking, searching, railing bring no answers.
Faith may console the faithful
Who take fewer chances
With punitive afterlife, but cancer's

Only answer comes to me in people's
Deep-down love and help and hope,
Their hanging on, their phone calls lasting hours,
Their prayers and smiles and messages
On cards and great bouquets of flowers,

And in the dawning sense that I can cope
With more than I had thought,
Being not alone, but caught
In unbreaking webs of gossamer support.
And when fear clings and haunts
And unintended words, more cruel than taunts,
Make optimism pale and every creed seem fantasy,

---

3. Bowker, *Problems of Suffering*, 1.
4. Previously published in Nesbitt, *Turn but a Stone*, 16; and D'Costa et al., *Making Nothing Happen*, 149.

> Another card or call, a country walk,
> A trip to town or comfortable talk
> Brings reassurance beyond any tried theodicy.
>
> And I can call this God,
> Or not, but must not set at nought
> The transformation that this cancer's wrought.

Poem Written in Mukteswar, June 1976

> There's either a worm
> or a very big germ
> that's making me writhe
> and wriggle and squirm.
>
> That God could invent
> a parasite meant
> to eat up my guts
> and never repent
>
> is a thought that defies
> the minds of the wise,
> whatever they try
> to hypothesise.

Floods 2014[5]

> Angry with England,
> you've flooded Somerset, demolished
> track at Dawlish, deluged Devon.
> Biblical's become a well-used word.

---

5. "UKIP [United Kingdom Independence Party] councillor has blamed the recent storms and heavy floods across Britain on the Government's decision to legalise gay marriage." London: BBC, January 18, 2014. See http://www.bbc.co.uk/news/uk-england-oxfordshire-25793358/.

In 1984, at York,
your anger left
less space for speculation.

Now, claims and counter-claims
of climate-change, and parliamentary
blame fill screens and screeds.

Newspapers overflow with:
dredging rivers (why not?)
building on flood plains (why?)
diverting necessary cash from foreign aid or wars
how to dry out houses
the pros and cons of sandbags . . .
victims, heroes,
neighbours . . .

Angry God, don't let your prophets,
preachers, politicians, pundits
drown out

a still, small voice.

THE AFTERLIFE

"The belief that there will be a worthwhile life after death is late in religious history."[6]

In the Ball Court, Chichen Itza

One player has lost his head. Blood
flows in seven streams—six serpents
and a twining plant. We photograph
the bas-relief. The guide explains:
Some say the cost of losing was

---

6. Bowker, *Oxford Dictionary*, xviii.

the captain's life. Not so, this head-
less player had led the winning side.
His prize: immediate entry
into Paradise.

Did relatives encourage him to play to win?
If so, no stranger than the anguished pride
of soldiers' widowed wives. We marvel
at the ring of stone that juts above our heads
and wonder how, thrusting with knees and hips
(not hands or feet), teams ever scored
a single goal. We try to get inside
the minds of men who played to win the match
but lose their lives, and recognise how hard
it is to disentwine courage, coercion,
faith and suicide.

Limerick

A Hindu who lived in Chennai
Met a Muslim from far-off Mumbai.
"After death we take birth
Again on this earth,"
He said. Said the Muslim, "Not I."

THE PHYSIOLOGY OF RELIGION

"It was a programme which captivated the young Freud, as he set out to make more systematic the explanation of even the most private and abstract features of human behaviour: all thoughts, including thoughts of God, must be ultimately reducible to physical-chemical activity."[7]

---

7. Bowker, *Sense of God*, 5.

Heaven

Their lives were dedicated to research.
Anaesthetised, they breathed their last and, as
their heartbeat ceased, they smelled the Promised Land—
the scent of foods galore, the cage companions
they had loved. Free, free to run about and stand up tall
(no humans, no laboratory stench)
they entered Paradise.

The watching humans monitored their brains' activity,
recorded elevated gamma oscillations and their highly activated
visual cortex and hypothesised:
visions of light and loved ones may well be explained
by increased brainwaves following cardiac arrest.

The headlines read: "Near death experience—
a surge of electricity in dying brain."[8]

WINTER

Yes," said Uncle Bolpenny, "I want to get ready for winter . . ."
"Ah, yes," said the Do It Yourself man. "You mean you want to seal the doors and windows so no cold wind comes through . . ."
"Oh, no," said Uncle Bolpenny, "I don't mean that at all. I mean I want to build a toboggan. That's what *I* mean by getting ready for winter."[9]

---

8. See Morelle, "Near-death Experiences."
9. Bowker, *Uncle Bolpenny*, 64.

Midlands Snow[10]

Walking new snowfall, not yet packed
on hardened ice that footfall nearly cracks,
the word I hear is your[11] word "thwock."
Thwocking (with concrete, tarmac, grass
now memories), I'm back with sledges,
snowmen, snowballs, when the world was
black and white. At eight a. m. today
ranges of recent roofs glow pearl and pink.
My legs recall their climb in Naini Tal[12]
to watch as Nanda Devi came alight.
I watch the TV weather with suspense:
will snowflakes on the map reach Birmingham?
Excitement topples more pragmatic fear,
and snow, like rainbows and elusive scents,
connects and quickens, and then goes.

PRAYER

"Prayer is presence, before One who elicits praise, thanksgiving, and joy, as well as penitence and sorrow."[13]

Prayer[14]

God make me gentle
Where the world is hard for living,
And where the world is harsh,
God make me kind for loving.

---

10. Previously published in D'Costa et al., *Making Nothing Happen*, 156.

11. "Your" here refers to Ian Florance, fellow "Gemini Poet." See Florance and Nesbitt, *Gemini Four*.

12. After part 2 of the Theological and Religious Studies Tripos at Cambridge, and after training as a teacher, I headed to Naini Tal in the Himalayan foothills to teach.

13. Bowker, *Oxford Dictionary*, xxiii.

14. Previously published in Nesbitt, *Turn but a Stone*, 28; and D'Costa et al., *Making Nothing Happen*, 147.

Examination Question[15]

"Hold us in the hollow of your hand;
Bless us with the radiance of your gaze;
Guide us, help us, succour and support;
Bring us safely to the promised land."

Does human tendency to anthropomorphise
initiate, inhibit or distort
theology? Discuss—while life allows—
but do not try too hard to understand.[16]

ANIMALS

My three verses[17] below John's are included in recognition of his interest in "attitudes to nature"[18] and, more recently, *An Alphabet of Animals*.[19] His poems whimsically celebrate creation and copulation, geese, cats, yetis, and yaks:

Praise him, you writhing ropes who softly slip
Through patterned shade with venom in your jaws,
Praise him, who move by wing or flitting fin,
On feet or hooves or predatory paws:[20]

---

15. Previously published in Askari et al., *Faith and Friendship*, 107 and D'Costa et al., 147.
16. Written long before reading: "Simpler it is by far / To see the river and the promised land / Than know what it would mean to understand." (From "Comprehension: 'Wittgenstein ask yourself: how does one lead anyone to a comprehension of a poem or a theme?'" [Bowker, *Before the Ending*, 34]).
17. The goose, python, and zebra verses figure in an "animals with attitude" series of calendars and postcard books, 2010–2013. (The illustrations are by Jenny Hare.)
18. Holm and Bowker, *Attitudes to Nature*.
19. Bowker, *Alphabet of Animals*.
20. Bowker, "All Creatures," in *Before the Ending*, 38.

Animals With Attitude

Augusta Goose, yes that's the name
In every gallery of fame.
My ancestors were geese of note:
Their honk saved Rome, as Livy wrote.

* * * * * *

My python (called Pythagoras)
Is ten yards long, but note: his mass,
Circumference and mental state
Are liable to fluctuate.
You'll see him swell and then unwind—
That's proof Pythagoras has dined.

* * * * * *

Zebra, zebra, black and white,
Speeding like a bird in flight,
Zebra, lightning-swift you sped,
White and black from hoof to head.

For My Tortoise, Joey[21]

For I will give thanks for my tortoise, Joey,
For his lizard skin and lozenged shell,
For his unlikely legs and bird-bright eyes,
For his emotional detachment.
For his hunger for campanula taught me
a multi-perspectival view of beauty.
For his escapology, not Aesop, taught me never to despair of slowness.
For his self-containment disclosed my species
aspiring to extrude its missing carapace.

---

21. Previously published in Florance and Nesbitt, *Gemini Four*, 104.

For he was never noisy, angry or in haste.
For he was untouched by rain or sun.
For he was perhaps impervious to love.
For he asked nothing, conceded nothing and departed without trace.

Thank you, John, for introducing me, long ago in lectures and supervisions, to the life of Al-Ghazali and to some unforgettable "Holocaust literature," and for remaining in touch over so many years. Your ongoing assignments have helped me, at some precarious times, along my own career path through the study of religions. Your publications will go on being inspirational companions.

BIBLIOGRAPHY

Askari, Hasan et al., eds. *Faith and Friendship: In Memory of David Bowen*. Bradford, UK: Bradford College, 2002.
Bowker, John. *An Alphabet of Animals*. Toronto: Key, 2010.
———. *Before the Ending of the Day: Life and Love, Death and Redemption*. Toronto: Key, 2010.
———, ed. *Cambridge Illustrated History of Religions*. Cambridge: Cambridge University Press, 2002.
———, ed. *The Oxford Dictionary of World Religions*. Oxford: Oxford University Press, 1997a.
———. *Problems of Suffering in Religions of the World*. Cambridge: Cambridge University Press, 1970.
———. *The Sense of God: Sociological, Anthropological and Psychological Approaches to the Origin of the Sense of God*. 2nd ed. Oxford: Oneworld, 1995.
———. *Uncle Bolpenny Tries Things Out*. Illustrated by Sarah Garland. London: Faber & Faber, 1973.
———. *Worlds of Faith: Religious Belief and Practice in Britain Today*. London: BBC, 1983.
———, ed. *World Religions: The Great Faiths Explored and Explained*. New York: DK, 1997.
D'Costa, Gavin et al. *Making Nothing Happen: Five Poets Explore Faith and Spirituality*. Farnham, UK: Ashgate, 2014.
Florance, Ian, and Eleanor Nesbitt, eds. *Gemini Four*. Henley-on-Thames, UK: Only-Connect, 2011.
Holm, Jean, with John Bowker, eds. *Attitudes to Nature*. Themes in Religious Studies Series. London: Pinter, 1994.
Morelle, Rebecca. "Near-Death Experiences Are 'Electrical Surge in Dying Brain.'" London: BBC, August 12, 2013. http://www.bbc.co.uk/news/science-environment-23672150/.
Nesbitt, Eleanor. *Turn but a Stone*. Norwich, UK: Hilton House, 1999.

Bibliography of John W. Bowker's Publications

I. BOOKS: SOLE AUTHOR

The Targums and Rabbinic Literature: An Introduction to Jewish Interpretations of Scripture. Cambridge: Cambridge University Press, 1969.
Problems of Suffering in Religions of the World. Cambridge: Cambridge University Press, 1970.
Jesus and the Pharisees. Cambridge: Cambridge University Press, 1973.
Uncle Bolpenny Tries Things Out. Illustrated by Sarah Garland. London: Faber & Faber, 1973.
The Religious Imagination and the Sense of God. Oxford: Clarendon, 1978.
Worlds of Faith: Religious Belief and Practice in Britain Today. London: BBC, 1983.
Licensed Insanities: Religion and Belief in God in the Contemporary World. London: Darton, Longman & Todd, 1987.
The Meanings of Death. Cambridge: Cambridge University Press, 1991.
A Year to Live: A Cycle of Meditations on the Transforming Power of the Christian Story. London: SPCK, 1991.
Hallowed Ground: Religions and the Poetry of Place. London: SPCK, 1993.
The Sense of God: Sociological, Anthropological and Psychological Approaches to the Origin of the Sense of God. Oxford: Clarendon, 1973. 2nd ed., Oxford: Oneworld, 1995.
Is God a Virus? Genes, Culture and Religion. Gresham Lectures 1992–93. London: SPCK, 1995.
What Muslims Believe. Oxford: Oneworld, 1998.
The Sense of God: Sociological, Anthropological and Psychological Approaches to the Origin of the Sense of God. 2nd ed. Oxford: Oneworld, 1995.
God: A Brief History. London: Dorling Kingersley, 2002.
The Sacred Neuron: Extraordinary New Discoveries Linking Science and Religion. London: Tauris, 2005.
Beliefs That Changed the World: The History and Ideas of the Great Religions. London: Quercus, 2007.
The Aerial Atlas of the Holy Land. Photography by Sonia Halliday & Bryan Knox. Buffalo, NY: Firefly, 2008.
Knowing the Unknowable: Science and Religion on God and the Universe. London: Tauris, 2008.

Before the Ending of the Day: Life and Love, Death and Redemption. Toronto: Key, 2010.
An Alphabet of Animals. Illustrated by Bryan Knox. Toronto: Key, 2010.
The Message and the Book: Sacred Texts of the World's Religions. New Haven: Yale University Press, 2012.
God: A Very Short Introduction. Very Short Introductions. Oxford: Oxford University Press, 2014.

II. BOOKS (EDITOR, PRINCIPAL AUTHOR)

World Religions: The Great Faiths Explored and Explained. New York: Dorling Kindersley, 1997.
The Oxford Dictionary of World Religions. Oxford: Oxford University Press, 1997.
The Complete Bible Handbook: An Illustrated Companion. New York: Dorling Kingersley, 1998.
The Cambridge Illustrated History of Religions. Cambridge Illustrated History. Cambridge: Cambridge University Press, 2002.

III. SELECT, REPRESENTATIVE ARTICLES

"The Origin and Purpose of St. John's Gospel." *NTS* 11/4 (1965) 398–408.
"Psalm CX." *VT* 17/1 (1967) 31–41.
"Haggadah in the Targum Onqelos." *JSS* 12/1 (1967) 51–65.
"Speeches in Acts: A Study in Proem and Yelammedenu Form." *NTS* 14/1 (1967) 96–111.
"The Correlation of Theological and Empirical Meaning." In *Marriage, Divorce and the Church*, appendix 2, edited by Hugh Montefiore et al., 96–112. London: SPCK, 1971.
"Merkabah Visions and the Visions of Paul." *JSS* 16/2 (1971) 157–73.
"Can Differences Make a Difference? A Comment on Tillich's Proposals for Dialogue between Religions." *JTS* 24/1 (1973) 158–88.
"Mystery and Parable: Mark iv.1–20." *JTS* 25/2 (1974) 300–17.
"Information Process, Systems Behaviour and the Study of Religion." *Zygon* 11/4 (1976) 361–79.
"'The Son of Man.'" *JTS* 28 (1977) 19–48.
"Art, Theology and Religious Systems: A Case for the Inquisition?" *Zygon* 13/4 (1979) 313–32.
"The Aeolian Harp: Sociobiology and Human Judgement." *Zygon* 15/3 (1980) 307–50.
"Religious Studies and the Languages of Religions." *RS* 17 (1981) 425–39.
"Did God Create This Universe?" In *The Sciences and Theology in the Twentieth Century*, edited by A. R. Peacocke, 98–126. Notre Dame, IN: University of Notre Dame Press, 1981.
"On Being Religiously Human." *Zygon* 16/4 (1981) 365–82.
"The Human Imagination of Hell." *Theology* 85/708 (1982) 403–10.
"The Burning Fuse: The Unacceptable Face of Religion." *Zygon* 21/4 (1986) 415–38.

"The Religious Understanding of Human Rights and Racism." In *Trevor Huddleston: Essays on His Life and Work*, edited by Deborah Duncan Honoré, 153–73. Oxford: Oxford University Press, 1988.

"Cosmology. Religion and Society." *Zygon* 25/1 (1990) 7–23.

"Christianity and Non-Christian Religions: A Neo-Darwinian Revolution?" In *God, Truth and Reality: Essays in Honour of John Hick*, edited by Arvind Sharma, 87–97. London: Macmillan, 1993.

"Science and Religion: Contest or Confirmation?" In *Science Meets Faith*, edited by Fraser Watts, 95–119. London: SPCK, 1998.

"Implicit Morality: An Empirical Ethical Perspective." *JIR* 1 (1998) 69–75.

"God, Spiritual Formation and Downward Causation." *Theology* 117/836 (2004) 81–88.

"Creation, Law and Probability: A World Religions' Perspective." In *Creation: Law and Probability*, edited by Fraser Watts, 181–88. Theology and the Sciences. Minneapolis: Fortress, 2008.

www.ingramcontent.com/pod-product-compliance
Lightning Source LLC
Chambersburg PA
CBHW051054230426
43667CB00013B/2287